Praise for
The Presumed Alliance

"A riveting narrative. . . . Vaca's well-researched book is essential reading for anyone desiring an understanding of the future of ethno-
graphic conflict in the United States."
—*Booklist*

"Nicolás Vaca has written a brave and pathbreaking book. For too long,
commentators have ignored important differences between the expe-
riences of Blacks and Latinos in the United States, to the detriment of
a full understanding of both groups. With grace and scholarly attention to detail, Vaca demonstrates that Latinos' interests are not always
identical to those of Blacks. Vaca shows that the presumed alliance between the two groups is less a fact than it is a product of wishful thinking on the part of civil rights activists."
—Linda Chavez, author of
Out of the Barrio and *An Unlikely Conservative*

"A hard and unnerving look at how changing demographics will forever
alter our country's dialogue on race."
—Jill Wolfson, *San Jose Mercury News*

"A frank discussion on the latest taboo subject in the race milieu: the
growing tension between Latinos and Blacks."
—Katherine Corcoran, *San Jose Mercury News*

"The most thorough analysis yet of Black/Latino relations. This is an
in-depth look at the shifting sands of ethnic politics."
—Bob Blauner, author of *Still the Big News:
Racial Oppression in America* and *Black Lives, White Lives:
Three Decades of Race Relations in America*

"A thought-provoking book."

—David Mills, *New York Post*

"The work puts the often conflicted relationship between Blacks and Latinos into the context of immigration and the dramatic growth in the Latino population. The topic of Black/Latino will certainly become more heated in the years to come, as Latinos are now the nation's largest minority. Vaca's narrative is provocative and often disturbing. It will no doubt illicit heated responses, which hopefully will lead to a better understanding."

—Rodolfo Acuña, author of *Occupied America:*
A History of Chicanos and *Anything but Mexican:*
Chicanos in Contemporary Los Angeles

"A thoughtful political/historical essay on the profound gulf that yawns between America's most populous minority groups."

—*Kirkus Reviews*

"Fascinating and complicated. . . . Vaca tears off the rose-colored glasses, bids farewell to political correctness, and handles the subject matter with genuine interest and expertise."

—*Hartford Courant*

"*The Presumed Alliance* explores conflicting perceptions with refreshing candor. Vaca demythologizes the idealized concept of the 'Rainbow Coalition' and calls on both [Latinos and African Americans] to reintroduce themselves to each other."

—Clarence Page

© James Fidelibus

A graduate of Harvard Law School, NICOLÁS C. VACA holds a Ph.D. in sociology from the University of California at Berkeley. He is a practicing attorney in the Bay Area and has been a visiting scholar at the University of California at Berkeley for the past two years. Vaca is also a contributing writer to the prestigious journal *California Lawyer*. He lives in California.

THE
PRESUMED
ALLIANCE

The Unspoken Conflict Between
LATINOS *and* BLACKS
and What It Means for America

NICOLÁS C. VACA

rayo

An Imprint of HarperCollins*Publishers*

FIRST RAYO PAPERBACK EDITION PUBLISHED 2004.

Designed by Nicola Ferguson

The Library of Congress has catalogued the hardcover edition as follows:

Vaca, Nicolás Corona.
    The presumed alliance: the unspoken conflict between Latinos and Blacks and what it means for America / Nicolás C. Vaca—1st ed.
        p. cm.
Includes bibliographical references and index.
ISBN 0-06-052204-6
    1. African Americans—Relations with Hispanic Americans. 2. Hispanic Americans—Social conditions. 3. African Americans—Social conditions. 4. Hispanic Americans—Politics and government. 5. African Americans—Politics and government. 6. Social conflict—United States. 7. United States—Race relations. 8. United States—Ethnic relations. I. Title.
E185.615.V33   2003
305.868'073—dc21   2003049224

ISBN 0-06-052205-4 (pbk.)

04 05 06 07 08 ❖/RRD 10 9 8 7 6 5 4 3 2 1

To my wife, Kris, without whom this work could not have been completed. To my children, Nicolás, Kristjan, and Melinda, who understood and accepted that time devoted to this endeavor meant time taken away from being with them.

CONTENTS

PREFACE

It was changed circumstances that inspired this book—my own and that of the Latino population. In the 1960s, relations between Blacks and Latinos were viewed through rose-colored lenses. It was the "brothers under the skin," "a house divided will fall," Latinos and Blacks united against the "white oppressor" perspective that expressly swept any differences between minorities under the rug. I recall standing in front of Dwinelle Hall at the University of California, Berkeley, circa 1963, listening to Malcolm X express his hatred for the "blue-eyed devil" while the handful of African Americans, Latinos, and Asian Americans in the audience clapped wildly in approval. And while not all minorities may have viewed whites as "blue-eyed devils," they held kindred views that allowed them to overlook any differences among themselves. And woe to those who questioned such a stance. In this day and age it is hard to recall how fervently such beliefs were held and how hot the criticism was that rained on those who dared to voice an objection to such a viewpoint. But it was there. After all, it was the ultimate refuge—people of color united against the "white establishment." Minorities, oppressed and disenfranchised—a kind of latter-day Rainbow Musketeers against the evil White Empire. And there were reasons to justify such a viewpoint: in the 1960s, Blacks were being denied the right to vote in the South, and only some 15 years earlier Mexican Americans were being segregated in schools throughout the Southwest. The emotions created by these facts blinded minority leaders, who likened their plight to that of the impoverished third-world countries, to the frictions that existed or could exist in the future between the coalesced minorities.

In this united ideological march for enfranchisement, Blacks took the lead, and the rest of the minorities supported them. The civil rights agenda was set by African Americans, and the rest acquiesced. There was reason for doing this. It was generally accepted that African Americans had suffered more than any minority group—more than the Chinese who had been barred from immigrating to the United States beginning in the latter part of the nineteenth century and extending into the first decades of the twentieth; more than the Japanese, who were also barred from immigrating to the United States as a result of the so-called Gentlemen's Agreement of 1908 and who were later interned in prison camps during World War II; more than the Mexican Americans, who had experienced harsh discrimination throughout the Southwest and even been "repatriated" to Mexico during the 1930s in an effort to reduce unemployment in the Great Depression; more than the Native Americans, who had lost their land and whose peoples' ranks had been decimated by the European invasion (including Spain). Indeed, in some sectors, African Americans were viewed as the only valid beneficiaries of any civil rights rewards.

In the late 1960s I appeared before the U.S. Commission on Civil Rights at a regional meeting held in San Francisco to complain that very little attention was being paid to the condition of Mexican Americans. My complaint was based in part on the fact that the summer before I had worked at the U.S. Commission on Civil Rights in Washington, D.C., as an intern. Before arriving in Washington I expected to encounter other Mexican Americans at the commission, but I discovered that I, a summer intern, was the highest-ranking Mexican American there. My statements before the commission invoked a strong negative reaction from Erwin Griswold, then dean of the Harvard Law School and chair of the hearing, who was visibly angry with me for raising this issue. I got the distinct impression that for Dean Griswold the only minority in the United States was the African American.

There was another reason why minorities were willing to let African Americans set the civil rights agenda. It had to do with numbers. From the very beginning, African Americans outnumbered all other minorities, and their numbers granted them an additional reason for assuming the leadership role. Without their numbers, any minority coalition would be weakened, and consequently not taken seriously.

However, things have changed—not intentionally, but naturally. Increased immigration, both legal and illegal, and exploding birthrates have swelled the ranks of both Asian Americans and Latinos. And as their numbers have grown in urban areas where Latinos and Asian Americans exist shoulder to shoulder with African Americans, conflicts have developed. There have been significant struggles over educational resources. Latinos and Asian Americans have fought to appropriate funds in order to respond to their unique linguistic needs, while Blacks have, in certain instances, opposed such actions. Struggles have also occurred in the workplace. African Americans have charged Latino immigrants who are fleeing abject poverty in third-world countries with taking any job under any circumstance at lower wages than Black workers. African Americans also complain that white employers prefer Latino immigrants as workers, not only because they are willing to perform the work in worse conditions and for lower wages but also because they are a preferred labor pool. White employers, it has been written, feel comfortable around Latino employees but threatened by Black employees.

Of all the arenas of struggle, certainly the fight for political power is in the heavyweight division. Political success brings access to the corridors of power, and access to power leads to economic opportunities. For this reason a significant part of the book is devoted to an analysis of various political struggles between Blacks and Latinos: the Los Angeles 2001 mayoral race, where Blacks voted for a white candidate over a Latino candidate; the refusal of Blacks to share power in Compton, California; the 2001 mayoral election in Houston, Texas, where Latinos left their normal party affiliation to vote for "one of their own"; and the troubled Black-Latino coalition that frustrated a Puerto Rican mayoral candidate in New York City.

For years I discussed these issues with close friends and fellow at-torneys—Anglo, Latino, and Black—as I waited for a book to appear that would address the conflict or at least go beyond pat analyses like "Interethnic conflict can exist, but it is believed that there is more of a basis for cooperation than there is for conflict"—and then drop the subject. I finally concluded that the likelihood of such a book was re-mote. A frank discussion of Black-Latino conflict could cause some people to misinterpret the intent of the author, and if the author's in-tent was misperceived, life could become very difficult for that person.

I know this because before becoming a practicing attorney I spent a significant amount of time in academia. I received an M.A. and a Ph.D. from U.C. Berkeley and I taught at the University of California at Santa Cruz. After that I spent four years back at Berkeley conducting re-search funded by the Ford Foundation. Over time I came to understand and accept that even in such an open forum intellectual constraints exist.

My inspiration for writing this book came from several sources. Principal among them was Ernesto Galarza, a legendary figure in Chi-cano academics. In my senior year at Berkeley, I was fortunate enough to be selected by him to assist him on research he was conducting on the economic development of Mexican Americans in Oakland. Ernesto would appear two nights a week in Berkeley and call me and his two other research assistants to meet with him in the motel room where he stayed. It was in the small, darkened room that we first discussed the nature of his project and where we would receive our assigned tasks. One evening I asked him why he was not a professor at some university. I told him that I thought that his numerous publications and reputa-tion in the academic community would certainly provide him with the opportunity for such a position. Ernesto responded that he felt "freer" working outside of the institutional setting, though those were not his exact words. That comment stayed with me because over the several months that I worked with him, I was impressed with his drive and his creativity, all of it emanating from that small room in a run-down motel.

I was also inspired by Octavio I. Romano, one of my mentors when I became a graduate student at Berkeley in the late 1960s. It was Octavio who introduced me to Carey McWilliams's book *North from Mexico,* an extremely readable history of Mexicans in the Southwest, which became a bible to me and countless other Chicanos who, at that time, hungered for a history that reflected our reality. I did not appreciate it at the time, but McWilliams, like Galarza, did not reside at a university. He was a lawyer. His work was such a departure from existing works on Mexican Americans that I failed to realize that perhaps his perspective was molded precisely by the fact that he stood outside the academic world. What he wrote about and how he wrote reflected a divergence from the common thinking.

My relationship with Romano grew during my time as a graduate student. Together we founded *El Grito: A Journal of Contemporary Mexican-American Thought,* a journal that published academic articles, poetry, fiction, and art. The mishmash of work that appeared in those pages was a reflection of the tremendous energy that existed within the Chicano movement. It was also a reflection of our independence from institutional constraints. Octavio was supremely proud of the fact that *El Grito* never relied on institutional support or advertising for its survival. It was supported exclusively by the sale of its quarterly issues (not always published on time). Because it was independent, we were never subject to external censure, but more importantly we never censured ourselves. The editorial meetings that lasted long into the night focused on the subject matter and quality of the submission under consideration, and never on the political correctness of its content. After founding *El Grito,* we established Quinto Sol Publications, which sponsored an annual literary prize and also published fiction. Those several years that I spent working on *El Grito* and at Quinto Sol were incredibly enjoyable and rewarding, and the experience has remained with me throughout the years.

So, as I waited for the book that would take on the hard topic, I recalled Galarza, I recalled McWilliams, I recalled *El Grito,* and I picked up the telephone and called Robert Blauner, my other mentor when I was a graduate student. Bob was responsible for my becoming a graduate student at Berkeley, and during my years there, he was and has been ever since a constant source of support and inspiration. With patience, wisdom, and warmth he shepherded me through the rigors of academic life, always supporting my ideas and theories and providing both a scholarly and a human sounding board. I believe I told Bob that I was thinking of returning to academics, though at the time that was only partially true because what truly possessed me was thoughts about "a book." Bob, as he always had in the past, responded immediately and sponsored me for two years as a Visiting Scholar in the department of sociology at Berkeley.

Fortune must have been smiling on me because at the end of my first year as a Visiting Scholar, by which time I had spent countless hours in the library researching articles on Latinos, my literary agent called and introduced me to René Alegria, director of the Rayo Imprint at HarperCollins. René and I spoke several times, and he suggested that I provide him with a proposal and an outline for the book that I envisioned writing. After several attempts, we reached a meeting of the minds and agreed that while the topic of a Black-Latino conflict could prove to be highly controversial, the 2000 Census showed that the tremendous growth of the Latino population made it a timely subject. And so this book came to be.

Because I dwell in two worlds—the academic and the legal—I have had a wealth of people to draw on to read and comment on the manuscript while it was still in its formative stages. And to the extent that this book has any merit in providing insight into the difficult problems of relations between Latinos and Blacks, it is in no small part attributable to the comments and guidance that I received from the following individuals: Guillermo Hernandez, whose comments, laced with his ever present humor, provided me with insight into various issues I had not perceived; Kevin Johnson, who patiently detailed his concerns with the manuscript and caused me to rethink and rewrite significant portions of it; Karen Kaufmann, whose comments regarding the chapter on Los Angeles caused me to essentially rewrite the chapter and add another chapter in order to provide balance to the book; Lorenzo

Trujillo, who took the time and care to edit the manuscript and provide me with comments that inspired some of the revisions; John Gonzales-Madrid, who took valuable time out of his legal practice to edit the manuscript and challenge me to more seriously examine some of the issues presented; Peter Allen, my longtime friend and editor of the *California Lawyer*, who took time to edit the first draft of the book and provide me with insights and comments that vastly improved the book; Mike Mooney from LexisNexis, who generously allowed me to use LexisNexis to access material in Houston, Miami, and New York; and finally Robert Blauner, my mentor and friend, whose encouragement was indispensable in completing the manuscript. While I remain indebted to these individuals for giving me guidance in regard to the structure and content of the book, the final product is ultimately mine, and only I am accountable for any errors that it may contain.

I also want to thank my agent, Andrée Abecassis, who never flagged in her support of the project even when I did. Her upbeat attitude and patience with my own frustrations saw me through the completion of the book. Finally, this book would never have seen the light of day but for the faith and encouragement provided by René Alegria at Rayo. It was his belief and trust in my ability to envision and write such a book that is the true spirit behind this project. I thank him for giving me this opportunity.

INTRODUCTION

Shortly after the 2000 Census released its numbers pronouncing that the Latino population at 35.3 million was closing in on the African American population at 36.4 million, the *Charlotte Post,* an African American newspaper published in Charlotte, North Carolina, asked one of its writers, Artellia Burch, to go out and get the reaction of Charlotte's Black population to this startling fact. The census had revealed that Charlotte's Hispanic population grew from 9817 in 1990 to 77,092 in 2000, a 685 percent increase over the last 10 years.[1] Little wonder that the *Charlotte Post* wanted to know what its readership thought about this.

Burch dutifully interviewed various Black residents of Charlotte and published her interviews in a piece entitled "When Worlds Collide: Blacks Have Reservations About Influx of Hispanic Immigrants."[2] The story contained quotes from Black residents which reflected some of the worst stereotypes of Latinos. For example, an African American computer technician unabashedly admitted that he was prejudiced against Latinos. He said, "I definitely think they are people to fear.... They travel in packs. They like to play stupid acting as if they don't understand English when you know they do. A group of them will sit around and talk to each other in their language. They could be plotting to kill you and you would never know."

The computer technician's mean-spirited observations of Latinos were not restricted to their potentially menacing ways. No, he was also concerned with the loss of jobs to the newly arrived immigrants. "They are taking over," he said. "They're taking all of our jobs. Slowly but surely. I just don't care to be around them. They make my skin crawl. I keep my ideas to myself. This might sound bad, but I don't go around making remarks about them to other people. So, only God can judge me."

Another respondent, an African American computer engineer, said that he was not surprised that Latino numbers were now nearly even with Blacks. Why not? Because "Hispanics come over here, start businesses, and multiply like rabbits. . . . It's no surprise they outnumber us because they have a baby every year." These and other equally disparaging observations from Black residents of Charlotte landed Burch in a firestorm of controversy. She was interviewed by Fox News, and the *Wall Street Journal*'s website had a link to her story. The controversy was so great that BlackPressUSA.com, which carried Burch's story on its website, felt compelled to remove it.

Burch's sin, if her story can be called that, was that she exposed what everyone believed was a well-kept secret. The secret was this: Because Latinos and Blacks have been exploited and suffered poverty and discrimination, and because they are both people of "color," it is commonly assumed that Blacks would not only *not* disparage the new Latino arrivals but would sympathize and understand the marginal nature of their lives. It was this presumed ideological alliance between Blacks and Latinos that Burch's story exposed in a very direct and graphic manner. It was the political incorrectness of the views expressed by her interviewees that caused the controversy.

When I committed to writing this book I did so with the knowledge that I too would likely become the focus of high-tension emotions. I got a taste of what I could expect one evening when I met with a couple of Latino attorney friends for drinks and what I thought would be an enlightened discussion about the subject matter of this book. One of the attorneys was of Peruvian heritage and the other was a veteran, like myself, of 1970s Chicano activism.

When we got together, I presented a broad-stroke synopsis of the book to my colleagues. Even before our first drinks arrived, the Chicano attorney became agitated and challenged the need for such a book, arguing, categorically, that all the book would do is exaggerate an already existing division between Latinos and Blacks. "Something that the *gringo* wants and which he can exploit." The words came out like well-rehearsed lines—no surprise to me since such a perspective had been in existence since the 1970s Third-World Strike Movement in the San Francisco Bay Area and was accepted gospel by many Chicano and Black activists.

I responded by telling him that the 2000 Census made the discussion of the relationship between Latinos and Blacks essential—that Latino birthrates and immigration, both legal and illegal, cranked up the Latino population to such a level that it almost equaled the Black population and was projected to outstrip it in the near future. Our population growth, I continued, was such that any dialogue on race relations in the United States could no longer be restricted to the Black-White dynamic but had to include Latinos as well and that a major component of that discussion had to address any problems between Blacks and Latinos. The Chicano attorney persisted with his assault and told me that what I should focus on is building bridges between Blacks and Latinos. How could we build bridges, I responded, unless we examined the basis of any conflict? The Latino attorney, perceiving that emotions were escalating, tried to calm the waters by telling the Chicano attorney that all I was doing was discussing what existed—I had not created the conflict, I was only addressing it. The Chicano attorney flicked the Latino's comments aside with a wave of his hand and continued with his barrage, his voice now two octaves higher than when we began our conversation. When it was clear that I would not come around to his position, he announced that he was leaving and that I should not expect any further calls from him. I was surprised by both the emotional level of our conversation and the dramatic manner in which it ended. Here was someone I had known for some years, with whom I had socialized on many occasions, who belonged to some of the same professional organizations that I did, but who had no compunction about terminating our friendship simply because of the subject matter of this book. If this was his reaction, what could I expect from those with whom I had no such ties?

The irony of the Chicano attorney's reaction was not lost on me. Neither Burch nor I were the first to address this issue. The troubled relationship between Blacks and Latinos had been broached before by Latinos, Blacks, and whites because the conflict between Latinos and Blacks had been perceived, and if not perceived then anticipated, by academics and laypeople years before Burch's article appeared. It had also been discussed in direct and uncompromising ways. An example of this was the division between Latinos and Blacks over immigration that manifested itself in the 1980s when Congress, concerned with controlling illegal immigration, began putting together what would later become known as the Immigration Reform and Control Act of 1986 (IRCA). A component of IRCA was an employer sanctions provision, which, for the first time ever in the history of immigration legislation, imposed federal civil and criminal penalties on employers who knowingly hired, recruited, or referred aliens who are not authorized to work by the Immigration and Naturalization Service.

When IRCA was wending its way through Congress, spokespeople from Latino and other minority groups warned that employers would be so afraid of violating the law that they "would not hire foreign-looking or foreign-sounding U.S. citizens or aliens who were legally authorized to work," thereby discriminating against Latinos and other minorities.[3] However, the NAACP and labor organizations supported the employer sanctions provision as a way of combating illegal immigration.[4]

The chickens came home to roost on March 29, 1990, approximately six years after passage of IRCA, when the U.S. General Accounting Office issued a report, the third in a series, concluding that the IRCA sanctions resulted in widespread discrimination against eligible workers who appeared to be foreign or who sounded foreign.[5] Latinos' worst fears were confirmed.

So when the Leadership Conference on Civil Rights (LCCR) held its meeting in Washington, D.C., in May 1990, Latino organizations once again faced off against Black organizations over employer sanctions.[6] For the Latino organizations it was a no-brainer. A federal report stated that the employer sanctions provision resulted in discrimination against Latinos. Therefore, Black organizations, whose members should certainly sympathize with Latinos about such discrimination, should join forces with Latinos in their attempt to correct this problem. Two Latino organizations, the National Council of La Raza (NCLR) and the Mexican-American Legal Defense and Education Fund (MALDEF), wanted the LCCR to support repeal of the IRCA employer sanctions, while the leaders of the LCCR wanted to take a more sanguine approach by first studying the issue more. This lukewarm response by the Black members of the LCCR infuriated the Latino groups. Charles Kamasaki, vice president of NCLR, stated, "We're not in a position to belong to a coalition that doesn't support our major civil rights issue. . . . Civil rights can no longer be viewed only in a black context. In the past, only parenthetically were other groups mentioned. That is going to change."[7]

Tensions rose between the Latino organizations and the LCCR leading to a threat by the NCLR to picket the Leadership Conference and organize a walkout of its fortieth annual dinner. Eventually only the picketing took place. The walkout was called off after the Latino organizations were assured by Black civil rights leaders that they would support repeal of the employer sanctions.

In July 1990, Dr. Benjamin Hooks, the executive director of the NAACP, kept his promise to the Latino organizations and pushed a resolution through the NAACP's national convention, held in Los Angeles, calling for a repeal of the employer sanctions provision of IRCA.[8] The passage, however, came after heated debate, which revealed the deep division between Blacks and Latinos on immigration. During the debate Charles B. Johnson of the Pasadena NAACP said, "We used [the sanctions] to keep undocumented aliens from taking the food from black children. If you withdraw those sanctions, then you open the door and you flood this state with a multitude of undocumented aliens who will take the jobs of blacks and other minorities."[9]

The events at the 1990 LCCR meeting no doubt greatly affected NCLR's perspective on coalition building with Black organizations. But it was the riots in May 1991 in the Mount Pleasant neighborhood of Washington, D.C.—riots that resulted from the shooting of a Latino immigrant by a Black female police officer—that convinced the leadership that they had to publicly voice their concerns.[10]

In the early 1990s the population of Washington, D.C., was approximately 65 percent Black, 28 percent white, between 5 percent and 12 percent Latino, and 2 percent Asian.[11] During the economic upswing of the 1980s, more Latinos than Blacks were employed in the construction industry. When the construction industry fell into the doldrums in the late 1980s, Latinos made an easy transition into the service industry, taking jobs as janitors, waiters, dishwashers, and laborers—jobs that had traditionally been filled by Blacks. This phenomenon left many Blacks feeling that "the Latinos are taking over."

Those who have studied this phenomenon have advanced two main reasons why Latinos were able to move into these low-level, dead-end jobs in Washington, D.C. The first reason is that many young Black males who are unskilled and lack education believe that they are above such jobs and that more money can be made through illegal activities.[12] The second reason is straightforward but chilling in its implication: whites prefer to employ Latinos because they feel uncomfortable around Blacks. Whether true or not, this observation was echoed in Los Angeles, where Black-Latino conflicts have permeated the groups' history together.

Whereas employers in the private sector in Washington, D.C., appeared to prefer Latino workers over Blacks, African Americans were entrenched in governmental positions. Latinos represented between 5 percent and 12 percent of Washington's population, but only 1 percent of its municipal (public) employees. More graphically stated, in 1992, there were 31,400 municipal employees, and of that number only 529 were Latinos. City agencies that were independent of the mayor's office had 19,723 employees, of which only 216 were Latinos. Of the 172 employees hired by Washington's city council, only 4 were Latinos.[13] These numbers led Keith Jennings and Clarence Lusane, two Black scholars, to conclude that "when considered with the fact that about 11 percent of the city's residents are employed by the District government, on the surface, a good case for hiring discrimination exists."[14]

If the underlying economic and social conditions of the Latinos formed the tinder, then the spark that ignited the flame of ethnic conflict was the shooting of Daniel Enrique Gomez by a Black rookie cop. The versions of how Gomez came to be shot were at odds with each other. The police contended that Gomez lunged at the officer, while the Latino community contended that Gomez was shot after he was handcuffed.[15]

As word of the incident spread, Latino youths began to riot. The riot extended to a second night of looting, burning, and violent confrontations between the police and Latino youths, who by now had been joined by Black youths. Frustration overwhelmed some Black residents. A Black radio host demanded that the mayor "round them up, herd them up, check their green cards, turn them over to immigration, and get them out of my neighborhood, out of my city."[16]

It was generally agreed that the principal cause of the riots was the frustration of a growing Latino population with the entrenched Black power structure. Washington elected its first Black mayor in 1974, but Blacks did not effectively begin to establish their power in the municipal government structure until Marion Barry's election in 1978. During Barry's first term of office, he hired thousands of Blacks into the civil service and let out millions of dollars in public contracts to minority businesses. His various social and summer programs also won him favor with the Black community. All of this occurred at the same time that the city budget was hemorrhaging red ink. By the time Barry exited in 1990, the city was being forced to cut both workers and services.[17]

It was at this very point that the Latino population, growing on a yearly basis, began to make its own demands for expanded social services and bilingual materials in the classrooms. Their demands, however, fell on deaf ears. Faced with shrinking resources, the Black politicians, like all other such politicians, saw no need to respond to a politically impotent constituency.

The lack of political representation in the district exacerbated Latinos' frustration. While Latinos represented between 5 percent and 12 percent of the population, their voting numbers were less than 1 percent. As a result, almost no Latinos had been voted into office to represent their community's interests. Even among Washington's advisory commissioners—elected representatives of neighborhood divisions to respond to local community issues—Latinos were underrepresented. In May 1992, one year after the riots, only 1 of the 323 elected commissioners was Latino.

After the Mount Pleasant riots, Raul Yzaguirre, president of NCLR, and Kamasaki could no longer keep quiet. In 1991 they delivered a paper at the Annual Meeting of the Political Science Association in Washington, D.C., entitled "Black-Hispanic Tensions: One Perspective."[18] The paper, which was subsequently published as an article in the Winter 1994–95 issue of the *Journal of Intergroup Relations,* critically examines the issues that divided the Latino and Black communities.[19]

> Hispanics understand the fundamental interests shared by the black and Hispanic communities. Both suffer disproportionately from poverty and discrimination. Hispanics recognize the legitimacy of black problems and concerns—after all, a significant number of Hispanics are also black. But Hispanics believe that blacks must also recognize the legitimacy of Hispanic problems and concerns. Blacks are now the nations's largest minority, but soon Hispanics will have that distinction. The authors believe that both communities, and the society as a whole, will be better off if blacks and Hispanics work in coalition. Growing tension between the two communities, however, threatens the ability of blacks and Hispanics to develop strong, sustainable coalitions.[20]

The purpose of the Yzaguirre-Kamasaki article was to identify and discuss the existing conflict between Latinos and Blacks in order that both groups might work together to achieve common goals. The themes of the article were the following:

1. Latinos have historically suffered as much as Blacks.
2. Blacks do not believe that Latinos are as deserving of civil rights protection as Blacks because Blacks have suffered more discrimination than Latinos and because Blacks contributed more to the civil rights movement than Latinos.
3. Latinos seek the same rights and privileges as all Americans, including Blacks.
4. Efforts by Latinos to obtain these rights had been met by a Black leadership that is "at best indifferent, and at worst opposed, to the interests of the Hispanic community." [21]

Yzaguirre and Kamasaki went on to identify five arenas in which Latino efforts to improve their situation had been met with indifference or opposition by Blacks.

1. *The 1975 Voting Rights Act Extension.* Latinos were included in the ultimate version of the bill over the objections of the NAACP.
2. *The 1982 Voting Rights Act Extension.* Some members of the LCCR succeeded in revising the language assistance provisions of the bill, which directly affected Latinos and other minorities, in such a way so as to reduce its coverage for these groups.
3. *The "English-only" movement.* Efforts by certain groups attempting to make English the "official" language of the United States (a clear effort aimed at Latinos and other bilingual groups) were only nominally opposed by the LCCR and other civil rights groups.
4. *Employer sanctions under IRCA.* During the bill's consideration in Congress, Latino groups requested that the LCCR oppose employer sanctions. Two member groups, the NAACP and the AFL-CIO, vetoed this request.

5. *Employment discrimination.* In the early and mid-1980s it was demonstrated that existing statutes and enforcement efforts did not provide adequate protection for Latinos against employment discrimination. Latino organizations made numerous requests to the LCCR to support requests for new enforcement programs, but these requests were rejected.

The reaction to this paper must have been as heated as my encounter with my attorney colleague. Yzaguirre and Kamasaki obliquely referred to the response when they wrote, "Since the initial publication of our paper in 1991, as you might imagine, we have received many interesting and powerful reactions."[22] However, when they were asked permission to reprint the article in 1995, they did so even though they understood that it could potentially result in political divisiveness.

Approximately a year after Yzaguirre and Kamasaki presented their paper, Jack Miles, using the riots ignited by the acquittal of the four white police officers charged with the beating of Rodney King as a starting point and Los Angeles as his ethnic laboratory, published an article in *The Atlantic Monthly* entitled "Blacks vs. Browns."[23] Miles presented a more far-ranging view of the Latino-Black tensions than did Yzaguirre and Kamasaki.

Miles found it somewhat ironic that the mainstream media framed the Rodney King riots as a Black-White phenomenon, completely neglecting the census data that had been released two weeks prior to the riots: In the 1980s the United States had admitted 8.6 million immigrants, 11 percent of whom identified Los Angeles as their final destination and 35.3 percent of whom spoke Spanish at home.

Something powerful was happening in Los Angeles, Miles observed, and at the heart of this something powerful was the Latino population. Miles quoted extensively from an editorial from a Spanish-language newspaper, *La Prensa San Diego,* in order to articulate what other Latinos were saying among themselves: During the riots it was Latinos who were the victims, not Blacks. In fact, it was Black-on-

Latino violence that characterized most of the crimes committed during the riots.

> Though confronted with catastrophic destruction of the Latino businesses, which were 60% of the businesses destroyed, major looting by Blacks and by the Central Americans living in the immediate area and a substantial number of Hispanics being killed, shot and/or injured, every major television station was riveted to the concept that the unfolding events could only be understood if viewed in the context of the Black and White experiences. They missed the crucial point: The riots were not carried out against Blacks or Whites, they were carried out against the Latino and Asian communities by Blacks.
>
> What occurred was a major racial confrontation by the Black community, which now sees its numbers and influence waning.

> Faced with nearly a million and a half Latinos taking over the inner city, Blacks revolted, rioted and looted. Whatever measure of power and influence they had pried loose from the White power structure, they now see as being in danger of being transferred to the Latino community. Not only are they losing influence, public offices, and control of the major civil rights mechanism, they now see themselves being replaced in the pecking order by the Asian community, in this case the Koreans.[24]

Miles concluded that in Los Angeles, not surprisingly, Blacks were competing more directly with Latinos than with any other ethnic group. The reason for this was simple: "The Korean population of Los Angeles County is just 150,000, a tiny fraction of the Latino population of 3.3 million."

Miles provided various examples of this competition. He pointed out that some school social workers who were monolingual were let go in order to make room for bilingual social workers who were needed to service Spanish-speaking residents in the district. Most of the social workers who were laid off were Black.

Miles even found evidence to support NAACP member Charles B. Johnson's assertion that Latino immigrants took jobs away from Blacks. According to the General Accounting Office, the unionized Black workforce previously used by janitorial firms in downtown Los Angeles had been almost entirely replaced with nonunionized immigrants. On the nitty-gritty of the competition between Latinos and Blacks, Miles wrote:

> If the Latinos were not around to do that [gardening, busboys, chambermaids, nannies, janitors, construction workers], nonblack employers would be forced to hire blacks—but they'd rather not. They trust Latinos. They fear or disdain blacks. The result is unofficial but widespread preferential hiring of Latinos—the largest affirmative action program in the nation, and one paid for, in effect, by blacks.[25]

In response to the knee-jerk reaction that Latinos and Blacks should not fight over peanuts, scraps left to them by the economic, political, and educational institutions, Miles asked simply, "But even if these communities make common political cause, do they have any choice about economic competition?" Put more bluntly, how do you explain to a Mexican immigrant that in order to establish cooperation and harmony between Blacks and Latinos, he must first sacrifice his ability to earn a living as a janitor to a unionized African American?

About a year later, on December 2, 1993, Toni Morrison, a Black author and Nobel Prize winner, wrote an article for *Time* magazine entitled "On the Back of Blacks."[26] While the piece was more of an editorial than an in-depth analysis and therefore less detailed than either the Yzaguirre-Kamasaki paper or the Miles article, Morrison was no less unequivocal about her view of the tension between Blacks and immigrants. Morrison recounts the last scene of Elia Kazan's film *America, America* in which newly arrived Greek immigrant Stavros Topouzolglou is given a job shining shoes at Grand Central Station. Mind you, the first hour of the film depicts the impoverished village in Turkey from which Stavros emigrated, accented by the burning of a church filled with Armenian women and children by the Turkish army. When Stavros finally makes it to the United States and is given his shoe-shining job, the audience is primed to identify and sympathize with him. Morrison, however, points out that in that scene a young Black man who also shines shoes at Grand Central Station attempts to solicit a customer. He is run off the screen with, "Get out of here! We're doing business here!" According to Morrison, Stavros is now set to become a true American—an immigrant, but also an entitled white who understands that, no matter his immigrant status, he stands above the long-suffering Black American citizen. And without this entitlement, Morrison concludes, Stavros's future in the United States would be in doubt.

Morrison did not view the final scene from the dewy-eyed perspective of the white audience. Instead she saw it as a visualization of racial oppression in the United States. "This is race talk, the explicit insertion into everyday life of racial signs and symbols that have no meaning other than pressing African Americans to the lowest level of the racial hierarchy. . . . Only when the lesson of racial estrangement is learned is assimilation complete." Morrison wrote

Is this true of Latinos? Have they learned the "lesson of racial estrangement"? I believe an argument can be made that they have. While the Black stereotyping of Latinos by some Black residents in Charlotte stunned and surprised some of the readers of the *Charlotte Post*, there is also hard evidence that Latinos also hold certain stereotypes of Blacks near and dear to their hearts. How do I know this? Apart from anecdotal evidence culled from years of interacting with Latinos on race issues, I recently became aware of a lawsuit filed by several Black employees against the Del Taco Corporation which appears to provide empirical evidence that such attitudes exist.[27] The lawsuit reads like a bad dream of Latino-Black relations and rivals, if not surpasses, the racial stereotyping by Blacks of Latinos published by the *Charlotte Post*.

The suit lists an amazing 42 causes of action against the defendants. The most disturbing of them are based on race discrimination—actions by Latino employees against Black employees. Examples of these actions listed by the complaint are:

> During the Scope of Plaintiff JOHNSON'S employment with Defendants, TONY ZAPADA, a Hispanic employee of Defendants used racial slurs against Plaintiff JOHNSON by calling him a "Myatte" (sic) which means a "Nigger" in English (sic); . . .
>
> ZAPADA further called Plaintiff JOHNSON and other African-American employees "Stupid." ZAPADA also incited other Hispanic employees to name-call on other African-American employees;
>
> Plaintiff JOHNSON personally advised PINEDA about ZAPADA calling African-Americans "Niggers." JOHNSON further notified PINEDA of Hispanic employees using racial slurs and harassing new African-American employees. PINEDA took no action to stop that harassment;
>
> During the scope of Plaintiff MOORE'S employment, Defendants' Hispanic employees used racial slurs and racial derogatory statements against him and his girlfriend IRENE RIVERA, a DEL TACO employee at Restaurant No. 152. Defendants' Hispanic employees called Plaintiff MOORE a "Nigger" and/or "Mayetta" (sic), which means a "nigger" in Spanish. Defendants' Hispanic employees further called Plaintiff MOORE a monkey and told his girlfriend who was pregnant by him that she was "carrying a monkey's baby."[28]

There you have it. Allegations against Latinos that appear to give credence to the fact that Latinos have learned the "lesson of racial estrangement" and who, according to Toni Morrison, have now secured their future in United States.

The foregoing examples demonstrate that, notwithstanding the reaction from the Chicano attorney who terminated his friendship with me because I dare to shine light on the tensions and conflicts that exist between Latinos and Blacks, I am not the first to make these observations.

So why do it now? Why dig up dirt, ruffle feathers, destroy the illusion of unbroken unity between Blacks and Latinos, bleeding the colors of the Rainbow Coalition by giving the dreaded *gringo* the ammunition my former friend told me I was providing? The simple answer is that the ethnic landscape has changed. What once was is no longer and will never be again. And this change requires a reexamination of relations between Blacks and Latinos.

When Yzaguirre and Kamasaki first presented their paper, it was no surprise that they focused on the 1990 Census, which counted more than 22.3 million Hispanics in the United States. This fact was essential. Without these numbers, Yzaguirre would be howling in the wind. He would not be taken seriously, but could only cajole, charm, or dazzle Black leaders into taking his Latino agenda seriously.

The numbers now belong to Latinos. And while it is tempting to exult in these numbers and become heady with the power that they will no doubt produce, the real challenge is how Latinos will handle the leadership role that the numbers will bestow on them. This challenge has arrived in California ahead of the rest of the nation. In many ways it is frightening how quickly it has come; even more frightening are the challenges that lie ahead. Consider the following:

1. In the fall of 2006, the majority of children entering the state's kindergartens will be Latino.
2. In the fall of 2014, the majority of children entering the state's high schools will be Latino.
3. By the fall of 2019, the majority of young adults turning 18 and eligible to vote will be Latino.[29]

In the blink of an eye California's Latinos will move from minority to majority. How they handle this responsibility will affect not only them but the rest of the state's residents.

Among the groups already affected, as the preceding discussion demonstrates, are African Americans. What this book attempts to present is the unvarnished truth about the relationship between Latinos and Blacks in various arenas and in various parts of the country as a result of the growth of the Latino population. What it presents, or perhaps how it is presented, may rankle and unnerve some readers, but there is no time to waste because the Latino tsunami that has engulfed California is sweeping across the nation, and sooner or later it will affect the rest of the country as well. If this book does nothing more, it should set the radar on the right frequency and aim it in the right direction. If it succeeds in doing that, I will consider it a success.

The Latino Tsunami

The Browning of America

> Since America's founding, blacks have had secure claim to being the nation's largest minority. But with the 2000 Census, that epoch has ended. America's Hispanic population now rivals its black population and will quickly surpass it.
>
> JONATHAN TILOVE
> *Newhouse News Service 2001*

Prior to the 2000 Census various political commentators, reporters, academics, and government entities predicted that while the number of Latinos in the United States would eventually surpass the number of African Americans, this phenomenon would not happen until some time in the very distant future. This fuzzy notion of eventual Latino numerical supremacy was reflected as early as 1980 in an article by Charles P. Henry, an African American scholar, who reported that according to the U.S. Census Bureau it would take more than 75 years—2055—for Latinos to surpass the African American population.[1] Even as recently as 1995, scholars, again relying on data produced by the U.S. Census Bureau, incorrectly predicted that by the year 2000 Latinos would represent only 11 percent of the U.S. population.[2] While this prediction turned out to be somewhat closer to reality, it was nevertheless wrong. Curiously, these predictions failed to take into account that from the 1970 U.S. Census on, the Latino population consistently demonstrated exponential growth, a pattern that did not mirror that of the general population.

The 1970 Census was the first census to identify the Latino population in a comprehensive way.[3] Prior to 1970 other methods, including country of birth, country of birth of parents, and mother tongue, were used to count only certain sectors of the Latino population. In 1980 and 1990 the U.S. Census obtained data on Latinos using self-identification questions that changed from one decade to the other.

The 1970 Census counted 9.6 million Latinos in the United States.[4] While this number was not alarming in the greater scheme of the U.S. population (which numbered 203 million) and also in comparison to the African American population (which at that time numbered 22.6 million), it would serve as a benchmark for the subsequent census numbers in demonstrating the incredible growth of the Latino population.[5]

When the 1980 Census was released most of the information describing the general population was of little interest (it had grown to 226.6 million). The African American population (26.5 million) had grown at a faster rate than the general population. Indeed, according to some scholars these numbers were expected. What was not expected was the incredible growth of the Latino population. The Latino population ballooned from 9.6 million in 1970 to 14.6 million in 1980, representing an increase of 52.1 percent over the prior 10-year period.

In 1990, the growth of the Latino population spiked off the charts, increasing by 7.7 million to 22.3 million. At the same time the African American population grew a mere 3.4 million, to 29.9 million, demonstrating a slower growth rate than in the prior 10 years.

It was, however, the 2000 Census that finally identified the Latino population as the tsunami that would eventually overwhelm the African American population and sweep across the entire country. Between 1990 and 2000, the Latino population had grown by an astounding 13 million to 35.3 million, representing 12.6 percent of the population. In comparison, the African American population increased by only 6.5 million to 36.4 million, representing 12.9 percent of the U.S. population.

And, of course, the phenomenal growth of the Latino population shows no sign of relenting. There is no better example of this than the fact that shortly after the 2000 population numbers were released the U.S. Census Bureau predicted that the Latino population would eventually surpass the African American population in the year 2005. It was wrong by two years: in January 2003, Latinos officially became the largest minority in the United States.

The projections for future years are even more astounding. According to the U.S. Census, not only will Latinos continue to outnumber African Americans over the next several decades, but the numerical superiority will be smothering. In the year 2020, African Americans will represent 13.8 percent of the U.S. population, whereas Latinos will represent 17.0 percent. By the year 2030, it is projected that African Americans will represent 14.1 percent of the total U.S. population, while Latinos will represent 19.4 percent. Skipping to the year 2050, it is projected that African Americans will represent 14.7 percent of the population, and the Latino population will skyrocket to 24.3 percent.[6]

While the projection of Latino growth is impressive, those numbers may well turn out to be far too conservative. The Census Bureau acknowledges that of the three components for predicting the future growth of Latinos—births, deaths, and international migration— international migration is the least predictable.[7] Historically, international migration, along with high birthrates, has been one of the most significant factors driving the tremendous growth of the Latino population in the United States.[8]

The U.S. Census Bureau based the immigration trend between 1999 and 2020 on five assumptions. First, increased immigration during the 1990s was the direct result of the Immigration Reform and Control Act (IRCA) of 1986, which made it possible for people to become legal residents and citizens. These new citizens then sponsored their immediate relatives. The Census Bureau concluded that this flow was transitory; it further assumed that migration from such sponsorships would crest between 2000 and 2010, then gradually decline to zero. "In particular, legal migration from Mexico is assumed to return to the levels of the early 1990s by 2010."[9] Second, there would be no change in U.S. immigration policy that would affect the number of immigrant visas available in those categories that have numerical limitations between 1998 and 2020. Third, the number of refugees arriving in the United States would drop between 1998 and 2020, except for an increase reflected by arrivals from the republics that used to be Yugoslavia. Fourth, illegal immigration from Mexico and Central America would not change significantly from those levels assumed for the 1990s base series. Finally, legal migration from places other than Mexico, Central America, and refugee countries will fluctuate, depending on events in the countries and the ability of those countries to supply immigrants.

Missing in this discussion is the possibility that there will be another amnesty program for undocumented residents or a guest worker program with Mexico.

Prior to the September 11, 2001, terrorist attacks, President George W. Bush and President Vicente Fox were seriously discussing various amnesty proposals for Mexicans residing illegally in the United States. While those talks are now on the back burner, Mexico continues to press for such a program. If time and events make a new amnesty program possible, then we will undoubtedly see a repeat of the process set in motion by IRCA. Once again the numbers of Latinos will swell, not only through legalization but also through immigrant visas granted to family members of newly legalized residents.

And what kind of numbers would those be? In November 2001, the Pew Hispanic Center estimated that in mid-2001 the number of undocumented Mexicans residing in the United States ranged from 3.4 to 5.8 million and the number of undocumented Central Americans ranged from 1.2 to 1.9 million, bringing the total pool of potential new Latino residents to between 4.6 and 7.7 million.[10]

As each year passes, the number of illegal Mexican and Central American immigrants in the United States increases,[11] and because of this undeniable fact, the numbers presented above are no longer reliable. However, assuming for the moment that the 7.7 million number is accurate, and that many of these immigrants would qualify for legal residency under a new amnesty program, then one begins to get the picture that the numbers predicted by the U.S. Census Bureau are totally unrealistic—and in fact significantly higher.

Now let us consider the possibility of a new guest worker program with Mexico. Between 1942 and 1964 some 5 million Mexicans were admitted into the United States as guest workers under the *bracero* program.[12] The Mexican workers were brought to the United States largely to perform work on farms in the Southwest. However, the program did not include any provision for legalization of the Mexican workers. Once their term ended, they ostensibly returned to Mexico.

The program ended in 1964, and since that time U.S. farmers have repeatedly lobbied legislators to reinstate it in one form or another. Most recently, the Agricultural Job Opportunity Benefits and Security Act of 1999 was introduced into the U.S. Senate, with a companion bill in the House of Representatives on March 22, 2000. These two bills included a provision that allowed for the legalization of workers who had been employed in agriculture for a certain period of time during the 12 months prior to the introduction of the bill. These bills did not pass, but similar proposals may succeed in the future.

What would a new *bracero* program mean for the growth of the Latino population? Like the legalization program, it would significantly increase the number of Latino residents. A study conducted by the Pew Hispanic Center arrived at this very conclusion, though it used a slightly different set of facts as the basis for its study. According to this study, approximately 1.2 million of the 2.5 million persons employed for wages on U.S. farms are undocumented. Using the criteria employed for the seasonal agricultural workers (SAWs) program under IRCA, an estimated 600,000 to 840,000 workers would be allowed to legalize their status. But more significantly, if the newly legalized workers left the farm workforce at the same rate as did the SAWs after they were legalized in 1987–1988, approximately 125,000 new workers would be needed each year for farmwork. The study also concluded that in order to replace all those who left all types of farmwork, at least 250,000 new workers would be needed each year if farm labor conditions did not change at all.[13]

Admittedly, not all farmworkers are Latinos, but historically Mexico has provided much of the labor used in U.S. agriculture, and there is little reason to conclude that this pattern will change.[14] It is reasonable to assume that a new *bracero* program would result in increased legal Latino immigration to the United States and in the process the Latino population would balloon.

If either a legalization program or a new *bracero* program (or both) is instituted by the United States, there is little doubt that the Latino population would increase in such dramatic numbers that the census projections would be irrelevant.

The growth in numbers of Latinos at the national level is impressive, but the numbers for certain states are even more compelling. This is particularly true in the Southwest, where Latinos have historically settled. It is therefore no surprise that the 2000 Census confirms that in California, Texas, New Mexico, and Arizona Latinos outnumber African Americans.

In California, Latinos number 10,966,556 and represent 32.38 percent of the population, dwarfing the Black population, which represents only 6.44 percent of the population. What is noteworthy is that between 1990 and 2000, the Black population declined from 7.03 percent to 6.44 percent. The Latino population, on the other hand, grew from 25.83 percent to 32.38 percent.[15]

In Texas the Latino population increased from 20.98 percent to 31.99 percent between 1990 and 2000 while the Black population, like in California, decreased slightly from 11.89 percent to 11.34 percent in 2000.[16]

Latinos in New Mexico constituted 42.1 percent of the total state population, representing the highest proportion for any state. In contrast the Black population in New Mexico decreased slightly from 1.78 percent to 1.69 percent.[17]

Between 1990 and 2000 Arizona's Latino population grew by 88 percent and now represents a little more than one-quarter of the total population. Between 1990 and 2000 Arizona's Black population increased by only 43 percent and represents only 2.9 percent of the population.[18]

In Colorado, Latinos represent 17.1 percent of the total population, while African Americans are only 3.68 percent of the population.[19]

The Great Plains states—Iowa, Kansas, Missouri, Nebraska, North Dakota, South Dakota—also experienced a major increase in Latino growth. While the overall increase in population for each state was below the national average of 12.4 percent, ranging from 0.5 percent to 8.9 percent, the Latino percentage increase exceeded the general population change in all of the states and Kansas and Missouri experienced almost 100 percent increase in their Latino populations.[20]

The Latino populations in large metropolitan areas have been growing steadily since 1980. They have even displaced African Americans as the Big Apple's largest minority. Between 1990 and 2000, the African American population of New York City declined from 25.2 percent to 24.5 percent. The Latino population increased from 24.4 percent in 1990 to 27.0 percent in 2000.[21]

Not only did New York's Latino population grow dramatically over the last 10 years but the composition of the Latino population also changed. While the Puerto Rican population declined from 50.3 percent of the total Latino population to 36.5 percent, the Dominican population increased from 18.7 percent to 25.7 percent and the Mexican population almost doubled its numbers. There were also great increases in the number of Latinos from Ecuador and Colombia.[22]

The 2000 Census also established that Latinos are now moving into nontraditional locations—locations where African Americans have long held a presence. Eighteen of the new Latino destinations, according to a Pew Hispanic Center report, can be categorized as locations with "hypergrowth"[23] because between 1980 and 2000, the Latino population grew by more than 300 percent. Cities with hypergrowth include Raleigh, North Carolina, which experienced a jaw-dropping 1180 percent increase; Atlanta, Georgia, saw a 995 percent growth; Greensboro, North Carolina, experienced a 962 percent jump; and Charlotte, North Carolina, had a 932 percent increase in its Latino population.[24]

These dry numbers, however, do not reflect the type of impact that Latinos have on small Southern towns, where their numbers have exploded. Take DeQueen, Arkansas, for example, a town where for decades the population was all white and where the principal source of work was a large poultry-processing plant. As the processing plant experienced a labor shortage from among its white residents in the 1990s, Latinos, mostly Mexicans and Central Americans, started to arrive and fill the waiting jobs. Initially only men arrived, but then wives, children, and extended families began to appear. By 2002, Latinos made up 40 percent of the 5765 population—a higher percentage than in Houston, Dallas, Phoenix, or San Diego.[25]

Another example of the impact that Latinos are having on small Southern towns is Siler City, North Carolina, where Latino immigrants, drawn by work at poultry companies and textile mills, have overwhelmed it in a short five-year period.[26] In 1990, this sleepy Southern hamlet with a total population of 4955 was recognizable only because, as viewers of *The Andy Griffith Show* knew, it was a shopping destination for Mayberry residents. In 1990 it had only 147 Latinos and 1270 Blacks.[27] In 2000, Siler City's total population had increased to 6966, but 2740 of the residents were now Latinos, outstripping the 1370 Black residents.[28]

The Latino arrival brings a new complexion to the traditional Black-White South. It also brings the same tensions that afflict Latino-Black relations in other states where Blacks and Latinos have a history of competing over jobs and resources.

"We've got many black people who believe that Latino people have come here and taken their jobs and taken over their communities, taken our women, taken our husbands—the whole nine yards. It goes back to the legacy of slavery. But how do you change that?" stated one Black resident of Mount Olive, North Carolina, where Latinos have arrived in large numbers to compete with Blacks for work in the local poultry-processing plant.[29] Latino residents counter such accusations with their own tales of how Blacks get the best jobs while they encounter discrimination in the workplace from whites and Blacks alike.

Sometimes the change from a Black-White dynamic happens overnight as it did in Greenwood, South Carolina, and thereby provides a case study of the impact that Latinos can have on the educational system and resources of such small towns. "One evening in 1994, Greenwood went to bed a town of two races, as it had been for 150 or so years," wrote Pat Butler, a reporter for *The State*, a South Carolina newspaper. "The next morning, residents awoke to find about 350 Hispanics, bused in from a grim Texas border town, living in a decaying apartment complex next to the Greenwood Packing meat plant. And more were coming."[30] As Butler notes, within 24 hours, Greenwood was tossed into the morass of a multicultural, multiracial society.

Four years after the first Latinos arrived, it is estimated that there are approximately 1000 Latinos in the city of 21,000. The town now boasts at least three grocery stores that cater to Latinos and at least two *cantinas*.

The impact that this overnight arrival had on the schools in Greenwood was felt immediately. Butler reports that on the first day on the job for the principal of the East End Elementary School, a man walked in and told her that he had 23 Latino children to enroll in the school. Prior to that day, the school had never had a Latino as a student and consequently had no experience in providing instruction to Latino children, many of whom spoke only Spanish. While the principal struggled during the first few years, she established a curriculum for the Latino students and has a full-time instructor and a part-time assistant to teach the Spanish-speaking students.

The impact of the Latino flood also reverberated in the neighborhoods and the job market. As in Los Angeles, where unionized janitorial services were replaced by nonunion Latino workers, in Charleston members of a largely African American International Longshoremen's Association local formed a picket line in front of a freezer operation to protest the cancellation of a union contract in preference for nonunion workers. And as in Los Angeles, the nonunion workers were Latino. Union members suspected that the workers were undocumented and complained to the Immigration and Naturalization Service. Word got out, as it has a way of doing in Latino communities, so by the time the INS arrived, the Latino workers had vanished and in their place were Black workers.[31]

The conflict between Latinos and Blacks in the South has even manifested itself in such traditionally Black strongholds as Georgia, where the Latino population grew from 108,922 in 1990 to 435,227 in 2000, an increase of almost 300 percent.[32] Some observers estimate that by 2010 Latinos will outnumber Blacks in the state.[33]

In 2001, Black legislators in Georgia initially defeated a bill supported by the governor to broaden the state's "minority" designation to include Latinos. The bill would have granted Latinos the right to be included in tax breaks to businesses that hire minority contractors. In opposing the bill, Bob Holmes, a member of the state's Legislative Black Caucus, stated, "We are not comfortable amending laws that originally were passed to aid racial minorities, such as African Americans and Native Americans, who have a long history of being discriminated against. There is growing competition between blacks and Hispanics, and in the South, it is going to get worse. We know that they have escaped from poverty, and we want them to have a better life here, but not at the expense of African Americans."[34]

After the actions of the Black legislators were strongly criticized, the bill was revived in the Georgia State Senate, approved, and sent to the House, where it was passed with votes that included those of the Black legislators who initially opposed it.[35]

Historically, Latino immigration begins with a "trailblazer" who crosses the border to seek employment and a better life in "frontier" cities of the United States. Once the trailblazer establishes a base and familiarity with his or her new surroundings, family and friends follow and a new immigrant community is formed. This was the pattern used by Mexican immigrants when they populated cities like Los Angeles and Houston and there is every reason to believe that all Latino immigrants will employ this tried and true method of immigration to new destinations in the United States, including Southern states.

How did the Latino tsunami come to be? How is it that in the year 2000 America awoke to an ethnic population the likes of which it had not seen in modern times? Certainly the Latino population did not mushroom to its current size overnight to surprise census takers and the general public alike. The answer, I believe, is very simple—the United States invited them. The invitation included making citizens of the residents of Puerto Rico and then encouraging them to immigrate to the United States; encouraging illegal immigration from Mexico; and accepting political refugees from Cuba, Nicaragua, and El Salvador.

If there is a complexity to the growth of the Latino population it rests on the fact that it is not made up of one single group. Quite the opposite. The Latino population comprises many groups, each bringing its unique characteristics to the pan-Latino formulation. Latinos know that Puerto Ricans are different from Mexican Americans and that Cubans are different from both. However, when all is said and done and the historical and cultural differences between various Latino groups are discussed, Latino leaders invariably resort to the umbrella terms "Latino" or "Hispanic," sweeping all differences under this label. The differences, however, are significant, not only in cultural terms but in raw numbers. The latter is best demonstrated by Table 1. The census demonstrates that while the U.S. Latino population is a mosaic of people from numerous Spanish-speaking countries, Mexicans, as a single group, represent the largest segment at 58.5 percent. The next largest Latino group are Puerto Ricans, who constitute 9.6 percent, while Cubans make up only 3.5 percent of the Latino population. Central Americans constitute 4.8 percent, and South American, 3.8 percent.

What the numbers make clear is that the Latino population in the United States is largely driven by Mexican immigrants and their progeny. Without the Mexican population Latinos would not have overtaken the African American population or present the enormous growth that is predicted for Latinos in the future. Furthermore, an

TABLE 1

ESTIMATES OF HISPANIC OR LATINO BY SPECIFIC ORIGIN
GROUP IN THE UNITED STATES BASED ON 2000 CENSUS

LATINO IDENTIFICATION	NUMBER	% OF TOTAL LATINO POPULATION
Mexican	20,640,711	58.5
Puerto Rican	3,406,178	9.6
Cuban	1,241,685	3.5
Dominican	764,945	2.2
Central American*	1,686,937	4.8
South American†	1,353,562	3.8
Other Hispanic/Latino‡	6,211,800	17.6
Total	34,305,818	

* COSTA RICAN, GUATEMALAN, HONDURAN, NICARAGUAN, PANAMANIAN, SALVADORAN, OTHER CENTRAL AMERICAN.
† ARGENTINEAN, BOLIVIAN, CHILEAN, COLOMBIAN, ECUADORIAN, PARAGUAYAN, PERUVIAN, URUGUAYAN, VENEZUELAN, OTHER SOUTH AMERICAN.
‡ SPANIARD, SPANISH AMERICAN, ALL OTHER HISPANIC OR LATINO.[36]

amnesty program could potentially legalize an additional 3 million or more undocumented Mexicans. For this reason any discussion of growth in the Latino population necessarily focuses on the Mexican population and its historical role in the United States.

If it is to understand the current and future nature of the Latino population, the United States must admit that it has historically extended what amounts to a standing invitation to Mexicans to cross the border in order to provide the much needed cheap labor that fuels the growth and development of large portions of American agriculture and industry. The corollary to this standing invitation is the expectation that Mexicans will go home when the work has been completed. But of course this has turned out to be an illusion. Instead, their presence here as workers has been the principal engine for the growth of the Latino population in the United States.

THE ORIGINAL MEXICANS

In a very lengthy and illuminating article about Latinos, Gloria Sandrino-Glasser, a Latina scholar, states that the history of Mexican Americans is unlike that of any other minority group. She contends that Mexican Americans became a minority not by immigrating (like Europeans) or by being brought to this country involuntarily (like African Americans), but by conquest.[37] Well, not really by conquest because she does concede that the "conquest" simply set the stage for the large-scale immigration from Mexico in the early twentieth century.

The U.S. annexation of Texas and the land in the Southwest ceded to the United States by the Treaty of Guadalupe Hidalgo in 1848 created a contiguous border, which made Mexican immigration a fact of life from day one of the conquest. Mexicans continued to reside in the ceded territory—these were the original Mexican Americans, or Chicanos. But their numbers were small compared to the current Mexican American population. Today large numbers of Mexicans voluntarily immigrate here because life is better in the United States than it is in Mexico. That was true shortly after 1848 and it is true to this day. It is, indeed, this fact that drives Mexicans to risk, and occasionally lose, their lives crossing the desert and mountains to reach the United States.

Over the years Mexico's economic and political chaos has pushed millions of its citizens into crossing its border. Over the years U.S. business has welcomed these workers whether they are here legally or illegally. Over the years this immigrant stream has replenished the Mexican American stock in the United States. A failure to understand and accept these unique facts about Mexican Americans is a failure to understand how they came to constitute such large numbers in the

U.S. 2000 Census and why those numbers will continue to increase exponentially in the years to come.

According to Latin American specialist Arthur F. Corwin, when the Treaty of Guadalupe Hidalgo was signed in 1848, ceding the states of Texas, New Mexico, Arizona, and California and parts of Colorado, Nevada, and Utah to the United States, the total number of Hispanics in these territories numbered between 75,000 and 80,000.[38] Carey McWilliams in his work *North from Mexico* concurred with these numbers.[39] Matt Meier and Feliciano Rivera, in their book *Mexican Americans/American Mexicans*, also estimated the number to be approximately 80,000.[40] And even if we accept the more generous figure of 116,100, calculated by Oscar J. Martinez for 1850,[41] as the total number of Mexicans in these territories at the time of the annexation, this number still pales in comparison to the 20.6 million Mexicans and Mexican Americans counted in the 2000 Census.

The first significant Latino immigration occurred in California in 1849, not long after California was ceded to the United States and gold was discovered.[42] It is estimated that between 1849 and 1850 more than 20,000 Mexicans entered California from the Mexican states of Zacatecas and Sonora. During this two-year period more people left Mexico for the American Southwest than during the entire Spanish and early Mexican eras.

However, as a result of the virulent nativism and jingoism that characterized Anglo-Mexican relations in the Southwest, anti-immigrant feelings in the mining areas where Mexicans (and other Latin Americans) had converged soon drove the Mexicans out of northern California. In a pattern that would repeat itself again and again, not all of the immigrants returned to Mexico. Some took to working for American employers, while others moved to southern California, where they began to establish Mexican communities.

After 1850 Mexicans continued to cross the border into California, and at a later date, they began making their destination the mining areas of Nevada and southern Arizona. In the late 1860s Mexicans began to appear in the mining locals of Colorado. All the while, the distance between Mexico's heavily populated central plateau and the U.S. border was being reduced by the construction of the railway under the reign of Mexican president Porfirio Díaz. Mexicans could now hop a train and, without great sacrifice, traverse the great desert and mountain barriers that had previously prevented them from journeying to the American border.

The stabilization of Mexico's political condition brought about by Porfirio Díaz's powerful grip on Mexico's political landscape and the joint effort by Mexico and the United States that successfully tamed Indian, Mexican, and Anglo renegades along the border also contributed to the narrowing of the border between Mexico and the United States. As Mexicans arrived and pushed up against the American border in the state of Sonora they found it a simple matter to cross the nonexistent frontier to work in the mines, lumber mills, railway spurs, and ranches in southern Arizona.[43]

As the peons pooled into a ready workforce in the various border towns, they became a seasonal labor source that would later be funneled beyond the border states to the rest of the United States, carried to their new destinations by the U.S. railway system.

How many Mexicans crossed the border between 1848 and 1900? No one knows. Migration from Mexico to the United States and back again went unrecorded for many years. What can be established through U.S. Census records is that in 1900 almost three-quarters of the total recorded Mexico-born population in the United States lived in Texas. A total of 8086 Mexicans resided in California; 14,172 in Arizona; 6649 in New Mexico; 274 in Colorado; and 71,060 in Texas.[44]

Corwin believes that the census takers missed 235,000 to 245,000 or more Mexicans in their count. The addition of these numbers would increase the numbers up to a "more realistic total of perhaps 335,000 to 350,000 Hispano/Mexican (or Chicano) people in the United States around 1900."[45]

One of the most important events in early U.S. immigration policy was the replacement of Mexican immigrant labor with Chinese labor. In the early 1850s mine owners and railway companies in the western states began importing Chinese to serve as inexpensive and controllable labor.[46] By the 1860s California was already relying heavily on Asian labor for certain agricultural activities such as clearing land and cultivation. By this date there were approximately 45,000 Chinese in California, with 20,000 working the gold mines and the rest distributed between work on the transcontinental railroad and miscellaneous work in San Francisco.

However, beginning in 1860 Chinese labor expanded its activity and began to appear on California farms. Chinese labor grew at such speed that by 1870 about 90 percent of the farmwork was performed by Chinese. By 1882, 132,300 Chinese resided on the Pacific Coast, working as laborers in mining, agriculture, and certain urban jobs.

While the number for the entire Pacific Coast was not significant as a percentage of the total population, nevertheless public resistance to Asian labor developed. A recession in 1871 left thousands of Americans without jobs. Trade unions began a campaign to halt any further Chinese immigration, and anti-Chinese racism fueled this movement. Not only were the Chinese immigrants considered inferior, but their culture was viewed as a threat to the American way of life. Historian Marion T. Bennett describe this view as follows: "The public protested the low Chinese health standards, peculiar customs, dress, color, language, and the fact that they were 'heathens.' The Chinese were regarded as unassimilable."[47] It was this type of sentiment that forced the eventual passage of the Chinese Exclusion Act of 1882, which effectively terminated immigration from China.

American nativists, however, did not have the same reaction to Mexican immigrants. They did not regard the difference between Mexican culture and American culture with the same degree of distrust. Moreover, the Mexicans were a familiar fixture in the Southwest, having been in the area since the late 1500s.

In addition to Anglo familiarity with Mexicans, white farmers and ranchers also perceived Mexicans to be ideal workers. American business believed that, unlike Asian laborers, Mexicans were not far from their real home and would therefore return. The railway system that brought them from the central plateau of Mexico could also just as easily take them back. Because the United States was only a place to visit and make money, the Mexican worker was viewed as someone who would always return, like a homing pigeon, to spend the money he had earned.

Mexican immigrants were also viewed as lacking ambition—they were considered to be docile and tractable.[48] It was also believed that their genetic makeup and climate of origin made them particularly well suited to working in the hot climate found in the Southwest. In 1909 it was discovered that for several years prior, Mexicans had performed most of the labor in the construction of the railway system in southern California, Arizona, New Mexico, and Nevada.[49]

Mexican laborers were also frequently seen as the only group who would do work that was looked down upon by other laborers. The reason for this was that even though the wages paid by American farmers and ranchers were paltry and the working conditions dangerous, they were still superior to the wages and conditions that existed in Mexico.

> Rural wages in Mexico hovered around $.12 a day for those working on the great haciendas. Those unwilling or unable to work for that wage had little else available to them in their native land. In the United States, on the other hand, employers paid markedly higher wages to their unskilled workers. Grubbers who cleared land in south Texas earned $.50 a day; a miner could earn well over $2.00 daily; railroad workers were usually paid $1.00 to $2.00 a day.[50]

The construction of the railway system, Mexico's economic chaos, and its inability to right its listing ship were a perfect match with the economic development of the American Southwest. American business needed cheap labor, and the dire economic conditions in Mexico provided an unending source.

Even before irrigation-based agriculture in the Southwest spawned its unceasing demand for cheap Mexican labor, and before the U.S. railway industry absorbed Mexican immigrants by the score, Mexicans

had crossed the border in significant numbers during the spring planting for the labor-intensive task of planting crops.

The popular and historically accurate image of Chinese laborers
performing the arduous, and sometimes dangerous, task of laying railway lines for the transcontinental railroad tells only part of the story of
the railways.[51] During the late nineteenth century and early twentieth
century it was Mexican labor that built the Southern Pacific and Santa
Fe railroads. In 1908 approximately 16,000 Mexicans were recruited in
El Paso to work on the railroads. "Two years later as many as two thousand Mexicans crossed the border into El Paso in a single month at the
instigation of the commissary companies."[52]

The United States commissioner general of immigration described
the appeal of Mexican workers by noting that they

> [m]et an economic condition demanding laborers who could stand
> the heat and other discomforts of that particular section. The peon
> makes a satisfactory track hand, for the reasons that he is docile, ig-
> norant, and nonclannish to an extent which makes it possible that
> one or more men shall quit or be discharged and others remain at
> work; moreover, he is willing to work for a low wage.[53]

So important was Mexican labor during this period that "the economic development of the American Southwest coincided with the
northward drift of Mexico's population. Railroads, using Mexican and
other immigrant labor, integrated the Southwest into the nation's industrial economy."[54]

The use of Mexican labor for the development of the railway system
had a further and dramatic consequence: it carried Mexican workers
beyond the border to fill all manner of unskilled jobs in the interior
states. For example, Mexican laborers were scooped up by coals mines
in Oklahoma once the workers had finished laying the track in that
state. Ten thousand Mexican immigrants were employed in the mines
around Trinidad, Colorado.

Eager for cheap Mexican labor, American business was not content to wait until Mexicans crossed the border in search of work. In an environment devoid of state or federal oversight, American and Mexican business entrepreneurs each worked their own side of the border. The division of labor was as follows: The Mexican recruiter would "hook" (*enganchar*) the *campesino* on a particular job that awaited him in the United States, enticing him with the promise of good wages and good working conditions. Once the worker was hooked, he would join other workers and cross the border under the leadership of a crew boss, who would deliver them to the American recruiter. The Mexican agent would be paid a fixed fee per head.

The largest recruiting agencies were those that specialized in obtaining workers for the railroads. Most of these agencies were located in El Paso, Texas, one of the most significant points of entry for Mexicans seeking work. These agencies moved large volumes of Mexican workers and operated businesses of considerable volume and profitability. In 1907 and 1908, for example, six employment agencies in El Paso supplied American railroads with more than 2000 Mexicans per month.

Lax enforcement of immigration laws against Mexicans during the first decade of the twentieth century made crossing the border a simple matter. Historian George J. Sánchez quotes an immigration inspector who went under cover in late 1906 and crossed the border into Mexico. When he returned to the United States, the immigration officer "asked a man ahead of me in Spanish, *'¿De dónde viene usted?'* (Where do you come from?) He asked me the same question and I answered, *'Yo soy Mexicano'* (I am Mexican), and he passed on."[55]

This laissez-faire attitude of the U.S. Bureau of Immigration could not be justified by existing laws. While there was no quota on the number of Mexican immigrants, statutes prohibited immigration of individuals who were deemed to be engaged in contract labor. According to Sánchez, because American officials believed that Mexican labor was needed in the Southwest, they turned a blind eye to the stream of Mexicans crossing the border.

Although its staff numbered no more than 60 men, the Immigration Bureau was responsible for patrolling the entire 1900-mile border.[56] But the Immigration Bureau was more concerned with apprehending illegal Chinese and Europeans than with controlling the migration of Mexican laborers. The commissioner-general of immigration fully supported President Theodore Roosevelt's view that the Mexican border should be sealed to all aliens except Mexicans.[57]

Between 1900 and 1910 the United States did not track how many Mexicans entered the United States or returned to Mexico, so we must rely on educated guesses to assess the numbers. By one estimate, as many as 60,000 Mexicans were entering the United States each year by 1907; and in direct contradiction to the homing pigeon theory, between one quarter and one third stayed on permanently.[58]

In 1910 the U.S. Census counted 221,915 Mexican-born residents.[59] Add to this number 107,866 U.S.-born children of Mexicans and 54,334 children of mixed parentage—a Mexican parent and an American parent—for a total of 384,105.[60]

However, even these numbers are suspect. Cardoso writes:

> It is possible that more than 500,000 border crossings took place from 1900 to 1910. This estimate seems substantiated by the few public announcements of the time. In 1910 the Mexican Secretary of Development thought that over 50,000 of his countryman left yearly for the United States. Victor S. Clark, after his extensive tour of the border in 1908, believed that the number of emigrants totaled 60,000 a year; the United States Commissioner General of Immigration estimated the number at 50,000.[61]

More to the point, Cardoso concluded that the 1910 Census was just the tip of the iceberg because census takers were paid on a per diem basis and did not always perform a comprehensive survey of the areas assigned to them. Moreover, Mexicans were not identified as a separate group and thus were frequently classified as white.

The political upheaval that culminated in the Mexican revolution of 1910 further spurred immigration between 1910 and 1920, and crossing the border continued to be an easy matter. The Immigration

Bureau allowed thousands of Mexican immigrants to cross the border, firm in its belief that once peace returned to Mexico the immigrants would flock home. So willing was the United States to accept Mexican immigrants that it enlarged the definition of "refugee" to include "those suffering from 'industrial depression and its attendant evils' because of the horrendous economic conditions brought about by the fighting."[62] The Mexican revolution was a godsend for farmers in the Southwest because agriculture continued to expand rapidly, bringing with it an increased demand for Mexican labor.

The Immigration Act of February 5, 1917, presented the first barrier to the legal immigration of Mexican workers and represented one of the major immigration laws until 1952.[63] The 1917 act, which went into effect just two months before the United States entered World War I, created an extensive list of aliens who were excluded, including those who could not read at least one language. It also imposed an $8 head tax upon entry.

The 1917 act also had the unanticipated consequence of increasing illegal immigration. Many of the poor Mexicans streaming into the border towns, fleeing poverty and hunger, were not going to be deterred by the imposition of certain requirements. After all, for years their compatriots had been crossing the imaginary line without much hindrance at all.

U.S. entry into World War I greatly expanded the need for production of agricultural products; at the same time, military service and higher wages in wartime industries were taking workers off the land, thereby creating a labor shortage. The response of the Southwest ranchers and farmers was to recruit more Mexican workers. However, the new immigration restrictions posed formidable barriers to the desperately poor and largely illiterate *campesinos,* and many were turned away at the border. Additionally, rumors circulated that aliens who came to work in the United States were susceptible to the draft. This rumor was taken so seriously that it produced an exodus of Mexican laborers back to Mexico. The loss of Mexican labor not only worried the farmers, it also caused concern to the government.

In an attempt to stem the flow of Mexican laborers returning home, various government agencies and officials engaged in a publicity campaign which had as its sole aim convincing Mexican laborers that the United States had no intention of inducting them into the armed forces. At the same time, the farmers and ranchers launched an aggressive campaign to convince the government that a severe labor shortage existed and that the only way to cure the shortage was to lift all restrictions on Mexican labor. The response of the Labor Department was the creation of the first *bracero* program, whereby Mexican labor could be recruited under a government-devised and -sanctioned program in order to meet the labor needs of American farmers and ranchers.

This program was carried out under the guise of the ninth proviso of the 1917 Immigration Act, which stated: "The Commissioner of Immigration with approval of the Attorney General could exact bonds to control admission of those otherwise inadmissible aliens who apply for temporary admission." On May 23, 1917, in response to a request from the Commission of Immigration, the secretary of labor waived, by departmental order, the literacy test, the head tax, and the contract labor clause as they applied to the temporary admission of Mexican agricultural workers.

Even though the requirements were lifted, the number of Mexican workers admitted under the first *bracero* program was insufficient to meet American industry's insatiable desire for cheap Mexican labor. During the first year of the program, 9401 Mexicans were admitted. The Southwest growers argued that these numbers were completely insufficient and the only true way to solve the labor shortage was to have an "open border" and allow Mexican workers "free and unrestricted crossing." Other business concerns joined in this chorus.

On June 12, 1918, the secretary of labor issued a departmental order that extended the stay of Mexican workers to cover the "duration of the war," and also allowed them to work on the "railroad tracks and lignite coal mines, as well as in agriculture." On July 10, 1918, less than a month later, the secretary of labor issued a second order that expanded the areas where Mexicans could work to include various types of mining and construction work performed on government projects in Texas, Arizona, New Mexico, and California. It also assigned more immigration officers to the border in order to "facilitate the entry of Mexicans."[64]

On December 15, 1918, a month after the United States had signed the Armistice, Secretary of Labor Wilson issued orders ending the first *bracero* program. The order stated that no new admissions would be allowed after December 18, and that those workers who had already entered into a labor contract were required to "enter the United States by January 15, 1919."

Southwest agribusiness reacted quickly. Sugar beet companies complained that they had significantly increased their acreage at the express urging of the Food Administration, and therefore it was now improper for the Labor Department to cut off the supply of Mexican labor they now needed to manage the crops.

Legislators from some of the western states also immediately urged the secretary of labor to amend the termination order. The pressure from these politicians was effective, and on January 2, 1919, Wilson issued an order extending "the admission of Mexicans destined for the beet fields until June 30, 1919."

On January 23, 1919, Wilson issued a further order that expanded the admission of Mexicans destined for all types of farmwork in the Rio Grande Valley.

When June 30, 1919, came, the Southwest farmers once again flexed their muscle and the Labor Department allowed the temporary admissions program to continue until January 1, 1920. Like a recurring dream, when the January 1 deadline came, the growers once again set up a wail about the labor shortage, and once again the Labor Department caved to their demands.

During the approximately three years that it was in effect, the first *bracero* program admitted 72,862 workers; 34,922 returned to Mexico, 15,632 stayed in the United States, 414 died, 494 were permanently employed, and 21,400 went on a walkabout and no one knew where they were.[65]

Unfortunately, these figures were not very accurate. The Immigration Bureau readily admitted, and to some degree accepted the fact, that employers were not careful about reporting the location of their workers. As to the numbers for workers who had ostensibly returned to Mexico, not only were employers lax about reporting the departure of their Mexican workers but there was never any government personnel to enforce the regulation.[66]

Between 1900 and 1920 the Mexican and Mexican American population of the United States jumped from 103,393 to 761,342.[67] This count was plagued by some of the same errors that have plagued all census counts of people of Mexican descent in the United States. How many more Mexicans were in the United States and not counted? No one knows. But based on the problems encountered in the past, the number was no doubt greater.

The first *bracero* program came to a close with the end of the Wilson administration, and once again Mexican immigrants were subject to the regulations of the 1917 Immigration Act. However, this did not end the immigration north. There was still a demand for labor, so for many Mexican immigrants, crossing the border illegally now became the accepted way of entering the United States. The numbers gathered by the U.S. Immigration Bureau during the 1920s were certainly incomplete, since they represented only legal immigrants. As Secretary of Labor James J. Davis admitted, "It is difficult, in fact impossible, to measure the illegal influx of Mexicans over the border, but everyone agrees it is very large."[68]

The Quota Acts of 1921 and 1924, designed to restrict European labor, made Mexican workers even more sought after. However, the 1924 act also required that all immigrants had to obtain a visa from the American consulate in their country of origin as well as pay a $10 fee. The fee was in addition to the $8 head tax. Predictably, these restrictions barred many Mexicans from legally immigrating to the United States. Needless to say, these new barriers did not deter determined Mexicans from crossing the border. Some entered on their own, while others employed the services of smugglers—precursors to the modern-day *coyote*.

In 1924, Congress responded by creating a 450-man Border Patrol to guard the Mexican and Canadian borders. This had an almost immediate impact on immigration patterns. Previously, Mexican workers returned home at the end of the harvest, assured that they could return the following year without any great difficulty. The vigilance of the Border Patrol now made the return more problematic and affected the flow of workers.

The Border Patrol's enforcement of immigration laws almost immediately met with resistance from the farmers and growers who relied on the ready pool of Mexican workers. So when the Border Patrol began sporadic raids to round up and deport illegal aliens, American farmers and ranchers criticized these actions as unnecessary harassment of their workers. And like their predecessors during World War I, they launched a vigorous campaign to safeguard their labor source. They deluged Washington with letters complaining about the enforcement of immigration laws and arguing that their "perishable" crops would rot in the fields if their Mexican labor was curtailed. This argument would be used repeatedly in the future.

Mexico's continuing economic and political turmoil, rapid economic development in the Southwestern states and elsewhere, and the cutoff of cheap alien labor from Europe and Asia all kept the immigration spigot from Mexico open. An accurate counting of Mexican immigrants and their offspring continued to elude the U.S. Census. "Actually there was no way, then or now, for either (American and Mexican) government to keep track of surreptitious movements to and fro," wrote Corwin about counting the number of Mexicans in the United States during the period between 1911 and 1930.[69] By 1930, the Mexicans and their U.S.-born children were estimated to be close to 1.5 million.[70]

The census figures also start to paint a different demographic picture of this population: Mexican Americans began to outstrip Mexican-born immigrants. Between 1930 and 1940, Mexican immigration, greatly affected by the Depression, experienced a significant decline and only 22,319 Mexican immigrants were admitted to the United States in comparison to 459,287 between 1921 and 1930. In addition to this decline in legal immigration, the U.S. Mexican population was diminished by the repatriation of Mexicans to Mexico. The 1930s saw as many as 450,000 Mexicans repatriated to Mexico. While there is evidence that many expatriated Mexicans returned to the United States, the Depression and the return of Mexicans to Mexico negatively affected the growth of the Mexican population during the decade.[71]

After the United States entered World War II in 1941, two factors combined to create a severe shortage in farm labor. From April 1, 1940, to January 1, 1942, the military draft reduced the farm population by 280,000. And higher-paying jobs in the defense industry drew more workers away from the farms.[72]

In response to this labor shortage, farmers in California, Texas, and Arizona, as they had in the past, looked to Mexico for a solution. And while their formal request in 1941 to the Immigration and Naturalization Service to allow them to recruit Mexican workers was denied, the United States' entry into World War II a year later produced a changed attitude. On May 12, 1942, the United States Employment Service, the agency then charged with approving the importation of Mexican workers to the United States, recommended to the INS that 3,000 Mexicans be imported to assist in the harvesting of sugar beets in California.[73]

In the spring of 1942, an interagency group was formed to examine the need for farm labor. In June 1942, the interagency group issued a formal request for Mexican labor to the Mexican government, and on July 13, 1942, negotiations between the two countries began.

By July 23, 1942, the two countries had signed a formal agreement for the Labor Importation Program, more commonly known as the *Bracero* Program.[74] It was officially launched on September 30, 1942, when 500 workers arrived in Stockton, California. This program, which would last more than 22 years, would bring 5 million *braceros* into 24 states. It would also set the groundwork for the avalanche of illegal immigration that would follow when the program ended in 1964.

For the United States the truly attractive quality of the *bracero* program harkened back to the supposed "homing pigeon" instinct that was attributed to Mexican workers at the turn of the century. But now instead of having to rely on the voluntary return of the workers, the government institutionalized, and therefore guaranteed, the procedure. The President's Commission on Migratory Labor described these advantages as follows, "[Growers] want a labor supply which, on one hand, is ready and willing to meet the short-term work requirement and which, on the other hand, will not impose social and economic problems on them or on their community when the work is finished. . . . The demand for migratory workers is thus essentially twofold: To be ready to go to work when needed; to be gone when not needed."[75]

In addition to bringing Mexicans by the thousands to the United States, the *bracero* program developed a shadowy twin brother not anticipated by the federal authorities—illegal immigration. For example, in 1945 the program admitted 49,454 *braceros*,[76] but in that same year the INS apprehended 69,164 illegal aliens.[77] While it is not possible to state that all the illegal aliens were Mexicans, it would appear that most were.[78] The number of illegal aliens apprehended represents only a fraction of those who actually managed to cross the border, particularly given the lax enforcement and limited resources that the INS had during this period. And while the *bracero* program ostensibly ensured that the Mexican laborers would return home once their work was completed, such was not the case for the illegal aliens who entered during the same period.

On November 15, 1946, the State Department informed Mexico that it wanted to end the *bracero* agreement because it believed that Mexican laborers were no longer needed. However, Southwestern farmers, comfortable with their Mexican workers, continued to besiege government agencies and officials, and the program was allowed to continue through a series of extensions.

During the entire run of the *bracero* program various events conspired not only to increase illegal immigration but even in some instances to sanction it. For example, Mexico included a clause in one of the extensions that illegal immigrants already in the United States should be given preference over newly imported Mexicans for *bracero* status. The provision initially allowed for the legalization of workers already in the United States at the time the agreement was signed, but the deadline for legalization was repeatedly extended to include even the most recent arrivals.

The provision had unintended consequences. Word spread among Mexicans that a surefire way to get a *bracero* contract was to cross the border illegally. As a result, more than 74,600 *braceros* were contracted from Mexico between 1947 and 1949, but almost twice as many illegal workers—142,000—were legalized. Again, in 1950 fewer than 20,000 *braceros* were contracted, while 96,000 illegal aliens—more than three times the number of *braceros*—were legalized and contracted to local farmers.[79]

The *bracero* program also sparked illegal immigration when *braceros* returned to their towns and villages and spread the word of work in the United States. Because there were always more willing immigrants than there were contracts available, many Mexican workers, following the traditions of their antecedents, simply entered the United States illegally.[80]

By the 1960s public sentiment began to turn against the program. The atmosphere that produced the Civil Rights Act of 1965 and the War on Poverty looked askance at procuring labor from Mexico for American business. In 1960, advocates representing growers' interests introduced amendments in Congress to extend the program for two years. The proposal was rejected and the program was extended for only six months.

In 1961, Congress passed a bill barring the use of *braceros* on power-driven machinery and in canning and packing activities. It also confined them to temporary employment. The program was extended under these conditions for only two more years. On December 4, 1963, the program was given one more year of life, and in December 1964 it finally ended.

As the program began to wind down in the 1960s, the number of illegal aliens apprehended on the U.S.-Mexican border increased dramatically. Between 1965 and 1970 the number of illegal aliens apprehended climbed from 110,371 to 345,353.[81]

The growth of illegal immigration after the demise of the *bracero* program was clear evidence that, as Calavita writes, "The contract labor system had further entrenched the interdependence of southwest growers and Mexican labor, exacerbating in the long run the dilemma that in the short run it helped resolve."[82]

For 22 years the *bracero* program brought more than 5 million Mexican workers to the United States—5 million Mexicans who took home (those who did return) stories of the opportunities available in the north; 5 million Mexicans who fed the unceasing need of American farmers in the Southwest. Small wonder that Mexicans' desire to cross the border and U.S. business's desire for cheap labor did not end with the program. Every year between 1977 and 1986, apprehensions of illegal aliens hovered around 1 million or more.[83]

The increase in the number of illegal immigrants to the United States during the 1970s and early 1980s concerned both the general public and politicians and engendered a restrictionist attitude on the part of the American public. A May 1982 poll conducted by the Merit Survey found that 84 percent of the public was concerned about illegal immigration.[84] By the 1980s these concerns were finally addressed with the passage of the Immigration Reform and Control Act of 1986 (IRCA), signed into law by President Reagan on November 6, 1986.

IRCA, with its goal of preventing further illegal immigration, contained two principal provisions. The first category allowed residents who entered the United States illegally prior to January 1, 1982, and remained in the United States since entering, to be granted temporary residence, which could later be converted to permanent residence status. The second provision applied to two categories of seasonal agricultural workers (SAWs)—a provision that took into account the ever-present need of American agribusiness. Farmworkers who worked at least "90 man-days of qualifying agricultural employment days" for three years in a row for the period ending May 1, 1984, May 1, 1985, and May 1, 1986, could obtain temporary legal residence, which could later be converted to permanent residence more quickly than the second category described below. Farmworkers who had worked "90 man-days of qualifying agricultural employment days" in the 12-month period ending on May 1, 1986, could obtain temporary legal residence, which could later be converted to permanent residency.

The farmworker provision of IRCA was truly a godsend for many undocumented Mexicans. Consider that a farmworker who had worked a mere 90 days in 1986 could jump to the front of the immigration line and obtain legal residency. The long wait endured by applicants sponsored by a legal resident relative—sometimes as long as 10 years for Mexicans—left many to watch with envy as the beneficiaries of IRCA moved ahead of them.

The second significant provision of IRCA was that, for the first time in legislative history, sanctions were imposed on businesses that hired illegal aliens. The purpose of the sanctions was to eliminate the magnet effect that U.S. business had on Mexican workers by punishing these businesses that hired undocumented workers.

What was the result of IRCA? Approximately 3 million aliens applied for temporary residence: Of the 1.76 million people who applied under the pre-1982 provisions, 1.2 million were Mexican. Of the 1.27 million who applied under the SAW provision, 1 million were Mexican. Clearly, the overwhelming number of illegal aliens crossing into the United States were Mexican.[85]

And what effect did IRCA have on illegal immigration? Initially, it reduced the number of apprehensions along the U.S.-Mexican border, but soon the numbers began to climb, and by the early 1990s the numbers once again reached 1 million or more apprehensions a year.[86]

By contrast, between 1994 and 1998 the total number of legal Mexican immigrants remained somewhat stable, peaking in 1996 at 163,572 and dropping thereafter.[87]

Peter Brimelow contends that "The current wave of immigration—and therefore America's shifting ethnic balance—is wholly and entirely the result of government policy. Specifically, it is the result of the Immigration Act of 1965, and the further legislation of 1986 and 1990."[88] But it is patently clear that even without the Immigration Act of 1965, the

Mexican population in the United States would have grown (and will continue to grow) by astronomical numbers.

What can we expect for the future? If we believe a report issued by Mexico's National Population Council,[89] we can expect a steady stream of illegal immigration. The report projects that Mexican immigration to the United States will continue at between 3.5 million and 5 million per decade until at least 2030,[90] doubling the population of Mexican-born residents in the United States. Since the current legal immigration of Mexicans to the United States is approximately 175,000 annually, these figures suggest illegal immigration will be between 200,000 and 300,000 per year for the next 30 years.

This projected illegal immigration combined with the demand for cheap labor and the toothless nature of the enforcement provisions of IRCA will sustain the custom and practice that has long developed between Mexican labor and American business. It is certain that the growth of the Latino population—and particularly, but not exclusively, the Mexican population—demonstrated between 1990 and 2000 will continue during the next decade. The Latino tsunami that is crashing over the United States portends that in many cities in the Southwest— places to which they have traditionally immigrated—Latinos may well become the majority. And in those cities, particularly in the South and the Midwest, where their presence is new, they will bring a new dynamic to race relations between Blacks and whites and in the process, no doubt, create friction and change.

Somewhere over the Rainbow Coalition

The Zero-Sum Game and Black-Latino Conflict

> We believe that political relations are based on self-interest: benefits
> to be gained and losses to be avoided. For the most part, man's poli-
> tics is determined by his evaluation of material good and evil. Politics
> results from a conflict of interests, not of consciences.
>
> **STOKELY CARMICHAEL AND CHARLES V. HAMILTON**
> *Black Power, 1967*

> In our communities today, it is we, blacks and Chicanos, who suffer
> from social, economic, and educational problems across the board,
> simultaneously, at the same time, and always, always, always by
> the same system. We must, therefore, move forward together, or not
> at all.
>
> **DANIEL OSUNA**
> *Latino activist*

Osuna's declaration that Latinos and Blacks have parallel histories of suffering at the hands of white America, and that they also share a history of struggling to obtain social, economic, and educational opportunities, is one of the grounds on which a presumed alliance between Blacks and Latinos is based. Occasionally, this approach is nestled in feel-good statements that have as one of their goals the binding of the Latino and Black psyches. "In the final analysis, to challenge the established order effectively and create a just and good society requires a cooperative effort by all progressive forces in the country. The factor of critical importance, then, is not the large numbers of a single group but the *cooperative engagement* of all progressive people in the struggle, and a collaborative concept in the context of maximum human flourishing" reads one such statement.[1]

In the academic world, Osuna's perspective is sometimes termed the "shared interest" perspective. In the lay world it is the cornerstone for the concept of the Rainbow Coalition popularized by the Reverend Jesse Jackson in his 1984 and 1988 presidential runs. Unfortunately, this squinty-eyed view of Black-Latino relations does not square with what has happened in the real world.

As Artellia Burch discovered in her foray into the collective consciousness of Charlotte's Black population, competition over jobs and housing has led to conflict between Blacks and Latinos. And Burch's anecdotal reporting has been confirmed by academic research, which has found, not surprisingly, that this conflict extends to the educational and political arenas.[2]

If the shared-interest theory of coalition formation was based on sound reasoning, then the existence of conflict between Latinos and Blacks should not exist, or if it exists, it should be rare and thus the exception. There is a better explanation for the persistent conflict that exists between Latinos and Blacks, and that explanation is provided by the Carmichael-Hamilton theory of coalitions.

Carmichael and Hamilton are a voice from a distant past where political correctness was less a consideration than assessing political reality. Carmichael, born in Port of Spain, Trinidad, moved to the United States in 1952. After attending high school in New York City, he entered Howard University in 1960, where he joined the Student Non-Violent Coordinating Committee (SNCC). In 1961 he became a member of the Freedom Riders, men and women who traveled to the deep South to test the 1960 Supreme Court ruling that outlawed segregation in all interstate public facilities. Because local police were unwilling to protect these protesters, they were attacked by white mobs in several locations. In Jackson, Mississippi, Carmichael was arrested and spent seven weeks in jail. After college, Carmichael returned to the South, where he focused his energies on SNCC's Black voter registration project in Lowndes County, Alabama. There he founded the Lowndes County Freedom Organization, an independent political party that used a black panther as its symbol.

In 1966 Carmichael became chairman of SNCC, and in August of that year he made a speech that ended with a call for "Black Power," a phrase that catapulted him into the national spotlight. Black Power emphasized independent political and economic development by Blacks as a necessary element of social change. In 1967, Carmichael collaborated with political scientist Charles Hamilton to write the book *Black Power*,[3] which elaborated Carmichael's theory on the meaning and intent of Black Power.

In that groundbreaking work, Carmichael and Hamilton described four conditions that had to be met before a coalition could be formed.

1. Parties entering into a coalition have to recognize their respective self-interests. Whether Blacks were forming coalitions with Asians, whites, or Latinos, it had to be understood that each group came to the table with different interests that are unique to its own group.
2. Each party must believe that it will benefit from a cooperative relationship with the other parties. What would be the use of joining forces with other groups if there is nothing to be gained from such unions?
3. Each party must have its own power base and have control over its own decision-making process. The decisions made by the group, therefore, are aimed at benefiting that group.
4. Each party must recognize that the coalition is formed with specific and identifiable goals in mind. Coalitions, therefore, are purposeful and can be either short-lived or long term, but they are not formed to achieve some vague goal.

The genius of the Carmichael-Hamilton paradigm is that it not only contains the elements necessary for the formation of a coalition but also indirectly provides the basis from which conflict between political groups emanates. Take, for example, the first two elements: that groups must recognize their own self-interest and believe that they will benefit by cooperating with each other. Time and again, when Blacks and Latinos come together, the result is more frequently competition (conflict) than cooperation.

Yzaguirre and Kamasaki found this to be true when they pushed for repeal of the employer sanctions in the Immigration Reform and Control Act of 1986. African Americans argued that undocumented immigrants would replace them at certain unskilled jobs without such sanctions. Therefore, arguably, it was in the self-interest of Blacks to support the employer sanctions provision under IRCA. The fact that illegal immigration has increased since the passage of IRCA, and employers have continued to hire undocumented immigrants, shows that the original position taken by Blacks—supporting sanctions—was closer to their self-interest.

While there are numerous other examples of how the Carmichael-Hamilton paradigm explains Black-Latino conflict, the case of municipal employment in Los Angeles demonstrates how the Rainbow Coalition model fails when the interests of Blacks are threatened by Latinos. Paula D. McClain, a scholar who has studied this phenomenon, poses the question: "Does the presence of one minority group affect the other minority group? Are municipal employment outcomes complementary, or do the successes of one minority come at the expense of the other?"[4] McClain's research found that the most significant factor in determining Black and Latino municipal employment was the size of the Black workforce. "The most significant predictor of limits to Hispanic municipal employment opportunities is the Black percentage of the work force. As the black share increases, Hispanic opportunities decline"[5] McClain, however, did not find that the converse was true: an increased Latino workforce does not appear have the same impact on municipal employment opportunities for Blacks. "Furthermore, in a small sample in which blacks are a plurality or majority, Hispanics seem to fare less well in municipal employment outcomes, while in cities in which Hispanics are a plurality or majority, the consequence to black municipal employment is not consistent."[6] What does this scholarly language mean? Simply, that an increase in the size of the Black workforce effectively prevents Latinos from obtaining proportionate representations in municipal employment, while an increase in the Latino population does not have the same effect on Blacks. In terms of the larger picture it means that as the Latino population grows, the potential for interethnic conflict increases.

McClain's conclusions, while astute and empirically correct, provide no clear insight as to why the existence of a large Black population bodes ill for municipal employment of Latinos, leaving the reader to conclude that this situation appears to come about organically without any proactive efforts on the part of Blacks other than simply competing with Latinos for the limited number of jobs available. This, of course, is not true and the historical competition between Latinos and Blacks for public sector jobs in Los Angeles County and the city of Los Angeles provides case studies of how Blacks have dominated the public employment sector and kept Latinos at bay.

Municipal employment in Los Angeles County and in the city of Los Angeles also demonstrates that Black dominance of this employment sector is predicated on a conviction that because of their civil rights struggle, only African Americans are deserving of these positions and that, once ensconced in these positions, they are unwilling to yield them to Latinos even when Latinos are underrepresented and Blacks are overrepresented. Ironically, the conflict that McClain predicted would happen sometime in the future was already raging in the Los Angeles area at the time that she published her article.

Between 1940 and 1990 Los Angeles County grew from 2.8 million to 8.9 million residents. The county's Black population grew most dramatically after World War II as a result of massive migration created by opportunities in the war industries. However, after the 1960s the Black population began to decrease relative to the total population as the Latino population grew dramatically. By 1990 the Black population of Los Angeles County stood at 931,449 while the Latino population had grown to 3,359,526.

TABLE 2

Los Angeles County Population:
White, Black, Hispanic, Asian-Other: 1940–1990

GROUP	1940	1950	1960	1970	1980	1990
White	2,620,450	3,796,190	4,897,580	4,798,872	3,977,480	3,647,555
Black	75,206	214,897	459,806	755,719	924,774	931,449
Hispanic	61,248	249,173	582,309	1,288,716	2,071,530	3,359,526
Asian-Other	52,911	57,582	123,638	201,704	436,241	963,642
Total	2,809,946	4,317,984	6,063,364	7,041,362	7,510,424	8,902,172

SOURCE: PHILIP J. ETHINGTON, SEGREGATED DIVERSITY: RACE-ETHNICITY, SPACE, AND POLITICAL FRAGMENTATION IN LOS ANGELES COUNTY, 1940–1994 (LOS ANGELES: UNIVERSITY OF SOUTHERN CALIFORNIA, 2000), P. 7, ADAPTED FROM CHART 2.2.

The Civil Rights Act of 1964 established that persons who suffer discrimination based on gender and ethnicity, in addition to race, are entitled to "affirmative action and equal employment policies and programs."[7] In California employers were bound not only by the 1964 Civil Rights Act but also by the additional legislative protections afforded under the Fair Employment and Housing Act of 1959 and Section 1135 of the California Civil Code, which prohibits discrimination against persons in California on the basis of ethnic group identification, religion, age, and sex. This applied to programs or activities conducted by the state or by any state agency, and funded directly by the state or receiving financial assistance from the state.

In 1972 the long arm of Civil Rights Act extended its reach to impose the requirements of equal employment and affirmative action in municipal entities. Municipalities were required to establish affirmative action programs to ensure that there was equal minority representation based on measurable objective standards.[8] However, even before 1972, Los Angeles County, in 1969, and the city of Los Angeles, in 1971, had already created equal-employment offices and adopted these equal-employment requirements into various of their local ordinances for all of those groups who fell under the protection of the Civil Rights Act. Latinos, because they constituted an ethnic and national-origin minority, fell under the protective umbrella of the act, and their inclusion was unquestionable.

> In 1970 a federal district court defined Mexican-Americans as "an identifiable ethnic minority." Three years later, the U.S. Supreme Court describing the problems of Mexican-American students in Denver, stated that blacks and Hispanos [Hispanics-Latinos] suffered identical patterns of discrimination ... the courts finally concluded that ethnic minorities as well as racial minorities could and did suffer discrimination.[9]

Los Angeles County chose to develop its respective affirmative employment programs based on parity with population representation. In other words, the goal was to have a municipal workforce that reflected the population distribution of minorities and women in the county.[10]

In 1990, the public sector labor force in Los Angeles County and the largest cities within its geographic penumbra totaled 262,350 and represented 5.9 percent of the county's entire civilian labor force. The county employed 85,000 people; it was also the single largest employer of women and minorities. And the city of Los Angeles alone had 45,000 employees.[11]

In 1970 Blacks constituted only 10.9 percent of the total population of Los Angeles County but 25.4 percent of its public sector workforce. By 1990 the Black population had dropped to 10.5 percent of the total, but it now constituted 29.8 percent of civil service.[12] In contrast, in 1970

Latinos represented 18.3 percent of the total population but only 6 percent of the county workforce. In 1990, the Latino population jumped to 37.8 percent yet its representation on the county workforce only increased to 21.4 percent.[13] In 1994, a report to the county board of supervisors stated: "African-Americans were overrepresented in thirty-three of the thirty-four county departments with the lowest level being 47.1%. . . . Hispanics were underrepresented in all thirty-four departments using either population parity or civilian force parity."[14]

In the city of Los Angeles, Jerry Yaffe, a sociologist who has written extensively on the overrepresentation of Blacks in Los Angeles County and the city of Los Angeles, pointed out that "in the City's government workforce, African American employees in 1973 were overrepresented at 21.9 percent. They remain overrepresented since that time, and in 1991 they occupied 22.4 percent of the city's workforce positions. Latinos in 1973 accounted for only 9.3 percent of the city's workforce and continued to be underrepresented through 1991 at 19.9 percent of LAC government positions. . . ."[15]

Yaffe, based on his research on the disparity between African American and Latino employment in both LACO and the city of Los Angeles, concluded that if an alliance in promoting minority employment did exist, such an alliance existed between Blacks and whites. Yaffe writes, "Decades of institutional and social traditions and beliefs served to create an almost collusive (though unofficial) alliance among whites and non-Hispanics regarding the lack of educational achievement and qualification of Hispanics. These fabrications provided the justifications and ambient factors for ignoring (and maintaining) the historic underrepresentation of Hispanics in local government employment."[16]

Yaffe also pointed out that Black employees aggressively worked against the enforcement of equal employment for Latinos in Los Angeles County. Yaffe noted that Blacks had openly advocated against inclusion of Latinos in the local government's implementation of federal, state, and county legal equal-employment requirements. It appeared that Blacks viewed municipal employment as their domain and one that they protected vigorously and aggressively.[17]

And what was the response of Latinos to this situation? Protests, of course. The Los Angeles County Chicano Employees Association (LACCEA) was involved in more than 20,000 cases of alleged discrimination against Latinos by various county departments—and prevailed in over 90 percent of them. And by the late 1980s Latinos were registering numerous complaints with the county Affirmative Action Office alleging discriminatory hiring practices. LACCEA claimed that for the preceding 20 years, the county had failed to bring representative numbers of Latinos into the workforce. At that time Latinos represented 18 percent of the workforce but 27.6 percent of the total population.[18]

In October 1987, these complaints prompted the federal Equal Employment Opportunity Commission (EEOC) to launch an investigation of county hiring practices. Of particular concern to the EEOC were the goings-on at the Los Angeles County–USC Medical Center where Latinos made up 18 percent of the employees whereas the patient load approached 60 percent.[19] Latinos were also upset with the hiring policies at Martin Luther King Jr. Hospital/Charles Drew Medical Center, where over one-third of the patients were Latino, but only 9 percent of the workers.

The LACCEA continued to register complaints with the county, and in February 1988, a study conducted by the L.A. County Office of Affirmative Action Compliance (OAAC) concluded that Latinos were "considerably under-represented."[20] The *Los Angeles Times* reported that "According to the statistics, the number of Latinos increased from 8,221 employees, or 13 percent of the county workforce in 1977, to 11,989, or 18.3 percent, a decade later. But the rising percentage for Latinos remains below the 27.6 percent 'parity' figure that is the county's hiring goal. The parity figure is derived from the county population figure for Latinos in the 1980 Census." The same article reported that "By comparison, blacks, Asians and Filipinos have already exceeded their parity figures."[21]

Latinos not only charged L.A. county with failing to provide the required affirmative action opportunities to Latinos that were clearly afforded to other minority groups, based on parity figures, but the

Chicano Employees Association charged that Blacks were overrepresented on the county employee rolls. LACCEA charged that "The black community gained these employment figures by the pressure put on the county by black political and organizational leaders. The black community had its members appointed and promoted to key positions in personnel, human resources and affirmative action." [22] If this statement is to be believed, then Blacks had specifically pressured white administrators to maintain their numbers while preventing an increase in Latino employment in spite of Latinos' numerical growth.

The struggle over equal representation revealed the raw nature of conflict between Latinos and Blacks over access to a finite number of public sector jobs. Clyde Johnson, president of the Black Employees Association (BEA), bluntly stated, "We're talking about a potential confrontation between Hispanics and blacks in the county workforce." A Latino consultant responded that "Latino issues were put on the back burners in the county, and no one saw the Latino community as a political threat. . . . Now you're seeing and will see more legal and political pressure against the county." [23]

Latinos had reason to be concerned. According to the *Los Angeles Times*, "[B]ased on the 1980 census, the number of Latino workers in the county is 18.3 percent or 11,989 employees. By comparison, while blacks are 12.6 percent of the county population, they represent 30.5 percent, or 19,947 employees, of the county government workforce." [24]

The rhetoric became so heated between Latinos and Blacks that the county board of supervisors delayed adopting the OAAC report in order to provide a cooling-off period for the two groups. By now Latinos were hailing the report as clear and convincing evidence of the county's failure to hire Latinos in proportion to their population figures—and damning evidence that it devoted more effort to hiring Blacks.

Blacks challenged the report by arguing that the affirmative action goals were falsely based on the 1980 Census figures, which counted *all* Latinos, including undocumented, necessarily creating an inflated number of Latinos eligible to work in the public sector. Undocumented aliens could not apply, and therefore their inclusion in the baseline population was unrealistic, they argued.

Blacks had further criticisms of the report. Clyde Johnson believed that the report should be discarded in its entirety and another study conducted by an outside entity. He further proposed a change in the rules, arguing that the county's affirmative action goals should be based on a minority's numerical representation in the *workforce* rather than on total population figures.[25] This had been a consistent position taken by Black leaders. As early as 1988, the BEA wrote a letter to the county board of supervisors that criticized the county's use of raw population figures for parity and argued that the basis for parity be changed. The rationale on the part of the BEA was clear: If Los Angeles County could be convinced to use civilian labor force numbers instead of raw population numbers, then the number of employable Latinos would necessarily drop because undocumented immigrants and individuals who did not meet the educational qualifications would be eliminated.

But in the summer of 1988, the board of supervisors unanimously voted to adopt the OAAC report and instructed its affirmative action officers to develop a plan to correct the lack of Latino parity in the county's workforce. In words that were all too reminiscent of white opposition to Black affirmative action, Mamie Grant, a Black leader, stated, "We support affirmative action but we do not support preferential treatment."[26]

In 1989 the EEOC concluded its three-year investigation stemming from complaints of Latino employees and charged that the county medical centers had failed to hire and promote Latinos on a basis equal to other ethnic or racial groups. As examples of this disparity, the report found that Latinos accounted for a minute 4 percent of the managerial staff at King Medical Center, whereas Blacks represented an astonishing 74 percent; Latinos represented only 12 percent of clerical workers at King, whereas Blacks represented 82 percent; Latinos represented 14 percent of registered nurses but held only 4 percent of nursing supervisor positions, whereas Blacks represented 20 percent of the nurses but held 29 percent of the supervisor positions. The report concluded that "the under-representation of Hispanics at (King Medical

Center) does not occur by chance.... Absent any other explanations, respondent would be expected to employ Hispanics and blacks in numbers that more or less approximate their availability in the relevant labor market." [27]

The conflict between Latinos and Blacks in Los Angeles County escalated almost on a weekly basis, so it should not have been a surprise that in the fall of 1990, Debrya J. Moore, a Black county employee, filed a complaint against the Latino affirmative action compliance officer Robert Arias, alleging he discriminated against her because she was Black. For good measure she further alleged that Arias was "in the business of fostering racial divisiveness and animosity between [the] two groups." [28] Moore's complaint alleged that Arias deliberately excluded her from "sensitive investigations," including an investigation of one of the complaints that led to the EEOC complaint. Arias denied the charges, a denial that was supported by a private attorney representing the county who also denied that there was any effort to keep Blacks from participating in the investigation.

The Black-Latino clash over parity spilled over to the county board of supervisors when Latino state senator Art Torres, in a rare intervention in county matters, said, "Discrimination occurs as a matter of rule rather than exception" when it came to hiring Latinos in Los Angeles County.[29] Torres recommended to supervisors that the county hire an independent monitor because the county's affirmative action office had not done its job. Despite the EEOC report and the glaring underrepresentation of Latinos on the workforce, Torres was nevertheless challenged by two supervisors, Peter Scharbarum and Mike Antonovich. Scharbarum claimed that no Latino had ever brought a complaint of discrimination to his attention, and Antonovich accused Torres of instituting "quotas."

The numbers, however, were hard to ignore. Since the passage of the 1964 Civil Rights Act Latinos had consistently been underrepresented in the county's workforce, and Blacks had been overrepresented. As an example, in 1965 Latinos were underrepresented by 5.6 percent but by 1990 the underrepresentation had jumped to an amazing 16.4 percent.[30] In contrast to the Latino underrepresentation in the county workforce Blacks were overrepresented in 1990 in the full-time workforce as well as in management positions.[31]

By March 1992, the county board of supervisors entered into a settlement of the EEOC claims. However, Gloria Molina, the only Latino member of the board of supervisors, objected to the settlement—and even went so far as to boycott the closed-door meeting where the settlement was reached—because under the agreement Latinos were to be hired and promoted in numbers that reflected the percentage of job applicants that they represented. As the *Los Angeles Times* reported, "If a third of the qualified applicants are Latino, a third of the hires must be Latino."[32] Latino leaders saw this as a deadly compromise. Raul Nunez, president of the Chicano Employees Association, called the settlement a "sellout" because it did not adopt the principal on which the county's affirmative action plan had been created—parity based on the raw ethnic population figures. Nor did it establish specific hiring goals for Latinos, making it possible for the county to drag its feet in raising the number of Latino employees. Jerry Yaffe, a longtime observer and commentator on the Black-Latino conflict, wrote about the plan:

> The plan is to change from population parity to civilian labor force representation, and for management levels, to occupational availability. However, these changes of direction in the middle of the stream will only serve to do the following: (1) avoid correcting of Hispanic underrepresentation, (2) minimize confrontations from other racial and ethnic groups, and (3) assure that the non-Hispanic work force retains positions of power and control.[33]

In commenting on the settlement, Clyde Johnson acknowledged that historically King Medical Center had almost exclusively hired Black employees largely because the neighborhood in which King was situated serviced a Black population. However, in recent years Latinos had begun to flood the area, and while he had no objection to hiring Latinos to service this new minority population, he did not want to do so at the expense of Black employees.[34] Just how the number of Latinos would be increased without reducing the number of Black employees was never addressed by Johnson or any other Black leaders. It was not addressed for good reason; there was no apparent answer other than to reduce the number of Black employees.

In February 1995, the Chicano Employees Association filed suit in state court, challenging the implementation of new affirmative action guidelines, which, the group contended, negatively affected Latino workers. The new guidelines replaced the raw population parity formula with one in which county labor force statistics would be the standard to measure progress in hiring and "county government employee statistics would be analyzed to measure progress in promotions."[35] Various Latino groups objected to the guidelines, which, they argued effectively, froze in place the existing racial overrepresentation of Blacks.

This problem continued to plague county health services. In early 1996, the L.A. County Civil Service Commission reported clear evidence that King Medical Center discriminated against non-Blacks.[36] And a year later the newly appointed director of the hospital was confronted with the undeniable fact that four years after the EEOC settlement, the number of Latino employees was still embarrassingly low. County documents produced in 1995 showed that Latinos were still underrepresented and Blacks significantly overrepresented in the hospital's workforce of approximately 21,000.[37]

The stonewalling by Black leaders in L.A. County provides a clear example of McClain's observation that a significant Black population has a negative impact on the hiring of Latinos in the municipal workforce. It is also an example of "Lester Thurow's 'zero sum' politics, where one group benefits or loses out—or perceives this to be the case—on the basis of the fortunes of other groups."[38]

Osuna's belief that Latinos and Blacks must move forward together or not at all crumbles in the face of harsh economic reality. The competition between Latinos and Blacks in Los Angeles County is but one of many examples of how zero-sum conflict trumps any idealized notion of Latino-Black cooperation.

Who's the Leader of the Civil Rights Band?

Latinos' Role in *Brown v. Board of Education*

> The fruits of the African American battle for civil rights are positions of power held by African Americans in the public and private sectors. And now we find ourselves in the position of defending that power against other people pushing for inclusion. Though we pride ourselves on our leadership role in civil rights, paradoxically, we guard the success jealously. "We're the ones who marched in the streets and got our heads busted. Where were they? But now they want to get in on the benefits."
>
> **BRENDA PAYTON**
> *Columnist for the* Oakland Tribune

There is a Black perception that Latinos have not suffered discrimination to the same degree and in the same manner as they and are thus are not entitled to the benefits of the civil rights movements. African Americans often assume that they were the pioneers in the area of civil rights. The actions of Martin Luther King, Roy Innis, and myriad other Black leaders would tend to confirm this belief. In addition to these inspirational leaders of the civil rights movement, Blacks reference the NAACP, the Congress of Racial Equality, and the Southern Christian Leadership Conference as leading examples of organizations that pushed for civil rights in the 1960s.

More specifically, African Americans point to their role in the passage of the Voting Rights Act of 1965 and the benchmark case of *Brown v. Board of Education* as demonstration of their leadership in the area of civil rights. While it is true that the historical deprivation of Black suffrage in the South was the impetus for passage of the Voting Rights Act of 1965, Latino civil rights litigation presaged the *Brown* decision by some eight years. Unfortunately, ignorance of Latino activism around this issue has led one scholar to conclude that the role of Latinos has been reduced to little more than a sidebar.[1]

The discrimination suffered by Mexican Americans in California and Texas and their response in the form of pioneering litigation gives Latinos a legitimate claim to being pioneers in the area of civil rights, as *Mendez v. Westminster* and *Delgado v. Bastrop Independent School District* make clear.

CALIFORNIA: *MENDEZ V. WESTMINSTER*

The insatiable appetite for cheap Mexican labor in the Southwest did not come without social consequences. In the beginning most Mexican workers were single men who came to the United States with the goal of earning money and sending it back to Mexico. But later immigrant male workers arrived with their families. Inevitably, this had an impact on social service agencies and the education system as well. The impact was two-way. Historian George J. Sánchez writes: "In the 1930s, three institutions most clearly framed the experience of Mexican American adolescents and young adults in Los Angeles: the family, the school, and the workplace."[2] Mexican Americans, Sánchez argues, had accepted that education was the path to success in American society. In 1938 the Mexican American Movement (MAM), an organization comprised of second-generation Mexican Americans, published a piece in its newspaper, the *Mexican Voice*, that stressed the significance of remaining in school. "Education is the only tool which will raise our influence, command the respect of the rich class, and enable us to mingle in their social, political and religious life. . . . EDUCATION is our only weapon."[3]

But education facilities for Mexican American students were not only separate but also unequal—this was the harsh reality. The creation of separate schools for Mexican American children existed throughout southern California. In 1913, Pasadena established a Mexican school. In 1921, the city of Ontario built its own Mexican school, and by 1928, the school was so overenrolled that another "Mexican" school had to be built. In 1924, Riverside built another "Mexican" school to accommodate the wishes of white parents to separate their children from Latino children.[4]

As the number of Mexican children who enrolled in school continued to increase, so did the degree of segregation. By 1927 over 65,000 Mexican American children were enrolled in California schools, and 88 percent were located in southern California with 50 percent concentrated in Los Angeles County. A study conducted in 1926 found that 80 percent of the Mexican American children were enrolled in 3 of the 14 elementary schools in East L.A. and 3 others had an enrollment of approximately 60 percent. The numbers had increased by 1939: each of the 6 schools enrolled more than 80 percent of their students from the Mexican American community. A survey conducted in 1931 discovered that 80 percent of school districts with significant Mexican student enrollment were segregated.[5]

The creation of separate schools for Latino children was not based on any statute or legal ruling. Up to 1947 California provided for the establishment of separate schools, but they were reserved for children of Native American, Chinese, Japanese, and Mongolian descent. Curiously, the statute did not mention Blacks or Mexicans. But even without a statutory basis, the school districts accomplished their goal of de facto segregation by two methods. The first was to gerrymander the school district. Gerrymandering was accomplished by arbitrarily creating school zone boundaries designed to include Mexicans only within those boundaries, thus assuring that the school that fell within that zone became a Mexican school. An example of how this gerrymandering was accomplished is reflected in a letter written by a "supervisory official" of the city of Los Angeles in 1933.

> Our educational theory does not make any racial distinction between the Mexican and native white population. However, pressure from white residents of certain sections forced a modification of this principle to the extent that certain neighborhood schools have been placed to absorb the majority of the Mexican pupils in the district.[6]

Such gerrymandering was not only the result of protest by white parents but also fit nicely into the pedagogy of the time. The segregation of Mexican American children was justified on several grounds, one being that they were naturally happier with their own kind. One educator described Mexican American students who sat in the same classroom as white students as "dull, stupid and phlegmatic." She contrasted this with the atmosphere in an all–Mexican American classroom, where the faces of the children "radiated joy, they had thrown off the repression that held them down when they were in school with other children."[7]

Another argument used by educators for segregated schools was the need to Americanize Mexican children. This push to assimilate the Mexican children could best be accomplished, educators argued, by segregating the students so that the special "assimilation" training that Mexican students needed would not hinder the white students' educational progress.[8]

An additional, and to many educators persuasive, argument for segregating Mexican children in separate classrooms or separate schools was the use and acceptance of standardized intelligence tests which ostensibly established that Mexican children were duller and slower than white students. The literature on the education of the Mexican-American in the early part of the 20th century emphasized their sub-normal intelligence. Study after "scientific" study established that Mexican children simply were not as intelligent as white students.

In 1931 B. F. Haught conducted a study that concluded that the "average Spanish child has an intelligence quotient of .79 compared with 1.00 for the average Anglo child." O. K. Garretson concluded that "retardation of the Mexican child . . . is from three to eight times as great as that of the American child. . . ."[9] Leo M. Gamble conducted a study on Mexican-American children and found that "the average intelligence quotient for the Mexican was 78.75."[10] William Sheldon of the University of Texas administered the Cole-Vincent and Stanford-Binet tests to Mexican and American students in Texas. His results "scientifically" established that Mexicans had only 85 percent of the I.Q. of the white students. Thomas Garth, a professor at the University of Denver, administered the National Intelligence Test to more than 1,000 Mexican and Mexican-American students in Texas, New Mexico and Colorado and discovered that the median I.Q. was 78.1.[11]

This group was joined by numerous other scholars—Helen L. Koch, Rietta Simmons, Kimball Young, Ellen A. McAnulty, F. C. Paschal, C. R. Sullivan, and Florence L. Goodenough—in concluding that the intelligence of Mexican children was inferior to that of American children.

By the late 1920s and early 1930s the segregation of Mexican and Mexican American children was a fact of life. As Charles M. Wollenberg, a scholar who has examined the segregation of Mexican children in California schools, observed, "In Orange County . . . over 4,000 students, a quarter of total school enrollment, were Mexicans or Mexican-Americans in 1934. About 70 percent of the Spanish-surnamed total attended the fifteen Orange County elementary schools which had 100 percent Mexican enrollment."[12] It is this background of de facto segregation of Mexican children in Orange County that led to the groundbreaking case of *Mendez v. Westminster*—a case that helped lay the groundwork for the ruling in *Brown v. Board of Education* eight years later.

THE SOCIAL CONTEXT OF
MENDEZ V. WESTMINSTER

Orange County's economy in the early 1930s and 1940s was almost exclusively based on agriculture. Crops such as oranges, lemons, nuts, beans, and vegetables dominated the region's industry. And like the rest of Southwest agriculture, the preferred labor for these crops was Mexicans. Over time the Mexican population, instead of remaining migratory, established permanent residency in various cities in Orange County. Gonzalez notes that in 1930, 17,000 Mexicans resided in these towns and cities.[13]

The Mexican population made an impact on the educational system as early as 1913 when a report revealed that school administrators had set aside a special room for "Spanish" children at one of the elementary schools. In time the number of Mexican children flowing into the school district forced the construction of a separate school building. Accompanying the physical segregation of Mexican children from white children was the creation of a separate curriculum for Mexican children. The school district emphasized manual training for the Mexican children, while it maintained academic preparation for white students.

In 1916, the Committee on Buildings recommended that a six-room building be constructed near the existing Fifth Street building, and that a separate two-room building be constructed to be used exclusively by Mexican children. Not only was there to be a separate physical facility for the Mexicans, and a different curriculum, but different criteria were used for selecting teachers assigned to the Mexican school and those assigned to the Anglo school. Responding to this resolution, the school board instructed the president to obtain bids for the construction of the building where all Mexican children would attend.

The proposed construction of the separate facility for Mexican children was criticized by both white and Mexican parents. The white parents did not believe that the construction was moving quickly enough, while the Mexicans demanded that it not proceed at all. In

1918, the all-Anglo Lincoln School PTA passed a resolution urging the school board to do something about the Mexican problem and advised that "segregation is eminently desirable from moral, physical and education standpoints." For its part, the Mexican community objected to the construction of the Mexican school. Pro Patria Club, a Mexican organization, objected strongly to the segregation of Mexican children and demanded they be returned to their respective schools.

Confronted with the two opposing parties, the superintendent of schools asked the city attorney to issue a legal opinion addressing the legal basis on which segregation of Mexican children could be justified. The city attorney conceded that the existing education statute did not provide for any basis for the creation of segregated schools for Mexican children. However, his opinion justified the creation of separate educational facilities for Mexicans based on language differences, age, and regularity of attendance. Based on this incorrect interpretation of the statute, the Santa Ana Board of Education passed a resolution that read, in part, "agreed that for the best interest of the Schools and especially for the great benefit to the Mexican children, to continue the Mexican school work at the present." [14] In other words, the school facilities would continue to be segregated.

Armed with what they believed was legal justification for segregating Mexican children, the Santa Ana Board of Education subsequently identified three schools as Mexican schools. Gonzalez writes:

> On 5 June 1919, the "plans and specifications for the [just permanent] Mexican school buildings were approved and the secretary was instructed to advertise for bids. . . ." The temporary arrangement evolved into the first Mexican school building in Santa Ana, named the Santa Fe School. Thus, the process of segregation, begun in 1912 with separate classroom, reached its completed form in 1920 with the establishment of a separate Mexican school. In 1921 the district added Logan, another Mexican school, and incorporated a third, Delhi, in 1924. [15]

Mexican children were not only relegated to separate school buildings, but the teachers hired to instruct them also were paid anywhere from $90 to $100 less per year than teachers assigned to the Anglo schools.

The unequal nature of the education provided to the Mexican children was exemplified not only by the separate curriculum developed for them (emphasis on manual training for the boys and homemaking for the girls) and the lower-paid teachers assigned to them, but also by the decrepit structures in which they received their segregated instruction. In 1928 Osman R. Hull and Willard S. Ford, two University of Southern California professors, conducted an educational survey of the Santa Ana school district at the behest of the school district. Hull and Ford described the Mexican schools as follows:

> The Delhi school is a wooden structure which is a fire hazard and poorly constructed [and] provides less than one-third of the required amount of light. . . .
>
> The Grand Avenue School . . . is a two story frame structure entirely unsuited to school use . . . it has been condemned for years.
>
> The most unsatisfactory school that is now being used . . . is the Artesia school. . . . It is a frame building with no interior finish. It has a low single roof with no air space, which makes the temperature in many of the rooms almost unbearable. Since no artificial light is provided in the building, it is impossible to do satisfactory reading without serious eye strain on many days of the year.[16]

Based on these findings, they recommended that two of the Mexican schools be demolished and new schools be constructed. The reaction of the Anglo community to this recommendation was swift and forceful. Harvey Gardner, a member of the advisory committee of the Chamber of Commerce, objected to the monies that would have to be used to build two new Mexican schools when, he argued, there were not "proper facilities for the American school children." The board, cowed by the fierce reaction of the Anglo citizens, rejected Hull and Ford's recommendation and instructed them to provide a new set of recommendations.

Ford and Hull, in compliance with the board's request, provided a revised plan: they recommended that only one school be torn down instead of two, and they reduced from $170,000 to $112,000 the amount of money designated for repairs to the Artesia school. However, even these reduced figures did not satisfy the board, so Ford and Hull were instructed to provide a third revised plan.

Once again, the plan proposed by Ford and Hull did not meet with the approval of the board and advisory committee, and the contract with Ford and Hull was then terminated. In their stead a committee was appointed to decide what to do about a Mexican school. Ultimately, the committee recommended a new Artesia school building with a budget of $65,000; a new kindergarten for Delhi at a cost of $500; and instead of building a new Grand Avenue school, the committee recommended that the vacant Logan school be restored and an addition be appended at a cost of $32,000.

After considerable debate and input from Anglo citizens, who objected to the proposal for a variety of reasons, not the least of which was a desire to relocate the Artesia school within the boundaries of a Mexican neighborhood, the committee's plan was adopted. In the 1929–1930 school year, the new Artesia school (which was renamed Fremont School) opened; Logan enrolled 232 students and Delhi enrolled 319 students. The total number of Mexican children enrolled in these schools represented more than one-quarter of the district's total enrollment.

While segregation of Mexican children continued into the 1940s, by the early 1930s theories regarding the benefits of segregation were coming under attack. George I. Sánchez, at that time director of information and statistics for the New Mexico Department of Education, argued that the results of intelligence tests administered to Mexican children had to take into consideration the child's environment. Wollenberg notes that "California educator Simon Treff asserted that Mexican students in mixed schools seemed to be less 'retarded' than those in segregated schools. Herschel T. Manuel of the University of Texas claimed that reading and arithmetic problems of Mexican-American children were caused primarily by poverty and bilingualism."[17] By 1937, some educators were "calling for an end to 'emotionalism' on the question of segregation; what was needed was more research."

It is generally accepted that soldiers who fought in World War II and returned to their towns were the impetus for many of the significant changes that occurred during the late 1940s in Mexican communities. Guadalupe San Miguel Jr., a Latino historian, writes:

> Despite these tremendous social and economic changes wrought by World War II, the status of Mexican Americans in the United States changed little . . . the majority continued to be denied equal opportunities, discriminated against, and treated as second-class citizens. . . .
>
> But change . . . was brewing within the Mexican American community. Much of this change was due to their experiences in the defense of American institutions and ideals. . . .
>
> The war experience gave Mexican Americans a new sense of dignity and responsibility. For the first time many of them were treated as first-class citizens and recognized for their contributions to the war effort.[18]

One of the issues that returning veterans confronted was the ongoing segregation in the school system. In 1943 Mexican veterans who returned to Santa Ana formed an organization, the Latin American Organization, whose main goal was combating school segregation. One of the first confrontations occurred on October 25, 1943, when Mrs. Leonides Sánchez and Mrs. Frank García appeared at a meeting of the Santa Ana Board of Education and argued that their children should be allowed to attend Franklin School, a largely Anglo school. The school board rebuffed the request, stating that while admitting that Anglo students were frequently transferred out of Mexican schools, the reverse was seldom the case. A year later Sánchez and Garica enrolled their children in the Franklin School, even though they had not been granted authorization to do so. The enrollment of the students was accomplished through a subterfuge, using false addresses that would allow the students to fall within the Franklin School zone. When this was discovered, the school board decided that, once the correct addresses for the two children were verified, they would be placed in the proper school—the Mexican school.

No sooner was the school board confronted with the Sánchez-García demand than an attorney representing Mr. and Mrs. William Guzmán and their son Billy Guzmán, along with several other parents, appeared before the board and requested leave to send Billy to the Franklin School. While the board initially indicated that it would study the problem and provide a response within 90 days, there was no change in the board's policy.

The struggle in which the Sánchez, García, and Guzmán families were engaged in Santa Ana was also going on in the town of Westminster. There, in 1944, Gonzalo and Felicitas Mendez attempted to enroll their three children in the school nearest their home—Westminster Elementary School. The school prevented them from enrolling on the basis of language deficiency. The Mendez family could have pursued the matter for their children alone, but the political atmosphere had changed by then. Instead, they organized a group of parents and petitioned the school board to end the segregation of Mexican children.

The superintendent maintained that Mexican children belonged in the Mexican schools, but that an exception would be made for the Mendez children: they would be allowed to enroll in Westminster Elementary School. Mr. and Mrs. Mendez rejected the offer and refused to allow their children into the school until such time as they could "regularly" enroll in the school. They were already of a mind to institute legal action, not only for the benefit of their own children but to challenge—and perhaps end—the existence of Mexican schools.

David Marcus was selected to represent the Mendez family. Marcus came to the Mendez case with an impressive résumé of court victories.

In addition to having prevailed in litigation to desegregate the San Bernardino public parks and pools, he also handled matters for the Mexican consulates in Los Angeles and San Diego.

On March 2, 1945, Gonzalo Mendez, William Guzmán, Frank Palomino, Thomas Estrada, and Lorenzo Ramírez filed a class-action suit in Federal District Court, Southern District, against the Westminster, Garden Grove, and El Modeno school districts, the Santa Ana city schools, and the respective trustees and superintendents of the school districts (*Mendez et al. v. Westminster School District of Orange County et al.*).[19] The American Civil Liberties Union and the National Lawyers Guild filed amicus briefs, attesting to the importance of the case.

The complaint alleged that the school districts had engaged in a systematic and purposeful segregation of Mexican children whereby the Mexican children "are now and have been segregated and required to and must attend and use certain schools . . . reserved for and attended solely and exclusively by children and persons of Mexican and Latin descent, while such other schools are maintained, attended, and used exclusively by and for persons and children purportedly known as White or Anglo-Saxon children."[20] The plaintiffs in the action argued that such segregated schools violated the Mexicans' constitutional rights under the Fourteenth Amendment and asked, as part of their relief, that the court issue an injunction abating the segregation of the schools.

Both parties to the lawsuit stipulated to the court that while the segregation was not based on race, segregation per se was practiced by the defendant school districts beginning with the time that the Mexican children entered school and advanced through the grades. The parties further stipulated that this was the case even though the children were qualified to attend public schools in their own school zone.

Having stipulated that the segregation of Mexican children was not based on race, the defendant school districts justified their actions on the special educational needs of the Mexican children. The court noted that the Mexican children were "required to attend schools designated by the boards separate and apart from English-speaking pupils; that such group should attend such schools until they had acquired some proficiency in the English language."[21]

The Mendez family responded that the use of language as a basis for segregation of Mexican children was a subterfuge used by the school districts to arbitrarily discriminate against children of Mexican descent.

The court was careful to note that the "separate" educational facilities provided to the Mexican children were "equal" to if not superior to that offered to the Anglo children. The court noted, "The record before us shows without conflict that the technical facilities and physical conveniences offered in the schools housing entirely the segregated pupils, the efficiency of the teachers therein and the curricula are identical and in some respects superior to those in the other schools in the respective districts."[22] By so noting, the court dismissed any potential argument that its decision was influenced by "separate but unequal" educational access for the Mexican children.

Having set the record regarding the various stipulations by the parties and the "separate but equal" nature of the educational facilities provided to the segregated Mexican children, the court then framed the question before it as follows: "Does such official action of defendant district school agencies and the usages and practices pursued by the respective school authorities as shown by the evidence operate to deny or deprive the so-called non-English-speaking school children of Mexican ancestry or descent within such school districts of the equal protection of the laws?"

In presenting their case, plaintiffs relied heavily on social scientists who testified that segregation of Mexican children had a detrimental effect on them. The social science testimony was persuasive, leading the court to write:

> The evidence clearly shows that Spanish-speaking children are retarded in learning English by lack of exposure to its use because of segregation, and that commingling of the entire student body instills and develops a common cultural attitude among the school

children which is imperative for the perpetuation of American institutions and ideals. It is also established by the record that the methods of segregation prevalent in the defendant school districts foster
antagonism in the children and suggest inferiority among them
where none exists.[23]

In addressing the districts' principal defense argument that the
segregation of Mexican children was based on their lack of English, the
court acknowledged that segregation of Mexican children could be justified on this basis, but that the facts before it did not warrant such a
conclusion and sided with the plaintiff's position that language skills
was a ruse for arbitrarily segregating Mexican children. As to the facts
before it relating to the Santa Ana city schools, the court noted that
"The tests applied to the beginners are shown to have been generally
hasty, superficial and not reliable." In other instances, the court noted,
the Santa Ana city schools simply used the "Latinized or Mexican
name of the child" to determine the child's language skills. Such methods "of evaluating language knowledge are illusory," the court wrote.

The court went further to undermine the districts' argument that
segregation of Mexican children in the elementary schools could be
justified because of deficiency in English, by first stating that such deficiency had to be established by "credible examination by the appropriate school authority of each child." Furthermore, the court noted, if the
segregation of a child was based on English-language deficiencies, then
"such segregation must be based wholly upon indiscriminate foreign
language impediments in the individual child, regardless of his ethnic
traits or ancestry." Meaning, apparently, if children of Italian descent or
German descent were appropriately tested and found to be deficient in
English, then they too could be segregated for the sole purpose of im-
proving their English.

At the end of the day, the court found that the school districts had,
by virtue of arbitrarily segregating Mexican children, violated their
rights under the Fourteenth Amendment and concluded that "the allegations of the complaint [petition] have been established sufficiently

to justify injunctive relief affianced all defendants, restraining further discriminatory practices against the pupils of Mexican descent in the public schools of defendant school districts."[24]

The decision by Judge Paul McCormick was hailed as groundbreaking. *La Opinión,* a Los Angeles Spanish-language newspaper, reported that McCormick's decision was a "brilliant judicial exposition." And Marcus hailed the results as "one of the greatest judicial decisions in favor of democratic practices granted since the emancipation of the slaves."[25]

The celebration was short-lived because the defendants decided to appeal. The appeal to the Ninth Circuit attracted the attention of a number of major organizations: the NAACP, the American Jewish Congress, the Japanese-American Citizens League, and the State of California attorney general, in addition to the ACLU and the National Lawyers Guild. Not only did the NAACP submit an amicus brief, but it considered the case to be of such significance that it sent Thurgood Marshall to argue before the court. The *New York Times* reported that the case was being closely watched and considered a test case for addressing the constitutional validity of the "separate but equal" doctrine.

The *Times* was correct. Christopher Arriola, an attorney who has written on the *Mendez* case, notes that the civil rights organizations saw *Mendez* as a test case to attack the separate but equal underpinning of *Plessy v. Ferguson.* The amicus brief filed by the NAACP argued that "fundamental law" invalidated racial classification. It also argued that segregation prevents the achievement of due process and equal protection. Finally, it argued that *Plessy v. Ferguson* did not prohibit a finding that school segregation was invalid since that case was restricted to public transportation.[26]

The court of appeals did not take the NAACP bait and refused to rule on the "separate but equal" issue. The court wrote, "We are not tempted by the siren who calls to us that the sometimes slow and tedious way of democratic legislation is no longer respected in the progressive society."[27]

The school districts did not choose to appeal the case to the United

States Supreme Court and the education commissioner of Orange County ordered that there be "some Anglo and Mexican children in every class." In the fall of 1947 the schools in Westminster, Garden Grove, El Modeno, and Santa Ana integrated their schools with few problems.[28]

While the impact of *Mendez* was not national in scope, its effect in California was both apparent and dramatic. In January 1947, a bill was introduced into the state legislature to repeal the state statutes that provided for the creation of segregated schools for Chinese, Japanese, Native Americans, and Mongolians. Some opposition was raised to the bill but it eventually passed, and on June 14, 1947, the bill was signed into law by Governor Earl Warren.

In Riverside, the school board members, reading McCormick's decision as writing on the wall, capitulated to the demands from the Mexican American community and integrated schools in the section of the city called Bell Town. Riverside closed an "all-white" school near a Mexican neighborhood, thus integrating a school that had previously been all Mexican. And the Ontario school board integrated a school in 1946.

Even though the effect of *Mendez* was not national in scope, its significance in preparing the ground for *Brown v. Board of Education* cannot be overemphasized. The use of social science testimony had a significant impact on McCormick and his decision. Gonzalez writes that Robert Carter, one of the NAACP attorneys, was so impressed with the effective use of social science testimony that he suggested to Thurgood Marshall that such an approach would be the only way to "overturn segregation in the United States." Gonzalez further notes:

> Later attorneys for the NAACP employed with success this particular strategy in the 1954 Supreme Court decision, *Brown v. Board of Education*. Carter . . . also felt that the *amicus curiae* that he and Marshall filed in the appellate court in support of the district court's *Mendez* decision was a "dry run for the future."[29]

A note in the *Yale Law Journal* concurred: "However, a recent District Court decision, affirmed by the Ninth Circuit Court of Appeals, has questioned the basic assumption of the *Plessy* and may portend a complete reversal of the doctrine."[30] This conclusion was given further credence by Lester H. Phillips in an article published in the Black journal *Phylon*: "The observations of the judges in both the district and the appellate courts relative to segregation suggest that this case must be ranked among the vanguard of those making a frontal attack upon the 'equal separate' canon of interpretation of the equal protection clause."[31]

It is, therefore, not an exaggeration to state that *Mendez* was the first stage in the process of overturning the "separate but equal" doctrine in the 1896 *Plessy v. Ferguson* case.

TEXAS: *DELGADO V. BASTROP INDEPENDENT SCHOOL DISTRICT*

The discrimination and segregation that Mexicans experienced was not confined to California, as Chicano historian David Montejano makes clear in his highly acclaimed book *Anglos and Mexicans in the Making of Texas: 1836–1986.*[32] The parallels between California and Texas are clear. Like California, Texas had no state statute that provided for the creation of separate schools for Mexican children. In the absence of a statutory basis on which to segregate Mexican children, educators in Texas relied on administrative decrees. Reminiscent of statements in California, Texas school officials—administrators, school boards, trustees, superintendents—justified the creation and maintenance of separate Mexican schools because Mexicans suffered from mental retardation, did not speak English, had poor hygiene, did not really appreciate education, and, frankly, were just inherently inferior. And when a well-meaning school administrator happened to ignore the common lore regarding Mexican children, he was reminded by Anglo parents of the imperative to keep Mexican and Anglo children separate. As an example, in 1919 Mexican children in the town of Pharr-San Juan in Hidalgo County were initially allowed to attend school with Anglo children. However, they were quickly transferred to a "Mexican church" for separate instruction after Anglo parents protested the mingling of the Mexicans with Anglo children.[33]

Herschel T. Manuel, a professor of educational psychology at the University of Texas, conducted a study of Mexican children in Texas and published the results in 1930. He found that Mexican children were segregated into inferior schools. He describes one school for Mexican children as a run-down building that had previously been a church, and in southwest Texas he found four Mexican children using one tablet and one pencil, which they rotated among themselves.[34]

By the late 1920s and early 1930s segregation of Mexican children was widespread and institutionalized in areas of Texas. For example, during the 1930s it was believed that more than 40 school districts had created separate schools for Mexicans, and by 1942 it was estimated that 122 districts in 59 counties operated separate schools for Mexican American children.[35]

While there had been individual challenges to segregation, the legal challenges were made with the help and support of a new statewide Mexican organization, the League of United Latin American Citizens, generally referred to by its acronym, LULAC. LULAC's membership was uniquely different from other Mexican organizations in that all of its members were either born in the United States or naturalized citizens. Its goals were also different. While the other organizations existed primarily to provide social services to the Mexican community, LULAC's goal was to enable Mexicans to take advantage of U.S. political, social, and cultural institutions. This was reflected in LULAC's constitution, which had as one of its goals: "to assume complete responsibility for the education of our children as to their rights and duties and the language and customs of this country." Conjoined with this goal was LULAC's avowed purpose of eliminating all discriminatory practices based on race.[36]

The 1928 claim of Amanda Vela was one of the first challenges to the segregation of Mexican children in Texas. In the case of *Vela v. Board of Trustees of Charlotte Independent School District*, Felipe Vela, a

Mexican American, had adopted Amanda Vela, a girl whose "race" was undetermined. Vela attempted to enroll Amanda in a school with white children. She was denied enrollment and transferred to the "Mexican school" by the board of trustees. Vela bypassed the local school board and made a direct appeal to the state superintendent of public instruction for a decision allowing his daughter to attend the "white school."

Much like the *Mendez* case, though not in a legal context, both sides agreed to certain facts. First, the parties agreed that the school district did not have any legal authority on which it could bar Amanda from attending the "white school." Second, the parties stipulated that Amanda did not live within the zone designated for the Mexican school, and that she was placed in the "Mexican school" simply because her parents were Mexican. Also, much like in the *Mendez* case, the local school officials defended their actions on pedagogical grounds, stating, "It is well understood that non-English-speaking children should be given special instruction and it is probably to the best interests of such children that they be placed in one room or in one school in order that the character of instruction given will be different from that given to English-speaking children."[37]

Like Judge McCormick in the *Mendez* case, the state superintendent of public instruction, S. M. N. Marrs, agreed that separation of Mexican children based on language difficulties could be used to justify segregating them into separate classes. In the case of Amanda, however, Marrs found that she not only spoke English well but was able to translate from Spanish to English and English to Spanish with great facility. As a consequence, he concluded, placing Amanda in the "white school" would not interfere with the progress of the white children and placing her in the "Mexican school" would disadvantage Amanda, since so many of the Mexican children did not speak English or, if they did, they did not speak it well. The school district, dissatisfied with the decision, appealed to the state board of education, but the board declined to reverse the state superintendent.

The first legal challenge to the practice of segregating Mexican children in the Texas education system was fostered by LULAC in 1930, two years after the Vela matter was resolved. *Independent School District v. Salvatierra* was a class-action suit filed against the Del Rio school district.[38] *Salvatierra* was also significant because it was a case of first impression, a fact the court acknowledged when it wrote, "The question of race segregation, as between Mexicans and other white races, has not heretofore found its way into the courts of the state, and therefore the decision of no Texas court is available in the disposition of the precise question present here."[39] Thus, its decision, if favorable to the plaintiffs, could be used to further challenge segregation in other school districts, but if favorable to the defendants could be devastating to any future challenges.

The Del Rio school district was composed of four school buildings and an athletic field, all of which were located on the same parcel of land. The white high school and two white elementary schools were at one end of the field and the Mexican school was located at the other end.

In 1930 the residents of Del Rio approved the sale of $185,000 in bonds to be devoted to the improvement of the existing school facilities. The school trustees earmarked the money to be used for constructing a new senior high school building, remodeling and enlarging the white elementary schools, and enlarging the Mexican school by adding five rooms, including an auditorium.

Mexican parents immediately objected to the plan not because of the quality or nature of the renovations to the Mexican school, but because such construction ensured the separation of the Mexican children from the white students.

The court, in deciding the case, concluded that the school district had not exceeded its administrative powers because the school board was not "arbitrarily" assigning Mexican children to the Mexican school. It also found that how Mexican students were identified as non-English-speaking for purposes of placing them in the Mexican school was not arbitrary or unconstitutional. Finally, it held that placement of Mexican children in the Mexican school was justified for additional pedagogical reasons. The first was the late enrollment and spotty attendance of the Mexican children. The second was, as in the *Mendez* case, the language issue. The school district argued that placing the Mexican children in the white school handicapped the Mexican students and thus they were better served by placing them in the Mexican school where their fellow students were more like them. Based on these grounds the court found that the school district had not violated any of the Mexican schoolchildren's constitutional rights.

The decision was a critical blow to LULAC and its zeal to eliminate segregation in the Texas school system. So devasting was the decision that LULAC concluded that, for the foreseeable future, the legal arena was not where the battle to end segregation in the school system should be fought. LULAC urged its members to take the battle to a different level and work informally with the various school districts to eliminate the discriminatory practices that they challenged in Del Rio.

While LULAC and the American G.I. Forum, another Mexican American organization that had as one of its goals the education of Mexican American children, continued to militate for equal educational opportunities for Mexican children, legal challenges to segregation in the Texas school system lay dormant until after the *Mendez* decision.

On April 8, 1947, the attorney general of Texas issued an opinion that prohibited segregation of Mexican children when such segregation was based solely on race. However, the decision provided an out to the local school districts by providing that separate placement of children could be justified based on language deficiencies and other needs, but only after these deficiencies and needs were determined by the administration of unbiased tests.

The attorney general's opinion turned out to be a paper tiger. It not only provided the school districts with an easy out—it also did not set forth a procedure to force compliance. The toothless nature of this decision was demonstrated when, several months after its passage, numerous challenges to school districts that continued to segregate Mexican schoolchildren were dismissed. A study of the Texas school system conducted by Virgil E. Stickland and George I. Sánchez found that segregation was practiced on "a purely arbitrary basis, determined solely by local custom, tradition and prejudice."[40]

Inspired by the *Mendez* case and assessing that the social and legal environments had changed, LULAC in 1948 assisted in filing a class-action suit against the Bastrop Independent School District. In *Delgado et al. v. Bastrop Independent School District of Bastrop County, Texas, et al.*[41] the complaint listed five arguments:

1. The defendants acted beyond the authority provided to them under the Texas constitution and laws of the state by separate placement of Mexican children.
2. Nothing in the Texas constitution permitted the segregation of Mexican children into separate schools and/or classes.
3. The segregation of the Mexican children was based on custom, usage and/or common plan.
4. The segregation of the Mexican children was condoned by the state superintendent of public education and state board of education.
5. The segregation of Mexican children denied them due process and violated their rights under the Fourteenth Amendment.[42]

As in *Mendez,* the court found that placing Mexican students in separate buildings was arbitrary, discriminatory, and illegal. The judge further wrote, "The plaintiffs, as aforesaid, by the acts of the defendants complained of, were deprived of their rights under the Constitution of the United States and the Laws of the United States to be free from discrimination solely because of their ancestry."

The *Mendez* decision, rendered in 1946, presaged the *Brown v. Board of Education* decision rendered by the U.S. Supreme Court in 1954 by approximately eight years, and the *Delgado* case rendered in 1948 presaged it by approximately six years. While *Brown v. Board of Education* provided the Supreme Court with the factual basis and legal arguments to declare state-imposed de jure segregation in public schools a violation of the Fourteenth Amendment, Mexicans in California and Texas had fought similar battles and laid much of the legal groundwork for *Brown*'s eventual victory.

One plausible reason can be advanced to explain why *Mendez* and *Delgado* have received so little attention from legal scholars and historians. The decision in *Brown v. Board of Education* was rendered by the Supreme Court, making it the law of the land. So while *Mendez* and *Delgado* had significant regional impact, the ruling in *Brown v. Board of Education* blanketed the United States, radically altering the educational policies of every state of the Union. It was therefore reasonable for the general public, and scholars as well, to view *Brown v. Board of Education* as the natural reference point for the elimination of the "separate but equal" doctrine in *Plessy v. Ferguson.* All other decisions were regarded as having lesser significance.

However, the struggle by Mexican Americans in the Southwest to overcome the pernicious effect of segregated schools was no less significant and meaningful than was the parallel struggle of African Americans in the South. And the detrimental, and in some instances devastating, effect that segregated schools had on Mexican American students was no less than their impact on Blacks in the South. On these grounds alone, the Latino struggle to eliminate the insidious quality of the "separate but equal" doctrine should receive the recognition that it deserves.

The Folly of Presumption

Black Voters and the Los Angeles 2001 Mayoral Election

> If [Jesse] Jackson wanted to forge a Latino and black political coalition . . . he should have been marching in Los Angeles alongside Antonio Villaraigosa in an historic attempt to be the first Latino elected mayor of that city. . . . Villaraigosa lost by about 40,000 votes. Ironically, when Harold Washington was first elected mayor of Chicago, he won by roughly 50,000 votes. In November 1983, Washington addressed a gathering of Hispanic leaders, and I heard him say it was the Latino vote that put him over the top. Wouldn't it have been nice if Villaraigosa could have said that about the black vote in L.A.? But Jackson wouldn't go near L.A., not with Magic Johnson and U.S. Rep. Maxine Waters rallying blacks to support the white candidate.

JUAN ANDRADE
President of the U.S. Hispanic Leadership Institute

In the late fall of 1999, Antonio Villaraigosa, then speaker of the California state assembly, decided, after more than a year of introspection and consideration, to run for mayor of Los Angeles. This "intense, energetic, handsome and plain-spoken" Latino did this even though he had been advised by numerous Democratic veterans, as well as by some of his most fervent backers, not to run. They asked him to be a good political soldier and wait his turn, assuring him that in time conditions would be right and then he would be the candidate of choice. Villaraigosa, however, did not listen. He was accustomed to hearing such negative advice during his political career, which he would ignore and go on to prove his detractors wrong by succeeding. His career as a state assemblyman was about to end as a result of term limits, and he was eager to continue his political career by becoming mayor of Los Angeles. He was convinced that he possessed the right qualities to lead one of the country's major cities into the new millennium.

After he announced his candidacy he was assessed by the *Los Angeles Times* as being decidedly nonethnic. While in Sacramento he had advocated for school reform, health care, and open space. Nothing particularly ethnic about that, the *Los Angeles Times* wrote, observing that such issues resonated not only with Latinos and liberals but with the entire California electorate. On the negative side, the *Los Angeles Times* noted that Villaraigosa was unabashedly liberal and blunt—the latter a real liability in the world of politics where sensibility and tact sometimes spell the difference between success and failure.[1] The concern was that his sometimes brash personality would strike a negative chord with white conservative voters. The paper also noted that Villaraigosa had low name recognition as a result of spending a great deal of time in Sacramento, California's state capital. This was not helped by the fact that his name, an amalgam of his surname and that of his wife, is nearly unpronounceable, even for some Spanish-speaking Latinos. Finally, the publication observed that while the Latino voting base was significant in Los Angeles, the time for a Latino candidate was still several years away.

Villaraigosa was also entering a crowded field that already featured a Latino candidate, Democratic state representative Xavier Becerra from Los Angeles. It also included James K. Hahn, the city attorney of Los Angeles. Not only was Hahn the only candidate to hold city office, winning five citywide campaigns over his political career, but he was also heir to a legacy that would turn out to be the difference between his success and Villaraigosa's failure in the mayoral race. Kenneth (commonly referred to as "Kenny") Hahn, James's father, was a legend among African American voters in South Central Los Angeles. If Clinton is sometimes regarded as the first African American president of the United States, Kenny was sometimes viewed as L.A.'s first citywide African American officeholder. Year after year Kenny delivered for his South Central Black constituents, and for that he was warmly regarded and repeatedly returned to office by Black voters. So when James Hahn began his campaign for mayor, he came to the game with a decided advantage. Taking the Black vote away from James would be a formidable, if not impossible, task. Challengers would not only be battling James but also vying with his father's ghost.

Villaraigosa thought from the very beginning that if anyone could do it, he could. He was Latino, a minority just like Hahn's Black voters, and he was convinced that his track record as a "coalition builder" made him the ideal candidate to draw Black voters away from Hahn's camp. Perhaps Villaraigosa did not truly appreciate the challenge he was facing. Already in January 2001, Hahn had secured the endorsement of such Black political luminaries as Congresswoman Maxine Waters and Los Angeles county supervisor Yvonne Brathwaite Burke. He had also received the support of former basketball star Magic Johnson, as well as that of Rev. Cecil L. Murray, the senior pastor of the influential First AME Church.[2] True, Villaraigosa would assemble his own list of Black supporters, including state assemblymen Carl Washington and Herb Wesson and state senator Kevin Murray, but, as time would prove out, Kenny's legacy ran deeper in the Black community than mere endorsements from Black candidates. Even though Villaraigosa cast himself as someone who could build a Black-Latino coalition, from the inception of the race it was clear that he was going to have a hard go of it.

As the deadline for filing papers for the mayoral race approached, Villaraigosa's friends and supporters once again beseeched him not to run. County supervisor Gloria Molina and Henry Cisneros, a former member of Clinton's cabinet, met with him several times and counseled him that if he ran against Becerra all he would do was succeed in splitting the Latino vote, thereby assuring that no Latino would win the Democratic primary or be in any runoff. Molina and Cisneros also lobbied Becerra with the same request.

Since neither Villaraigosa nor Becerra would voluntarily back away, Molina and Cisneros devised a novel plan to convince one of them to drop out. Their idea was this: Each candidate's ability to raise funds and obtain endorsements, as well as his citywide popularity, would be measured by some neutral body. The "loser" in this assessment would be asked to step down. By some accounts, Villaraigosa agreed but the proposed plan fell apart when Becerra refused to go along with it.[3] Frustrated with Becerra's recalcitrance, Molina and Cisneros broke off all discussions.

Predicting that both candidates would fail as a result, Cisneros stated: "I think it's quite likely that neither one can make the June election runoff, if both are in the race. . . . That is really a shame for Latino ambitions in Los Angeles."[4]

Early in February, the Villaraigosa and Becerra campaigns became embroiled in a scandal that revealed the effect that monetary contributions can have on the wise judgment of politicians. It would also prove to be a scandal with legs—it would stay with Villaraigosa long after its initial revelation and far into his mayoral campaign.

It was discovered that Villaraigosa and Becerra, along with Cardinal Roger M. Mahony, had written letters to President Clinton in support of Carlos Vignali Jr., a Los Angeles cocaine dealer whose sentence President Clinton commuted on his last day in office. Villaraigosa wrote his letter five years prior to the commutation. Nevertheless, he felt compelled to apologize for sending it, insisting that the letter had nothing to do with the $2,795 the Vignali family had donated to his past campaigns.[5] This sum was only slightly less than the $3,500 the family had contributed to Becerra. The letters were viewed as clear lobbying efforts by both candidates, even though Becerra protested that all he was doing was urging the White House to make certain that justice had really been served in Vignali's case.

About the same time that the news was breaking about the Vignali imbroglio, Villaraigosa managed a significant breakthrough by winning the backing of the Los Angeles County Federation of Labor, AFL-CIO, by a single vote. It was a hard-fought battle in which Hahn worked hard to keep the union neutral. However, the union, which increasingly represented Latino workers, wanted to be responsive to its membership, and the AFL-CIO was also beginning to flex its muscle after several big electoral wins. Miguel Conteras, the union's treasurer, was positively ebullient about Villaraigosa's endorsement, making it a "bet the farm" commitment by promising to rally hundreds of volunteers to work phone banks and walk neighborhoods.[6]

During this heated contest, Kenny's specter loomed large: Maxine Waters and Yvonne Brathwaite Burke joined Hahn in his efforts to keep the union neutral. Their argument, at least on the surface, was that the union should back a winner—someone who was certain to make the runoff. It was also an early manifestation of the problems that Villaraigosa would encounter with Hahn's Black supporters.

In February Hahn launched a series of television spots that highlighted his work for Los Angeles as an insider—first as city controller and then as city attorney. Hahn, who was widely recognized as being less than dynamic, countered his milquetoast personality with an emphasis on the solid nature of his service to the city.

His television spots appeared to have the intended effect. Five weeks before the election, Hahn appeared to pull ahead of the pack. In a poll conducted by the *Los Angeles Times,* the numbers broke down like this: 24 percent of the votes favored Hahn; 12 percent for commercial real estate broker Steven Sorboroff; 12 percent for Villaraigosa; 11 percent for city councilman Joel Wachs; 10 percent for Becerra; 8 percent for state controller Kathleen Connell. Among Black voters, Hahn was favored by 58 percent.[7]

Hahn understood that having the Black vote behind him was not enough to put him in the mayor's office. What he needed was a coalition. Coalitions are never the sole domain of minority voters—indeed, they are a thing apart from color and ethnicity. If his father's legacy helped him clinch the Black vote, then his long term as the city attorney of Los Angeles helped to guarantee the white conservative vote. In the 10 years that he had been city attorney, Hahn had doled out over $29 million to outside law firms to represent the city in a variety of cases. It was only natural, then, that some of these law firms would come to his aid. O'Melveny and Meyers, for example, contributed $25,000 to his campaign—small change compared to the $2.9 million in business that Hahn had sent their way. Other law firms contributed similarly, and several partners in some firms held their own fund-raising events.[8] Hahn was managing to operate successfully in two entirely opposite worlds—the everyday, workingman's world of his father's Black constituents and the rarefied world of successful white businessmen.

Villaraigosa's image, on the other hand, was undergoing a severe and not too flattering remake. With the Vignali matter still dogging him, and with less than a week before the election, Villaraigosa found himself the victim of a truly diabolical plot. In a recorded telephone call to potential voters, someone who identified herself as "Gloria Morina" and who sounded surprisingly like Gloria Molina—but wasn't—announced that the call was an emergency. The caller stated that it was time to break the silence about Villaraigosa. It was time to reveal that Villaraigosa opposed increased penalties for rapists and that he twice opposed legislation to increase penalties for child pornography. The recorded message went on to say that people should vote against Villaraigosa in order to ensure the safety of women and children.[9] Of course, all of Villaraigosa's opponents denied that they were behind the call. The call was not only disturbing in its content, it also seemed to confirm, at least to some degree, the image that Villaraigosa was acquiring among certain Los Angeles voters.

Not only was Villaraigosa being painted as soft on crime, but his stated goal of forming a coalition with Black voters was quickly slipping away. In a second *Los Angeles Times* poll released days before the election, Hahn had increased his rating among Black voters by 7 percent: now 63 percent of African Americans stated they expected to vote for Hahn. What was truly startling, state controller Kathleen Connell received the next most favorable rating, with 12 percent of the Black respondents stating they favored her. Villaraigosa garnered only 7 percent in the poll. Clearly, his goal of creating a Black-Latino coalition was failing.[10]

If Villaraigosa had accompanied Hahn on one of his frequent so-journs through South Central, he could have witnessed the true futility of his efforts to win away Kenny's legacy. "During a lunchtime program in an auditorium at the Watts Labor Community Action Committee, elderly African American women swapped stories about the Hahn family. As Hahn walked through the room, one person after another reached to clasp his hands," the *Los Angeles Times* reported.[11] The af-fection that the Black residents of Watts showed Hahn also translated into support at the polls. A Black voter who approached Hahn said, "Hahn, right? I'm so appreciative of your father and the work that he did. You've got one vote."[12]

At the same time, Villaraigosa and Becerra were fomenting tremen-dous excitement in the Latino community. For the first time, people believed that a Latino could be mayor of Los Angeles. But the reality was that, for all of their population numbers—which in 2001 stood at between 43 and 47 percent of the total Los Angeles population—they did not translate into votes. Indeed, in the 1997 mayor's race, Latinos represented only 15 percent of the electorate. Many were unable to vote because they weren't citizens or had not registered. And a *Los Angeles Times* poll found that 37 percent of the Latinos planned to vote for one of the four white candidates.[13]

At the eleventh hour of the election, Villaraigosa found he still could not distance himself from the Vignali fiasco, thanks to radio ads paid for by the Morongo Indians. Accusations flew as to who was really behind the ads. Parke Skelton, Villaraigosa's campaign consultant, al-leged that it was Assemblyman Tony Cardenas, a supporter of Hahn. Skelton described Cardenas as the principal legislative proponent for the Morongo and other Indian tribes that had been successful in push-ing to expand gaming in California.[14] Cardenas denied the accusations and the Morongo Indians also denied that he was in any way involved in the ads, the Morongo Indians stood fast in saying that they alone were responsible for them. No matter who the instigator was, the ads did not help Villaraigosa.

On April 10, Los Angeles voters went to the polls and made Villaraigosa and Hahn the top vote getters among the pack of candidates, giving Villaraigosa 30 percent of the vote and Hahn 25 percent. Latinos swelled with pride at the fact that a Latino was so close to the highest citywide office in Los Angeles. The *Los Angeles Times* described one of the day-after celebrations: "Veterans of political struggles past, people old enough to remember the days when the idea of Chicano power was a seemingly impossible dream, all came to Villaraigosa's Union Station celebration to see 'one of our own' move one step closer to becoming mayor by making the runoff." [15]

The "one of our own" sentiment should have been expected. Latino voters knew instinctively, if not through readings, that Los Angeles began as a Mexican town. After all, wasn't Los Angeles first named El Pueblo de Nuestra Señora la Reyna de Los Angeles de Porciuncula? A real mouthful, but one that dripped with Mexican history. And for 20 years the mayor of Los Angeles had been an African American—so wasn't it the Latinos' turn? Shouldn't it be "one of our own" sitting in that office? And shouldn't African Americans help put him there?

The level of anticipation and frustration that Latinos felt in the spring of 2001 could not be understood without an examination of modern-day Los Angeles politics and the long period of time that Latinos had stood outside the halls of power, noses pressed against the glass as they watched, unable to fully participate in the comings and goings of the political process.

Carey McWilliams, in his classic work *North from Mexico*, took great glee in deflating the myth that Los Angeles was founded in 1791 by Spanish grandees and *caballeros*. The true founders of the City of Angeles, states McWilliams, were "Pablo Rodríguez, who was an Indian; José Variegas, the first *alcalde* of the *pueblo*, also an Indian; José Moreno, a mulatto; Felix Villavicencio, a Spaniard married to an Indian; José de Lara, also married to an Indian; Antonio Mesa, who was a Negro; Basilio Rosas, an Indian married to an Indian; Antonio Navarro, a mestizo with a mulatto wife; Manuel Camero, a mulatto." McWilliams notes that the twelfth founder was simply identified as a *Chino*, and was probably Chinese. [16]

Even though it could be argued that Los Angeles' founders were multiethnic, after 1848 the population took on a different complexion as white migrants began to flood into the city. In spite of the already significant Mexican and Asian populations in Los Angeles at the time of their arrival, the largely white and Protestant migrants were intent on replicating the homogeneous nature of the American heartland. To this pool of white immigrants was added white immigrants from the South. The development of a white power structure was so successful that by the 1920s the white immigrants had formed a power structure that controlled most of the public offices and closed political opportunities to minority groups.[17]

Just as the arrival of Anglos in Los Angeles overwhelmed the existing residents, the white residents of Los Angeles soon witnessed a challenge to their own strength as a growing number of Mexicans, Asians, and Blacks left the South in search of industrial jobs in Los Angeles. Between 1920 and 1930 the Mexican population grew from 30,000 to 97,000, the Black population jumped from 15,500 to 39,000, and the Japanese population grew from 11,600 to over 21,000. Only the Chinese population remained relatively unchanged, numbering 2,000 in 1920 and 3,000 in 1930.[18]

The flow of Blacks to Los Angeles increased significantly during World War II. Los Angeles was transformed into a major site for aircraft and shipbuilding, which necessitated a constant flow of labor. By 1960 Blacks represented 13.5 percent of the total L.A. population. By the 1950s and early 1960s the Black community was organizing for political power. The Latino residents, also growing in numbers, proved to be less adept at exercising their political power. And the Asian community, no doubt affected by the relocation of Japanese Americans during World War II, lagged even further behind.

The growth of the African American, Latino, and Asian populations was matched by the growth of the Jewish community. Jews not only populated the downtown area and West Los Angeles, but also spilled out into the San Fernando Valley.[19] In addition to establishing pockets of residency in areas outside of Los Angeles, Jews also created economic centers away from downtown Los Angeles.

The significance of the Jewish population extended beyond their numerical growth and business centers to the political arena. Raphael J. Sonenshein, a political science professor and longtime observer of Los Angeles politics, points out that the high literacy rate among Jews produced a higher percentage of the electorate than their population.

Despite their economic base and voting numbers, Jews were excluded from the dominant social, political, and economic life of Los Angeles. The combination of their exclusion and their liberal activism in the community led to a natural alliance with the similarly disenfranchised Blacks. In the early 1960s, this liberal ideology and shared political interest led to the formation of a political coalition, which, in conjunction with Black mobilization, led to the successful election of three Black members to the Los Angeles City Council.

Tom Bradley, a well-known Black political figure, was the focus of the biracial coalition, and he made plans to challenge Mayor Sam Yorty for office. Bradley lost his first bid for the mayoralty, but his second run in 1973 proved to be successful. As a result of Bradley's election as mayor, Blacks and Jews, the mainstay of his coalition, were rewarded with appointments to city commissions.

Bradley's coalition was based on the strong political and personal ties among Black and white activists who had worked together and learned to trust one another since the early 1960s. Any participation on the part of Latinos in the Bradley coalition was secondary to the role played by Jews and other white liberals.[20]

It is also important to note two events regarding the Latino role in Los Angeles politics prior to the election of Bradley as mayor. The first involved the District 9 city council position, which had been occupied by Edward Roybal, the only Latino on the Los Angeles City Council. District 9 was almost equally divided between Latinos and Blacks, and because of Roybal's long tenure and visibility, that district had long been considered a Latino district. In 1962, Roybal resigned his position as city councilman and ran successfully for Congress. The City Council then faced a difficult choice in selecting a replacement: either Gilbert Lindsay, the Black deputy to then county supervisor Kenneth Hahn, or Richard Tafoya, Roybal's first cousin and aide to Mayor Sam Yorty. This was a clear zero-sum situation, with Blacks trying to obtain their first seat on the City Council and Latinos trying to retain the only seat they had.

It was the white council members from districts with Black constituencies who took the lead, championing Lindsay to replace Roybal. Joe Hollingsworth, a white council member from District 10, who had been appointed by the City Council at a time when Blacks thought that an African American should represent his district, nominated Lindsay and also ushered in a procedural move that accelerated his selection. On January 28, 1963, the City Council appointed Lindsay as one of its board members, making him the first Black to hold office in Los Angeles.

Tafoya was outraged, but the Black leadership was pleased with its success and made plans to organize a Black united front to vote for Lindsay in the upcoming municipal elections. That Lindsay, an African American, was battling with Tafoya, a Latino, for the district that had previously sent a Latino to the City Council did not appear to concern the Black leadership. They were determined to maintain the position even at the expense of going against Roybal's cousin, and even after Roybal had been the principal voice in City Council speaking out on behalf of Black representation.

In addition to running Lindsay against Tafoya, African Americans fielded candidates in two other districts—Tom Bradley in the Tenth District and Bill Mills in the Eighth District. The *Eagle*, a Black newspaper, urged the Black community to unite behind their candidates.[21] Ceding the council seat to Tafoya did not appear to be a consideration.

On election day, Bradley won District 10, but both Lindsay and Bill Mills were forced into runoff elections. Even though Bradley's position was secured, the Black leadership did not find it necessary to change their position and support Tafoya in the runoff, thereby assuring that at least one Latino and one African American would sit on the City Council for the first time in the history of L.A. Instead, Blacks went all out to make certain that Lindsay defeated Tafoya. Bradley, who would later attempt to woo Latinos to support his mayoral bid, even sent one of his key aides to the Lindsay campaign to help him in mapping out the precincts. There would be no attempt at coalition building to save the one council seat that had historically been occupied by Latinos.

The effect of this election was devastating for Latinos in Los Angeles. It would be more than 23 years before another Latino sat on the City Council. On the other hand, it was a boon to African Americans—the three seats they won would be occupied by Blacks for the next 30 years.

Black dominance of minority politics in Los Angeles was exacerbated by the consequence of the 1965 Watts riots. The three-day riots were sparked by the arrest of two Black men and their mother by the California Highway Patrol in South Los Angeles on August 11, 1965. In all, 31 African Americans were killed, 1032 persons were hurt, 3438 adults and 514 juveniles were arrested, and there was $40 million in property damage.

The riots focused attention on the African American community of South Los Angeles. Black Leaders thought that the impact of the uprising would make the white power structure more attentive to the needs of this community, but Latinos and whites generally agreed that the riots would not help race relations. Both groups feared personal attacks by Blacks.

As it turned out, the riots did lead to allocation of antipoverty funds. Sonenshein notes that "Some Latino activists expressed resentment at the great attention being paid to Blacks in the wake of the riot, especially in the allocation of antipoverty funds. The obvious lack of Latino political influence was remarkable considering that Latinos outnumbered Blacks in the county."[22]

While the riots gave Mayor Sam Yorty a platform for appealing to an existing conservative base, it inspired African Americans to push for more political representation at the local level. It also had the effect of uniting African Americans against Yorty, giving him only slightly higher ratings than police chief William Parks.

In the aftermath of the 1965 riots, divisions were created that car-

ried forth into Tom Bradley's 1969 mayoral race. Yorty and his administration were pitted against the alliance of African Americans and white
liberals. Sonenshein describes Latinos as being in the middle. Exactly
what Sonenshein means is unclear, but it would appear that Latinos
were not an integral part of the Black-White coalition: "Persistent attempts would be made to incorporate Latinos into this coalition, but it
would be a long, frustrating process. As often as cooperation, conflict
appeared between Los Angeles Blacks and Latinos over antipoverty
programs, the Watts riot, police practices, and Sam Yorty."[23]

This schism was apparent not only in the zero-sum game of antipoverty programs and the funds they distributed but in the eventual
defeat of Bradley by Yorty in 1969. Sonenshein observed that coalition
among Blacks, liberal whites, and Latinos had not yet formed. Not only
was Jewish support for Bradley not as strong as was expected, but Latinos had voted for Yorty in numbers close to those of white conservatives.

Sonenshein explains Bradley's failure to attract Latino voters in the
1969 mayoral race by presenting a list of possible reasons for this disaffection ranging from class status to areas of residence, with poor Latinos favoring Bradley over Yorty. However, Sonenshein glosses over the
level of trust that existed between white liberals and Blacks, developed
as a result of their long history of working together.

Beginning with the Tafoya-Lindsay fiasco, which disenfranchised
Latinos for 23 years, and followed by the conflict over antipoverty program funds, Blacks and Latinos had a substantial history of *not* working together and *mis*trust. Sonenshein alludes to this fact when he
writes, "As far back as the battle over the Ninth District council seat in
1963, Los Angeles Blacks and Latinos had been competitors as well as
allies. With three council seats for Blacks and none for Latinos, the argument that both were politically excluded rested on shaky ground.
Liberal money and support had been flowing to blacks, most notably
Bradley, creating resentment among even liberal Latino activists."[24]

In 1973, Bradley finally prevailed and became mayor of Los Angeles.
Like his election to City Council in 1963 and his 1969 mayoral cam-

paign, Bradley succeeded largely on a Black–white liberal coalition. So-nenshein's attempts to explain the failure of Latinos to coalesce around Bradley during his 1973 election are somewhat ambiguous.

> On the other hand, the Latino vote may be a class vote. Los Angeles may have a basis for a Black-Latino coalition that is quite different from the sort of coalition that could be made with whites. This Latino class vote gets pulled out of voting analysis as an "ethnic vote," but it may be important in class terms. In the search for a white working-class base for black politics, observers may tend to miss it. If there is a working-class Latino base for the biracial coali-tion, its members probably have different priorities than those of white liberals.[25]

Whatever meaning can be drawn from this statement, the fact remains that Latinos did not vote overwhelmingly for Bradley during his 1969 and 1973 mayoral runs, and the reasons for this reluctance can be exca-vated from the historical relationship between Latinos and Blacks in the political and economic arenas.

Latinos also demonstrated their disaffection for other Black candi-dates when their votes helped defeat two Black candidates to the school board.[26]

Approximately one year later, Bradley helped elect two Black allies to the City Council, increasing the number of Black City Council mem-bers from two to four. Bradley also invited David Cunningham, another Black candidate, to run for his now-vacant City Council seat in District 10. Cunningham ran against a Japanese American candidate, George Takei, who had been chairman for Bradley's 1969 and 1973 mayoral campaigns. Cunningham defeated Takei in December, and like the Latino community, the Asian community would not have one of their own on the council until 11 years later, when Michael Woo won the 1985 election. It was a victory, however, that would come without much Black support.

The coalition that swept Bradley into power retained its base, allowing Bradley to successfully repel opponents in 1977, 1981, 1985, and 1989. It remained, however, a largely Black–white liberal coalition, with only moderate support from Latinos. As long as Blacks and white liberals stuck together, the coalition was unbeatable. While the coalition welcomed the participation of Latinos, it was clear that their role continued to be secondary to the Black-white liberal coalition.

In time the biracial coalition came unglued. Bradley's victory in the 1985 mayoral election surpassed anything that he had experienced in his previous mayoral victories. For the first time he won all 15 council districts. The victory, however, masked changes that were occurring— changes that would eventually lead to the end of Bradley's political career.

In 1985, several events occurred that began to erode the coalition. The first was Bradley's approval of Occidental Petroleum Corporation's plan to drill in the Pacific Palisades area. The decision was apparent confirmation that Bradley had changed from someone committed to quality of life, something highly prized by a certain sector of the white liberals, to someone allied with industrial development.

Bradley damaged his Jewish alliance by not denouncing Nation of Islam leader Louis Farrakhan's anti-Semitic posture immediately when Farrakhan visited Los Angeles. A group of Black leaders had convinced him that they could get Farrakhan to tone down his rhetoric. When Black and Jewish leaders finally convened over the Farrakhan incident, "there was little common ground and much animosity."[27]

The mayor's personal reputation as someone above reproach was tainted when it was reported that Bradley, who received an annual stipend from Far East National Bank (FENB), used his influence to restore city funds that had been removed from the bank. It was alleged that Bradley, at the behest of the FENB president, not only restored a $1 million deposit to the bank but added an additional $1 million. Proof supporting this allegation was "A notation on the treasurer's record 'per the mayor' had been whited out."[28]

James Hahn, Villaraigosa's eventual mayoral opponent, began an investigation of the changes and subsequently issued a report that charged Bradley with ethical improprieties but did not indict him. As these facts were given wide publicity by the newspapers, Bradley's vulnerability became evident. Gloria Molina, then a member of City Council, criticized Hahn for not proceeding with criminal charges, attesting to Bradley's damaged public stature. And while the scandal eventually faded away, Bradley was never able to recover the full trust of the public.

In the 1989 mayoral race, the fracturing of the Black–white liberal coalition was further complicated by the entrance of two challengers in the nonpartisan primary: Nate Holden and Baxter Ward. Neither candidate was considered to be a real threat, not only because of Bradley's long history of success at the polls but also because both candidates did not have much money to spend on the campaign. Bradley had amassed over $1 million, and by the time the campaign ended, he had spent over $2.6 million, compared to $266,723 spent by Holden, his closest spending competitor. However, even with such an enormous expenditure, Bradley won very narrowly, with 52 percent of the vote.

Of the seven districts that Bradley carried, five were predominantly Black and two had white liberal majorities. The three districts in which Bradley was defeated were overwhelmingly white. The districts in which he broke even included two Latino districts, and one mixed Latino-white district. These numbers reaffirmed that Bradley's victory, narrow as it was, rested on his original biracial coalition—Blacks and white liberals. Latinos were almost equally divided but had low voter turnout.

The demise of the coalition, the financial scandal, and the riot that followed the beating of Rodney King in 1992 were the apparent reasons that convinced Bradley not to seek another term in 1993. This allowed Michael Woo, a onetime member of Bradley's political camp, to run against Richard Riordan, a Republican businessman. The Black–white liberal coalition that had so successfully catapulted and maintained Bradley into political prominence did not serve the same purpose for Woo, who was defeated by Riordan.

The 1997 mayoral race revealed the ethnic fault line of the Los Angeles voting public. Riordan, who had successfully created an image as a moderate, was then challenged by Tom Hayden, a Democratic state senator. During his four-year term, Riordan had successfully defined his administration not by political party affiliation but by policy issues and programs that he believed benefitted Los Angeles. President Clinton rewarded his crossover administration by providing federal funds to the city. Riordan, however, alienated Black voters when he refused to renew Black police chief Willie Williams's contract.

Riordan defeated Hayden by a 2-to-1 margin. However, the true significance of the 1997 mayor's race was the emergence of the Latino vote. In 1997, Latinos made up 33 percent of L.A.'s adult population, but only 14 percent of the registered voters. Furthermore, of this small percentage, only 8 to 10 percent of them actually voted. In comparison, even though Blacks constituted only 13 percent of the population, they represented 18 percent of registered voters. But in 1997, Latinos outvoted Blacks 15 percent to 13 percent. Not only that, whereas Blacks voted in overwhelming numbers for Hayden, Latinos voted in greater numbers for Riordan.[29]

Now in the year 2001, Villaraigosa stood toe to toe with Hahn, battling to be the first Latino mayor of Los Angeles in modern times. He hoped it would come about with the help of African American voters. Where he got that notion was a mystery. Certainly it was not from the numbers in the April 10 primary. When all the ballots were finally counted, Hahn got 71 percent of the Black vote and Villaraigosa got only 12 percent. A political realist would have called Villaraigosa aside and advised him to forget about the Black vote—it was lost to him. But why was it lost to him? Madison Shockley, a member of the board of directors of the Southern Christian Leadership Conference, tried to tell him. As she related in the *Los Angeles Times,* for all his willingness to work with the Black community, Blacks had a hard time "seeing a common agenda with the Latino immigrant community. Many blacks view it as a zero-sum political calculation: Their gain is our loss."[30] Her advice to Villaraigosa was to outline to the African American community an agenda that could be shared by both groups: "Villaraigosa must

show blacks a way that African American culture, community and political participation will not be destroyed by the burgeoning Latino
presence." The dilemma was great for Villaraigosa. What could he do to
assure Black voters that he was not going to take away what Kenny had
given to them as the Latino population mushroomed before their very
eyes. Nothing, as it turned out.

Earlier Sonenshein had spoken in much the same manner as
Shockley. Even though Sonenshein allowed that "the most likely rainbow coalition is between Blacks and Latinos," he also observed that,
upon closer examination, Los Angeles rainbow coalitions look less
promising than advertised. "Ethnic conflict and economic competition
significantly undermine the potential of such alliances." [31]

During the runoff, Villaraigosa continued to pursue the Black vote.
He met with the congregation of one of L.A.'s largest and best-known
Black churches, announcing new endorsements from Black leaders—
Bishop John Bryant of the African Methodist Episcopal Church, Bishop
E. Lynn Brown of the Christian Methodist Episcopal Church, Bishop
Leon Ralph of the Interdenominational Church of God of America, and
J. Benjamin Hardwick, president of the Western Baptist State Conven-
tion of California—in an effort to counter Hahn's own growing list of
supporters among Black religious and community leaders. [32] Villa-
raigosa emphasized repeatedly his ability to create coalitions and
stressed how important the Black vote was to his mayoral run.

Less than three weeks before the mayoral runoff vote, Susan Anderson, a Los Angeles writer, presented an upbeat analysis of Villaraigosa's
chances for successfully wooing the Black vote. She pointed out the obvious split among Black community and religious leaders' support for
Villaraigosa and Hahn as proof positive that Hahn did not have the
Black vote in his back pocket. She also underlined Villaraigosa's long
history of involvement with the Black community, beginning with his
high school days when he was involved with the Black Students Union
and continuing to his days as co-chair of the Black-Latino Roundtable
during the 1980s and his long association with coalition builders such

as AGENDA executive director Anthony Thingpen and Community Coalition head Karen Bass.[33]

However, Anderson contrasted Villaraigosa's potential appeal to the Black voters with Kenny's proven track record with the Black community. "Hahn's black supporters have many reasons to stick with their candidate, among them, the unmatched family legacy—'We know him,' say many. . . ."

Anderson's somewhat academic approach to the division among Black voters was made flesh and blood in a piece written by Steve Lopez for the *Los Angeles Times*. In a scene that might have come straight out of the recent film *Barber Shop*, Lopez recounts an encounter between Kevin E. Hooks, a Black 30-year-old owner of an entertainment marketing company and supporter of Villaraigosa, and Tony Wafford, another young Black supporter of Villaraigosa, and some of the denizens of L.T.'s Barber Shop, a Black barbershop in South Central Los Angeles. Their combined attempts to win converts to Villaragosa's camp was met not so much with a virulent dislike of Villaraigosa but with a near-religious fervor in support of Hahn, based almost solely on his father's legacy. "His father didn't have no crooked in him," Hooks is told by one of the elders of the L.T.'s shop. And Lawrence Tolliver, the owner of the shop, lectures Hooks and Wafford that "The Bible tells me that the fruit don't fall far from the tree, and Ken Hahn was a strong tree!" To which Wafford responds, "You pick up fruit, you knock it, you squeeze it. . . . Jim Hahn's daddy's dead, I'm telling you! Is a dead white man better than a live Mexican?" The question was never quite answered, but Tolliver provides the last word. "The bottom line [is that] 90% of the black community is going to vote for Hahn . . . [and] when the white man goes into the booth in the Valley and has to decide between a white man and Mexican . . ." Tolliver does not complete his sentence but it is obvious to everyone in the barbershop which box will be checked by the white voter.[34]

As Election Day approached, the generation gap between older and younger Black voters began to surface. "There is no empirical evidence on this, but we suspect that more and more younger black voters will be attracted to the Villaraigosa campaign," Michael Preston, a USC political scientist, told the *Los Angeles Times*.[35] Preston's statement was given credence by the fact that Villaraigosa's Crenshaw district office was staffed by dozens of volunteers, two-thirds of whom were African American. Another anecdotal indication of the generational division was exemplified by Melina Reiman, a doctoral candidate at USC, who stated that she brought young Black undergraduate and graduate students to hear Villaraigosa present his views on the mayor's race. "Every single person I've brought to hear him speak and hear what he says on the issues has become a supporter," she stated. In contrast, she pointed out that older Black voters insist that she must vote for Hahn, but few of them can give her any specific reasons why she must do so. "The only reason I would get is, 'Wasn't his daddy Kenny Hahn?' "

In the final week of the campaign Hahn revived Villaraigosa's ill-fated letter to Clinton on behalf of Carlos Vignali by running a television ad. It reinforced Hahn's attack on Villaraigosa that he was an unknown candidate who could not be trusted. The ad itself smacked of the Willie Horton commercial run by George Bush against Michael Dukakis in 1988. The Hahn ad depicted a razor blade cutting cocaine, a copy of Villaraigosa's letter to the White House, a grainy photograph of a smoking cocaine pipe and Villaraigosa. As the ad runs, a voice describes the letter and the campaign contributions and states that Villaraigosa "falsely claimed that the crack cocaine dealer had no prior criminal record." The ad ends by stating that "Los Angeles can't trust Antonio Villaraigosa."[36]

On Election Day Hahn was carried into office on the unlikely shoulders of a Black–white conservative coalition. Hahn received 59 percent of white voters, an astounding 80 percent of the Black vote, but only 18 percent of the Latino vote. Villaraigosa received 41 percent of the white vote, 10 percent of the Black vote, and 82 percent of the Latino vote. The predictions and speculation that surrounded Hahn and his Black supporters came true.

While Hahn's father's legacy no doubt proved to be a significant factor in gaining support among Black voters, there were other reasons why Black voters came out in such astounding numbers for Hahn. The *Los Angeles Times* reported, "The anti-Latino anxiety won't show up on any exit pool. But it does in candid conversations. 'I got heat from blacks,' says one African American legislator who endorsed Villaraigosa. 'They asked, Why do you support him? He'll throw us all out.' "[37] This candid comment is understandable in the context of Black politics in Los Angeles. Tom Bradley was mayor for five terms, and during that time Blacks were able to make substantial gains when they were appointed to commissions, received public contracts, and increased their employment both in the city of Los Angeles and in the Los Angeles County public sector. Again, these gains were obtained during the reign of the Black–white liberal coalition, with Latinos and Asians playing a secondary role. This long-term relationship gave Blacks a history and a level of comfort with white liberals that they did not have with Latinos. In addition, unlike the white liberals, Latinos were now in direct competition with Blacks over jobs, housing, and educational opportunity. The interests of the Black voters conflicted directly with the interests of Latinos.

There was another unspoken reason that prevented Villaraigosa from getting the Black vote—a reflection of the candid statement translated into political terms. The fact that at the time of the election Los Angeles was 11.2 percent Black and 46.5 percent Hispanic, reflecting a 15 percent decrease of the Black population since 1990 and a 24 percent increase in the Latino population, frightened many Black politicians, who saw their voting power waning in the state. It was reportedly for this reason that Congresswoman Maxine Waters backed Hahn—"out of fear that Hispanic gains in political power come at the expense of black political power."[38]

Congresswoman Waters had a reason to be concerned. By the time of the mayoral race in Los Angeles, Latinos had eclipsed African Americans as political players in the state, moving from 7 percent of the electorate in 1990 to 14 percent, while Blacks stayed at 7 percent. By the time of the mayoral election, Cruz Bustamante had been elected as the first Latino to a statewide office, and the new state legislature had a record 26-member Latino caucus, while the Black caucus was reduced to 6. Waters must also have been aware that approximately 20 years before, Willie Brown, now mayor of San Francisco, was speaker of the State Assembly, Tom Bradley was beginning his third term as mayor of Los Angeles, Lionel Wilson was mayor of Oakland, Wilson Riles was ending his third term as the state's superintendent of public instruction, and Mervin Dymally was lieutenant governor.

In the aftermath of the election, a flood of statistics provided a glimpse of the future. Take, for example, the Los Angeles mayoral races: in 1993 Latinos cast only 10 percent of the votes; in 1997, they cast 15 percent; in the 2001 mayoral primary, they cast 20 percent; but in the 2001 runoff, they cast 22 percent of the vote. Furthermore, their registered numbers were far greater. More than 315,000 Latinos were registered to vote on Election Day, but only 128,267 actually voted, according to the William Velasquez Institute. Consider that 186,733 Latinos did not vote and Villaraigosa lost by only 40,000.[39] Clearly, if Latinos had shown up at the polls in anything close to their registered numbers, his victory would have been assured.

What do these numbers mean for the future? A Latino optimist would argue that as the number of Latino voters continues to explode, it may be possible for Latinos to form effective alliances with the Jewish liberal vote and this alliance alone would provide a Latino candidate with the votes necessary to gain office.

While it is easy to compare the alliance that helped propel Bradley into office and keep him there with a potential Latino–white liberal alliance that could help elect a Latino mayor and keep him or her in office, such a comparison neglects the dynamics of the growing Latino population.

It is just as likely that as the number of Latinos grows in the general population and on the voter rolls, Latinos will conclude that they do not need to form alliances but can instead act on their own—a posture not unlike that advocated by Stokely Carmichael and Charles Hamilton at the inception of the Black Power movement.

From 1973 to 1993, for 20 long years, Tom Bradley, an African American, held the highest position in Los Angeles city politics. During that time, Latinos were largely excluded from the corridors of city politics.

In 2001, Villaraigosa stood on the brink of being the first Mexican American mayor of Los Angeles in over 130 years. His election would have represented a monumental moment in the history of Los Angeles politics and a sign of a new era for Latinos in California politics. In order to be ushered into that position, Villaraigosa needed the help of Black voters—the very voting block with whom Latinos ostensibly have a symbolic and ideological basis for support. When the dust settled, it was this "friendly" vote that turned against the Latino aspirant and voted in lockstep with white conservatives to deny Villaraigosa his historic moment.

What does this mean for the future of Latino-Black relations in the Los Angeles political arena? A statement from Roger Wilkins, a veteran Black civil rights leader, may be instructive. Before the mayoral race Wilkins noted, "As the Hispanic population grows, as it remembers the predominant place in the racial dialogue blacks traditionally held and remembers its feeling of exclusion, it's going to be hard for them to modulate their feeling of potency from numbers. That's going to cause real stress for blacks."[40] And so it may.

Passed By and Shut Out

Blacks Trapped in Miami's Latino Vortex

> [Native whites] are racists by tradition and they at least know that
> what they're doing is not quite right. . . . Cubans don't even think
> there is anything wrong with it. That is the way they've always re-
> lated, period.
>
> **Black Miami resident**

On Martin Luther King Day in 1989, in the middle of Miami's Overtown district, a run-down predominantly Black neighborhood,
William Lozano, a Latino police officer, shot and killed Clement Lloyd,
a Black motorcyclist. The gunshot to Lloyd's head sent the Kawasaki
Ninja motorcycle careening into an oncoming car. Allan Blanchard,
Lloyd's passenger on the motorcycle, died from head injuries suffered
when the motorcycle slammed into the car.[1]

Lozano's version of why and how he shot Lloyd was quite different
from that of the other eyewitnesses to the incident. Lozano, who the
Los Angeles Times described as "white," was an immigrant from Bo-
gotá, Colombia, and had been on the Miami police force for three years.
He painted a picture of imminent danger to himself. According to
Lozano, Lloyd was being pursued by another police officer. Lozano,
who was several blocks away taking a report from a crime victim, became aware of the chase when he heard it over his radio. Lloyd was
coming directly at him, Lozano avowed, so he was forced to shoot him
in order to avoid being struck by the motorcycle. Witnesses disputed

this account, stating that they saw Lozano next to a patrol car in the company of another policeman. Another man was standing next to Lozano, talking to him about a registration sticker that had been stolen from his license plate. Moments later, the witnesses continued, Lozano "looked up," threw his pen and notebook into the patrol car's open trunk, and took up his gun. "He crouched, then kind of tiptoed out into the street. . . . He crept into the street, almost to the center line, holding his pistol with both hands. Just when the motorcycle came by, he fired. Boom! He meant to kill him," declared a Black witness who refused to identify himself for fear of police retribution.[2]

Moments after the incident occurred a crowd of at least 100 Black residents gathered around the downed motorcycle. When police officers tried to remove Lloyd's body, the milling crowd began to throw rocks and bottles. The police called for backup, and when the supporting officers arrived they did so in full riot gear. This exacerbated the already agitated crowd, and what might have remained a minor disturbance escalated into three days of rioting.

Although the shooting was the trigger event, the true reasons for the rioting were more fundamental and historic. In 1989 unemployment in Overtown and Liberty City, another Black enclave, was as high as 44 percent when those who had given up looking for work were included. The Black poverty rate for Dade County was 35 percent for the adult Black population and 40 percent for Black children. The schools Black children attended were regarded as some of the most segregated in the South, and the dropout rate was 30 percent. Additionally, the African American community was encased in a state of fear and violence, evidenced by the fact that while Blacks made up only 20 percent of Dade County's population, they were 33 percent of the robbery victims and 44 percent of the perpetrators.[3]

These facts were sufficient to stir the emotions of the African American community in Miami on the night of the motorcyclist's killing. The deadly combination of poverty, crime, and drug use were the same elements blamed for other Black riots in the late 1980s and early 1990s. In Miami, however, there was something else added to this already volatile condition. That something else was an intense frustration felt by African Americans at being passed over and shut out by the Latino population of Miami. African Americans viewed themselves not only as indigenous to the region but also as the leaders and thus rightful beneficiaries of the advances made during the civil rights movement of the 1960s. However, beginning in the 1960s with the arrival of Cubans in significant numbers, they stood witness to a transformation of Miami that eventually engulfed them in a Latino maelstrom. Not only did Latinos end up controlling most of Miami's major political, economic, and educational institutions, but their leaders appeared to have little regard for the history of suffering that Blacks had been subjected to or appreciation for their pioneering role in the civil rights movement. In Miami, African Americans confronted something they had not seen before in other parts of the United States—a power structure that felt no apparent guilt or empathy for their plight, or any desire to extend special privileges to them as a disenfranchised group.

This sense of powerlessness and frustration was expressed in graphic terms after the Lozano/Lloyd incident. "What I want to know is how come it's always the Cubans that's shooting the niggers," asked one Black resident. This sentiment, though misplaced on this occasion because Lozano was Colombian, was echoed by a Black former police officer, who declared, "The Cubans will shoot a nigger faster'n a cracker will."[4]

Adding insult to injury, only a week before the shooting, Miami had opened Bobby Maduro Stadium to indigent Nicaraguan refugees who were fleeing the communist Sandinista regime and streaming into the city. This act of compassion stood in sharp relief to the treatment that Blacks received at the hands of the Cuban power structure. "Black Americans for years have been sleeping under the expressways or on the sidewalk, and now the Nicaraguans show up and they get a baseball stadium," observed a Black resident of Miami.[5] The message to Blacks was clear: Not only did Miami's Cuban population sympathize with these new arrivals, whose situation was not unlike their own flight from Castro's Cuba, but their future integration into Miami's power structure seemed assured.

The conditions that led to the 1989 rioting had been brewing for years. Blacks were outsiders looking in. Miami's thriving Latino middle class made their bilingual world almost impenetrable to Blacks, and in most instances, Cuban American voting power rendered the Black vote almost meaningless. But whereas in other cities the conflict between Latinos and Blacks generally took place in the shadow of a larger white community, in Miami Latinos had actually usurped the role of whites and Blacks appeared destined to remain a minority, unable still to challenge the existing power structure.

MIAMI IN THE EARLY YEARS

Migrant Blacks from the Bahamas and the American South created Miami's tourist industry. Blacks "built the railroad, the villas, and the hotels and later staffed them with porters, maids, waiters, and gardeners."[6] They came in such numbers that by 1910, 42 percent of Miami's 5000 residents were Black.

But Southern sensibility required that this workforce cloak itself in invisibility once its work was done so as not to rankle the white tourists. As a result, Blacks were kept in their own quarters and their free movement was controlled by force and intimidation. The northwest section of Miami was given the none too original name of Colored Town, which was later changed to Overtown. It was common knowledge in the Black community that any attempt to move out of the squalid conditions of Overtown would be met with violence.[7]

The forced restriction of Blacks to Overtown did have some positive consequences. In 1910, through the beneficence of Overtown's first and only millionaire, a park, a library, and a school were built. The city's largest Black newspaper, the *Miami Times,* was published in Overtown. Numerous Black civic organizations developed and flourished within

Overtown's confines—the Civic League of Colored Town, the Negro Uplift Association of Dade County, and the Colored Board of Trade.

During the 1930s Liberty City, another Black neighborhood, came into being through the diligent work of a Black Episcopal minister and the Greater Miami Negro Civic League. They convinced the *Miami Herald* to publish a series of articles on the squalid living conditions in Overtown. The articles were read in Washington, D.C., and as a consequence President Franklin D. Roosevelt's Public Works Administration built the first housing project in the Southeast: Liberty Square, an apartment building in Miami that consisted of 34 units.

By 1950, Miami was home to 172,000 residents. It remained a largely segregated Southern city with a small but prominent Jewish community and a large annual tourist population. Blacks continued to perform work in the hotels and other low-skilled service industry–related jobs. In 1960, whites represented 80 percent of the population, Blacks 15 percent, and Latinos 5 percent. These numbers would undergo a radical change during the coming decade.[8]

THE CUBANS ARRIVE

Prior to Castro's ascension to power in January 1959, Cuban immigration to the United States was insignificant. In 1960, the U.S. Census counted 79,156 Cuban-born persons living in the United States. However, "if the refugees who arrived during 1959 are subtracted from these, the prerevolutionary Cuban population in the country can be estimated at no more than 30,000."[9] Between 1959 and 1980 more than 800,000 Cubans fled Castro's Cuba. Alejandro Portes and Robert L. Bach, two scholars who have studied the Cuban population in the United States, estimate that 85 percent of this number came to the United States mainland or Puerto Rico.

It is generally accepted that Cuban immigration to the United States occurred in five significant waves. The first occurred between January 1959 and October 1962. After Cuban dictator Fulgencio Batista

and his supporters fled Cuba, there was an exodus of landowners, in-
dustrialists, and managers of American businesses that the new Cuban
government had expropriated. This group was later joined by a significant number of professionals and merchants. It is estimated that during this time frame 215,000 Cubans fled the island.[10]

The second wave of Cuban immigrants occurred between November 1962 and November 1965. The Cuban missile crisis, which resulted
in the confrontation between the USSR and the United States, halted
all direct flights from Cuba, forcing those who wanted to leave to take
clandestine routes or come in via third countries. While the Cuban
government did not allow the resumption of direct flights to the United
States, in September 1965 it announced that those Cubans who had ex-
iled relatives living in the United States could depart from the fishing
port of Camarioca. The second wave of immigrants totaled 74,000.

The third wave left Cuba between December 1965 and April 1973.
Shortly after Cuba announced the departures from the port of Camari-
oca, it signed a "memorandum of understanding" with the United
States that allowed two daily flights from Varadero Beach in Cuba to
Miami. More than 340,000 new exiles arrived via this route.

The fourth wave occurred between May 1973 and April 1980. The
Cuban government voided the terms and condition of the "memorandum of understanding," and in so doing also terminated the daily
flights. Once again, Cubans who wanted to leave the island had to do so
secretly or travel to a third country. The number of exiles declined during this period to fewer than 3000.

The final period of Cuban immigration, and perhaps the most controversial, occurred between May and September of 1980. It also represented the largest Cuban exodus in a single year. This was the famous
Marielito boat lift, which was inspired by the occupation of the Peruvian embassy in Havana in April 1980 by Cubans seeking political asylum. Initially the Cuban government announced that those wishing to
leave Cuba could do so only via flights to Peru and Costa Rica. Shortly
thereafter, the government amended its edict and announced that anyone who wished to leave Cuba could do so through the Port of Mariel.

During the five-month period it is estimated that 124,769 Cubans arrived in the United States.

Unlike their Mexican, Central American, or South American counterparts, the Cuban exiles were granted special status, allowing them to enter the United States with none of the restrictions that are imposed on other immigrant groups. Furthermore, the Cuban Adjustment Act of 1966 gave automatic legal residency to any Cuban, no matter how he or she entered, after only a year and a day in the United States. The value of this exception is apparent: Refugees fleeing other Communist countries must apply for political asylum and undergo a lengthy process and provide convincing evidence of persecution. The Cuban Adjustment Act also allowed Cubans to apply for federal assistance, including SSI, food stamps, and Medicaid, immediately after becoming legal residents. It is reported that more than 500,000 Cubans immigrated to the United States under the Cuban Adjustment Act.

The effect on Miami was felt almost immediately. In 1962 there were only a few Cuban businesses in Miami. Most were holdovers from the previous anti-Batista exiles. In 1967 Cuban-owned businesses numbered 919, but by 1978 the number had increased to 8000. And by 1985 there were 13,000 Cuban-owned businesses.

The new Cuban population also fueled growth in other industries. Between 1969 and 1977, the number of manufacturing firms had increased twofold and construction firms had tripled. Cuban-owned industries included textiles, leather, footwear, furniture, and cigar making. In the service sector Cuban-owned businesses included "restaurants . . . supermarkets, private clinics, realty offices, legal firms, funeral parlors, and private schools."[11]

By the early 1980s Cubans had not only come to influence the economic sphere of Miami, but they were also major players in Miami's political and cultural life. In 1981 Dade County counted 1.7 million residents, of whom 39 percent were Hispanic, 44 percent white, and 17 percent Black. These numbers translated into a real political presence: The 1981 Miami mayoral race featured two Latino candidates—Puerto Rican–born incumbent Maurice Ferre and his challenger, Manolo Reboso, who was Cuban-born. Equally significant, when Ferre won, it was his fifth two-year term. In other words, Miami's mayor had been a Latino since 1971.[12]

The *Miami Herald* now printed a daily Spanish-language edition, which quickly reached a circulation of 60,000. In order to service the growing Latino population, three television stations and seven radio stations in south Florida broadcast in Spanish. There were also six Latino theaters, two Latino ballet companies, and a Latino light opera company.

By 1981, African Americans had begun to express their frustration and discontent. Not only did they resent the more prosperous and established Cubans, but they also feared that with the recent arrival of the Marielitos, they would lose the few low-skill jobs still available to them. Their feeling of economic marginality was no doubt heightened by the fact that Latinos were creating economic beachheads in the traditionally Black areas of Miami. In Liberty City, the departure of white businessmen opened the door for Latino businessmen, posing a definite threat to struggling Black entrepreneurship. "The only things blacks have in Miami are several hundred churches and funeral homes. After a generation of being Southern slaves, blacks now face a future as Latin slaves,"[13] commented a former Dade County school superintendent.

While they were not major players in the political arena, African Americans could console themselves with the knowledge that they were still pivotal in certain political circumstances. In the 1981 Miami mayoral race it was their vote that helped return Ferre as mayor. Reboso, who had been a participant in the ill-fated Bay of Pigs invasion, the attempt of Cuban exiles to invade and recapture Cuba, played the Cuban American card hard and frequently. Ferre, perhaps sensing that Reboso's Cuban heritage as well as his hands-on anti-Castro credentials had already sewn up the Cuban vote, made his pitch to white and Black voters. In the end Reboso drew 70 percent of the Cuban vote, but Ferre was returned to office with 95 percent of the Black vote and half the white vote. More than half of the African American voters went to the polls. In comparison, only 38 percent of the white voters, perhaps disillusioned by both Latino candidates and their own diminishing role in the electoral process, decided to exercise their vote.

This was the picture in the early 1980s—Latinos, in raw numbers as well as politically and economically, were on the rise and African Americans were doing all they could to retain their position. The 1980s would prove to be a decade filled with strife and conflict, pitting African Americans against the growing Latino power.

RIOTS IN THE EARLY 1980S

The 1989 shooting of the Black motorcyclist was not the first time that the actions of a Latino police officer had triggered a riot among Miami's Black population. In 1980 riots broke out in Liberty City after an all-white jury acquitted four white police officers charged with the beating death of Arthur McDuffie, a black insurance executive. The three-day riot resulted in 18 people dead and between $50 million and $100 million worth of property damage.

And on December 28, 1982, a similar incident involving a Cuban American officer and a Black man also resulted in riots. The official position of the Miami police department was that Luis Alvarez, a Cuban American police officer, entered a video arcade in Overtown to demonstrate to Louis Cruz, a Cuban American police trainee, how to conduct a "routine check." In fact, Alvarez had left his assigned posting in a Latino community and went to Overtown on his own initiative. Why he did this was never made clear. Alvarez claimed that he approached a man named Johnson, who was playing an arcade game, because he had spotted a suspicious bulge under his shirt. In order to disarm Johnson, Alvarez put his own gun to the back of Johnson's head and instructed him not to move. According to Alvarez, Johnson turned suddenly, making Alvarez believe that he was reaching for the gun, and it was then that he shot him between the eyes.[14] Other witnesses, including Johnson's cousin, stated that Johnson made no threatening movements. Johnson lay in a coma for 24 hours before he died.

The 1982 incident pointed to the changing ethnic composition of the Miami police department and of the city as a whole. Between 1981 and 1983 the police department had expanded from 640 to 1039 members. This expansion was in response to one of the highest crime rates in the nation. Of the new officers, 82 percent were minority, but the breakdown favored Latinos. At the time of the Johnson shooting, the Miami police force was 44.2 percent white, 39.2 percent Latino, and 16.6 percent Black. In 1983 the population composition of Miami was 15 percent white, 58 percent Latino, and 27 percent Black.[15]

The shooting touched off three days of rioting in Overtown during which time another Black man was killed by a police officer, more than 25 persons were injured, and 45 more were arrested. T. Williard Fair, president of the Miami Urban League, expressed the anger that Blacks felt when he stated, "Blacks already believe that Cubans have gotten preferential treatment at our expense."[16] Black leaders openly stated that Latino officers were insensitive to Black residents. They pointed to another police shooting two months before Johnson's death: Another Latino police officer, Ernesto Urtiaga, killed a Black suspect after he was stopped near a stolen truck.

Alvarez stood trial for the shooting of Johnson, but for Black residents of Miami the trial must have been déjà vu. As in 1980 when all four police officers were acquitted, an all-white jury, after two hours of deliberation, acquitted Alvarez.

The Miami police department, with the 1980 and 1982 rioting still fresh in their minds, prepared for the verdict by setting up perimeters around Miami's Black enclaves, while the highway patrol closed off some interstate exits. The response of the Black citizens of Miami did not, however, reach the levels of either of the earlier riots. Youths in Liberty City threw stones at a white motorist, set trash on fire, and threw burning furniture into the streets. The tempered response may have been because the U.S. Justice Department was conducting its own investigation to determine if federal charges could be brought against Alvarez. Alvarez was suspended until the federal investigation was completed. In the end no federal charges were brought. The U.S. attorney announced that there was not enough evidence to charge the Latino officer.

MORE NEW ARRIVALS

The futility that Miami's African Americans felt at being unable to draw attention to their economic and social plight was exacerbated by the support that the Cuban Americans gave the Nicaraguan *contras*— the American-backed forces who were fighting the Sandinista government. South Florida had become home to many of the *contra* leaders and field commanders. Adolfo Calero and Arturo Cruz, two members of a trio that ostensibly directed the *contra* strategy, bought homes in Miami, and six of the seven leaders of the United Nicaraguan Opposition's advisory committee moved into south Florida.[17] Even though many wealthy and middle-class Nicaraguans had settled in the Miami area in the late 1970s, particularly after the fall of Nicaraguan dictator Anastasio Somoza Debayle, the real crush of Nicaraguan immigrants began in the mid-1980s when the U.S.-sponsored *contra* war brought disorder to Nicaragua's economy. However, unlike their predecessors, the new arrivals were workers and *campesinos*.

The Nicaraguan fight against the communist Sandinistas rang a bell of sympathy and understanding in Miami's Cuban population. Cuban American doctors would treat soldiers fighting for the *contra* forces at reduced prices, while Cuban-owned radio stations in Miami's "Little Havana" regularly held telethons to raise donations of cash, clothing, medicine, and food.[18] By 1986, as many as 70,000 Nicaraguans lived in Miami, dominating several neighborhoods.

By 1989, the almost daily arrival of Nicaraguans finally began to concern Dade County officials. The Nicaraguan population had grown to 100,000, with the expectation that it would soon grow by another 100,000. In large part, this was based on a ruling by a federal court in Texas that issued a temporary restraining order barring the INS from forcing immigrants to stay at their point of entry until their requests for asylum were completed.[19] This ruling opened the door for Nicaraguans to leave Brownsville, Texas, and head for their destination of choice. For many Nicaraguans that choice was Miami.

As the Nicaraguans started to arrive in Miami, once again the Black residents expressed a fear that they would lose jobs to the new arrivals and that services would be diverted to the new immigrant group. When Officer Lozano shot and killed Clement Lloyd, it was the television images and newspaper photographs of the new immigrants being housed in Bobby Maduro Stadium that Miami Black citizens were viewing.

The African American community was also angry with the treatment that Haitians were being accorded. While Latino groups were being welcomed with opened arms, Haitians were been met at sea and returned to Haiti. Nor were they being granted political asylum in the same numbers as Nicaraguans even though they were fleeing a dictatorship every bit as repressive and cruel as that alleged to be found in Nicaragua. From 1985 through 1988, 1196 Haitians applied for political asylum but only 12, or about 1 percent, of the applications were granted. During that same time 15 percent of the 41,683 applications by Nicaraguans were granted.[20] African Americans could not help but feel resentment at this separate and unequal treatment.

BATTLE LINES DRAWN IN 1989

By 1989 the ethnic lines had been clearly drawn and the terms of engagement defined. Latinos held economic and political power and appeared to care little about the condition of disenfranchised African Americans. "There are many in the black community who are unemployed who cannot feed, clothe or house their families," stated the head of the Dade County Office for Minority Business Development. A Black minister observed that Latinos control much of the city's wealth and political power but are doing little to extend a helping hand to African Americans. "What happens in Miami is Latins look out for Latins. That's the bottom line."[21]

Blacks also expressed frustration at the treatment of Black citizens at the hands of Latino police officers. "Many in this community believe that there is a vendetta being carried out by Hispanic cops against African-Americans. Prejudice is widespread in the Police Department," expressed one prominent Black resident.[22]

Latinos responded to these accusations by blaming the Black residents of Miami for their social condition. A local Spanish-language TV station conducted a poll that found that a majority of Miami's Latinos believed that Blacks themselves were responsible for their plight. "Black people should do more to help themselves. . . . We worked for everything we have. They should too," pronounced Alida Suarez, a Cuban American.[23]

This was the antipathy that existed between the two groups when Lozano was arrested and charged with two counts of manslaughter. This was the antipathy between Latinos and Blacks when Lozano's trial began in October 1989. The Black community was holding its breath and waiting to see if this time justice would finally be done. Miami was prepared for the worst if Lozano was found not guilty. When the jury filed into the courtroom approximately 400 riot police had been spread throughout the Black neighborhoods. Sharpshooters manned their positions from rooftops in anticipation of rioting or looting.

In a little over eight hours of deliberation the jury found Lozano guilty. The verdict was cause for celebration. As word of the verdict reached Overtown, "young blacks danced in the streets to Public Enemy's rap song 'Fight the Power' while others drove about honking their car horns in celebration."[24] However, though the verdict eased the immediate tension, it did little to ameliorate the long-standing friction between Latinos and Blacks. One reporter noted that "Overtown residents are angry that Hispanics and Central American immigrants find jobs easily while blacks face high unemployment."[25]

Lozano returned to court the following month for sentencing, and though the prosecutor asked for 12 years, the judge gave him 7 years. The judge further ruled that he could remain free on a $10,000 bond until his appeals were completed. Black residents were outraged. "If he were black, he'd be in jail right now," declared a Black resident of Over-town.[26] The president of the Southern Christian Leadership Confer-ence angrily denounced the sentencing. "Seven years and bail after two men are dead is a slap in the face. . . . We have black men in jail for stealing a loaf of bread."[27]

The deep divide between Latinos and Blacks was further revealed in 1990 when Nelson Mandela visited Miami. Mandela announced that he would visit Miami Beach, the only city in Florida on his itinerary, as part of his effort to raise funds for his anti-apartheid struggle in South Africa. In fact he was going to Miami Beach for the sole purpose of ac-cepting a check from the American Federation of State, County and Municipal Employees, which had been a longtime supporter of the African National Congress's battle against apartheid.

The African American community was delighted with his visit. Mandela had reached international status after his release from prison only four months before his scheduled visit. Almost immediately there were rumblings of discontent from Cuban Americans. The Cubans were furious with Mandela because of his consistent support for Fidel Castro, which was accented by a nationally televised interview the week before showing Mandela thanking Castro for his help during the ANC's battle against apartheid. Hard battle lines were drawn over this issue.

Five Cuban American mayors in Dade County were so incensed with Mandela's visit that they issued a statement condemning him. The statement was signed by Xavier Suarez, Miami's mayor. Suarez and two other Cuban Americans on the Miami City Commission also decided to abandon a city resolution honoring Mandela.[28]

The African American reaction came in the form of an ultimatum. "We're demanding a proclamation to honor Nelson Mandela, and if we don't get it by 5 p.m. Wednesday they will not get one black vote again. We're tired of this racism, and we're not going to tolerate it anymore," vowed Ray Fauntroy, the executive director of the Southern Christian Leadership Conference. "We're really disappointed by these actions that serve not only to exacerbate deep wounds but to further entrench the racial polarization that has our city in its grip," stated the publisher of the Black newspaper the *Miami Times*.[29]

The Cubans' responses were equally strident. "We don't care for the black leaders. . . . We care about Cuba. Our cause is Cuba," stated a Cuban resident. And Victor DeYuree, a Cuban American on the city commission, made the Cubans' stance on Mandela unequivocal. "I think the black community, after living with us for 30 some odd years, is well aware of our No. 1 issue and that's Fidel Castro. There is no compromise in the Cuban community when it comes to Fidel."[30]

As the date for Mandela's visit approached, the police devised a strategy for keeping the two groups apart and thus diminishing the possibility of violence. First, it activated a rumor-control hotline, something that was generally reserved for hurricanes or potential riot situations. It also confined the opposing groups to opposite sides of the enormous Miami Beach Convention Center and enlisted 130 police officers and security guards from the U.S. State Department to patrol the convention center.

When Mandela finally arrived in Miami Beach and walked into the convention center, he also walked directly into the Black-Cuban conflict that had been brewing since his visit was announced. Inside the center all was cool and gracious, but outside thousands of Black Mandela supporters and hundreds of Cuban Americans hurled insults and menacing gestures at each other. Cuban Americans called for Blacks to return to Africa where "they belonged," and Blacks responded by chanting "Lozano."

The Cuban reaction to Nelson Mandela's visit was a further wake-up call to many Blacks in Dade County. H. T. Smith, a Black lawyer, dedicated himself to convincing Black organizations to boycott Dade County. He promised to persuade one Black organization a week to boycott Miami as a convention site or remove Miami from its list of sites. The first such organization to comply with Smith's request was the National Bar Association, with 13,000 members. By the ninth week of the boycott, Smith estimated that Dade County had lost more than $17 million in convention business.[31]

The success of the boycott inspired its leaders to expand its scope to address the lingering problems that Blacks had suffered over the years. Smith and his supporters insisted that Blacks be awarded a fair share of the tourism jobs and vendor contracts. They also demanded a review of the U.S. immigration policies that ostensibly discriminated against Haitians.

In June 1991 the Miami Court of Appeals overturned Lozano's conviction. The three-judge panel reversed the decision because they believed that jurors had been fearful that an innocent verdict would cause rioting. The court wrote, "We simply cannot approve the result of a trial conducted, as was this one, in an atmosphere in which the entire community including the jury was so obviously . . . so justifiably concerned with the dangers which would follow an acquittal." [32]

Once again Miami prepared for an outbreak of violence in the Black communities, but this time not much happened. H. T. Smith explained it this way: "The message was this: We won't burn our own community this time. . . . We will not destroy our neighborhoods this time." [33]

Shortly after the decision was rendered, two Latino police officers were involved in the shooting of another Black man. On June 27, 1991, Jorge García and Serafín Ordoñez responded to a call involving a man who was shooting in the street. When they arrived, a man identified as Charlie Brown was shooting. García and Ordoñez fired and wounded the man. Other witnesses, including Brown's mother, dispute this account, stating that Brown had dropped his gun and was walking toward the police with his hands up when they shot him. [34]

As word spread, rioting broke out in Overtown. The police arrested 25 people, one building was burned, and a store was partly looted. The response, perhaps because Brown did not die, and also perhaps because the residents of Overtown had tired of massive rioting, was muted compared to the 1980 and 1982 rioting.

In May 1993, the African American community finally ended its two-and-a-half-year boycott of Dade County's convention business. What had been termed the "quiet riot" cost Dade County about $50 million in lost business. It also gave notice to the tourism industry that for all of the problems that it had endured over the years, the Dade County Black population could still wield power.

The end was brought about by a coalition of Blacks, non-Latino whites, and Latino leaders who agreed to provide assistance to the Black community. Corporations and banks promised to help Black businessmen start or expand a minimum of 10 businesses each year, put together a consortium of Black owners for a hotel, and assist Black businesspeople to qualify for the financing, bonding, and insurance that are needed to bid for work.

After several delays and a change in venue, in May 1993, Lozano was retried for Lloyd's death. When the jury returned a not-guilty verdict there was an expectation that violence might once again erupt. The expectation died quietly—only minor incidents were reported. By now it seemed that the African American community had resigned itself to not receiving justice through the legal process. "That man [Lozano] got away with murdering two people," stated one Black Miami resident.[35] And celebrations by Latinos, particularly Colombians, seemed to confirm that the antipathy between Latinos and Blacks was still prevalent in Miami.

The end to the boycott brought about through the use of the quiet riot was hailed as a new beginning with the stated goal of trying to lure back 200 Black professionals who left Dade County out of frustration and resentment at being locked out of the economic and political power structure.

The new beginning, it turned out, was not different from the old past. In 1997 Black Miami residents spoke about being passed by instead of being displaced by the Latino community. Nowhere was this more evident than in the political process, where Blacks had declined to 25 percent of registered voters while Latinos had grown to 50 percent. In Dade County, where 2 million Latinos live, the two prior mayoral elections and Miami City Commission seats were drawn along racial lines, with the Black candidates losing despite near unanimous support from the Black voters. Of the five city commissioners, four were Latino and one was white. Miami had also proven inhospitable to

Black professionals who felt left out of the job market because they could not speak Spanish.[36]

In 1997 Latinos had increased their dominance in Miami. Out of a population of 375,000, 62 percent were Latino, 25 percent were Black, and 12 percent were white. These numbers were significant when racial tension between Latinos and Blacks revolved around the appointment of a replacement city commissioner. On July 29, 1997, Humberto Hernández, a city commissioner, was indicted in a federal bank fraud and money-laundering probe that resulted in his suspension from his post. After being suspended, Hernández appeared in Spanish-language radio stations to complain that he was singled out because he was Latino and that his replacement should be a Latino. Unfortunately for Hernández his argument was weakened by the fact that not only were three of the five commissioners Latinos but the seat that he held was previously occupied by Miller Dawkins, an African American who also lost his seat after having been indicted in a federal bribery probe.[37] When Blacks lost the Dawkins seat to Hernández, many argued that they were disenfranchised.

In the year 2000 the Black-Latino conflict continued to manifest itself. The flash point was Elián Gonzalez, the young Cuban boy who was brought to Miami after his mother drowned en route to the United States. His Cuban father wanted him returned to Cuba to be with him. The Cuban American community was on fire with emotion that such a thing would happen. In their eyes Elián was not going back to his father, he was going back to the hated Castro, and they wanted him to stay in Miami with his relatives.

In this instance the Cuban Americans stood alone. Most Americans believed that Elián should be with his father, and none of Miami's other ethnic groups sided with the Cuban Americans. Not surprisingly, the group with the least sympathy for the Cuban American position was Miami's African American residents. H. T. Smith, the veteran Black activist who spearheaded the quiet riot, expressed the differences between Cuban Americans and Blacks when he said, "What Cuban-American leadership fails to understand is that they are the majority political power behaving as a minority." This observation was echoed by one of the Cuban demonstrators, who proudly stated, "We've been around here for 41 years and have learned how the system works."[38]

In December 2002, a study was conducted that concluded that more than half of Miami-Dade County's residents believe that race and ethnic tensions are a serious problem. The survey of more than 1000 residents was commissioned by the Miami-Dade County Community Relations Board and focused on perceptions and beliefs about race, ethnicity, and religion. The survey found, not surprisingly, that the greatest tension existed between Blacks and Cubans.[39] For most long-time Black residents of Miami, no such report was needed. All they had to do was call on their collective memories to confirm that friction between Latinos and Blacks was a long-standing problem. All they had to do was look around and see the power wielded by Latinos in Miami.

Since the arrival of the Cubans in the early 1960s, African Americans have seen their fortunes diminish. The successful Cubans zoomed past them, pulling other Latino groups in their slipstream. Once in power, Latinos have held tightly to the reins and because they did not feel responsible for the plight of African Americans, they did not appear compelled to extend a helping hand. Friction, violence, and deeply troubled waters have resulted from this relationship and it is a friction that promises to continue into the future.

When Blacks Rule

Lessons from Compton

Latinos of Compton have plenty of reasons to lament. The city is being run and operated without their input and participation. Even though they represent such a large portion of the area's population they experience systemic exclusion.

As a resident of 25 years in Compton, I found it very painful to know that blacks in power can be just as insensitive to minorities as whites have traditionally been toward their race.

FRANK M. SIFUENTES
Letter to the Los Angeles Times

Beginning in the late 1940s and 1950s the city of Compton, California, a hamlet adjacent to Los Angeles, began to change complexion. The largely white city began to experience an influx of African Americans who, barred from many sections of Los Angeles, found that Compton was open, if not necessarily receptive, to them. The good citizens of Compton conceded the west side of town to the newly arriving Black residents, reserving the east side to themselves. Not only did the white citizens of Compton maintain their grasp on the east side, but they also held tightly to the city's political and economic structure. The persistent attempts by African Americans to break into the corridors of power included standard tactics of the period, including frequent picketing at government offices. But for all their attempts, Blacks were unable to break the stranglehold that the white citizens had on Compton's political and economic power centers.

Things began to change in 1965 after the rioting in nearby Watts. Whites in Compton, fearful that the same thing might happen on the west side, began to flee, leaving the city in the hands of the Black residents. As the white citizens left, they were replaced by Blacks, and the political vacuum created by their departure was filled by the deserted and the newly arriving African Americans. By 1968 Blacks, now with an overwhelming majority population, had gained control of the city council and the school board and also replaced most of the white employees at city hall and in the schools.

African Americans might have continued their monopoly on Compton's political, educational, and economic structures, unchallenged by any group, if the city's ethnic population had not started to change in the late 1980s. Unfortunately for the Black population of Compton, by now accustomed to holding the reins of power, Latinos started to appear in significant numbers. In 1980, the U.S. Census listed the African American population at 73.2 percent and Latinos at only 21.6 percent. However, by 1988 the Latino population had grown to 32.0 percent.[1]

This demographic shift presented the Black power structure with a dilemma: How should they react to the growing presence of a new "minority" group who was demanding inclusion in Compton's political and economic structures? Should they recall their own experience in trying to break into the white power structure during the 1950s and early 1960s and reach out to the new group to incorporate them into the governance of the city? Or should they view Latinos as challengers to the gains they fought so hard to achieve and hold them at arm's length? As it turned out, they chose the latter, and in so doing provided valuable insights to those who believe that Black-Latino alliances are both natural and to be expected.

Three areas of conflict arose beginning in the late 1980s and continuing to the present. One battlefront was over educational resources and representation on the school board. The change in student demographics made this an early and significant issue. Between 1984 and 1989 the Latino student population in the Compton school district increased by 17 percent, while the Black student enrollment decreased by 16 percent. By the 1988–1989 academic year, 12,393 Latinos and 13,447 Blacks were enrolled—an almost equal division between the groups.[2]

The increase in Latino student enrollment, however, did not see a concomitant increase of Latinos in the school administration. In 1989, only 3.6 percent of the 1385 teachers and administrators were Latino, while Blacks held 77 percent of those positions. Latinos also pointed out that Compton had only 30 teachers who held credentials for teaching bilingual education, while the Spanish-speaking student body of the school district numbered 7500. Based on what they saw as an obvious disparity, and one that they did not consider to be accidental, Latinos charged Blacks with discrimination.

The second arena of conflict was public sector jobs. Latinos charged Blacks, who occupied almost all of the public sector jobs, with "systemic discrimination," pointing out that only 9.7 percent of the 514 full-time city jobs were held by Latinos while Blacks held 78 percent of the jobs. The same battle that was being fought in Los Angeles County was being replayed in Compton. The accused Blacks, unaccustomed to being in such a position but also veterans of similar battles with whites, responded with the party line that their administrators "are recruiting [Latinos] and they've done a tremendous job as far as recruiting goes."[3]

The third turf war involved representation on the city council, where no Latino had been elected in 20 years. Latinos were severely handicapped in this area. While their numbers were increasing on a yearly basis, many of the new residents were undocumented immigrants who were unable to vote or legal residents who paid little or no attention to the political process. In 1989, Martín Chavez, a Latino candidate, acknowledged this weakness when he pointed out that of Compton's 40,000 registered voters, only 1800 were Latino.

Even though Latinos lacked the voting numbers to effectively challenge the existing Black power structure, they still lobbied for their share of public sector jobs, bilingual personnel in city hall and schools, and city improvements to their neighborhoods. The city responded to their clamor for equal access by creating a Committee on Hispanic Affairs, which consisted of Latino leaders and city staff members who were appointed by the city council to work on Latino hiring concerns.

In April 1989, the Committee on Hispanic Affairs presented an affirmative action plan to the city council that had as one of its goals tripling the number of Latinos hired over the next five years.[4] The city accepted the recommendation but remained noncommital on its implementation. There appeared to be two reasons for the city's lack of commitment. The first was based on bitter feelings harbored by some Black leaders who remembered a time when Latinos were in relative positions of power but allegedly refused to extend a hand to Blacks. In an interview with the *Los Angeles Times,* Maxcy D. Filer, a city councilman, pointed out that Manual Correa, the only Latino member of the Compton school board, was on the city police force when Blacks were trying to break into the employment rolls there; that Joe Ochoa, a Compton Latino activist, was on the Compton Personnel Board when Blacks were lobbying for government jobs; and that Ray Gonzales, a deceased Latino leader, was a school board member when Blacks were fighting to be hired as teachers. "I don't remember any of them fighting for Blacks. Where were they when I was walking a picket line in Compton," he told the reporter.[5]

The second reason reflected a deeply ingrained perspective held by some Blacks and which was also expressed by Filer, when he openly conceded that there were very few Latinos working for the city of Compton. "But if you go and look at the factories between Alondra [Boulevard] and Artesia [Boulevard], 98% of those working there are Hispanic."[6] What Filer appeared to be saying was that because Latinos were being hired in the private sector (with the implication that Blacks were being passed over by employers in favor of Latino workers), Compton was justified in discrimination against Latinos in public sector employment.

In the summer of 1989, the Compton school district was plagued with problems: low student scores on state tests; loss of teachers to neighboring Los Angeles County because of better wages offered by that district; buildings in great disrepair, leading some parents to charge that they were unsafe; and a Latino student population with special needs that were going unmet. Latinos continued to assail the school board for its failure to respond to the needs of its growing Latino population by failing to hire more bilingual teachers and Latinos in administrative positions.

Curiously enough, in the spring of 1989, Pedro Pallan, a longtime Latino activist, was removed from his position as personnel commissioner of the Compton school district on the grounds that he was not a resident of the district. Pallan was convinced that the true reason for his removal was his outspoken criticism of the district for its failure to hire sufficient numbers of bilingual teachers and its discrimination against Latinos. After consulting with counsel, Pallan filed a lawsuit to regain his position. Four years later, the court would agree with Pallan, concluding that the school district had wrongfully dismissed him. But for four years Pallan was prevented from actively working with the personnel commission to correct the discriminatory practices in which, he believed, the school district engaged.

Matters were made more difficult for the school district when in the fall of 1989 Ted D. Kimbrough, who had been superintendent since 1982, was allowed to terminate his contract with the district in order to assume the position of superintendent for the Chicago school district. It was generally agreed that Kimbrough, who in 1987 had been selected Superintendent of the Year by the Association of California School Administrators, had created order and brought professionalism to the school district. Wiley Jones, the director of the Compton teachers union, opined that before Kimbrough arrived in Compton, the schools were "deplorable" but now they are just "bad."[7]

The summer of 1989 also saw 30 persons file as candidates for five open seats on the seven-seat Compton school board. Manuel Correa was the only Latino incumbent on the school board who was running.

Gogornio Sánchez Jr. was the only Latino challenger. In November 1989, five incumbents, including Correa, were returned to the school board.

The 1990s began with a clear notice to the Black leaders of Compton of the shifting ground beneath their feet. The 1990 Census figures were out, and citywide the Black population had dropped from 73 percent in 1980 to 66 percent in 1990, while the Latino population shot up from 21 percent to 30 percent. By 1990, the number of Latino children in the Compton school district had become a majority. The 1990s, however, also began with a sobering reminder to the Latino community that even though their numbers had been increasing on a yearly basis, they remained powerless. Blacks controlled every public institution in Compton as well as the chamber of commerce and the Democratic Party machine, and they displayed no inclination to share that power with their brown brethren. "Here we are, a truly minority community and the blacks are not giving us an affirmative action committee in either the city [government] or the school district. There cannot be equal employment opportunity without an affirmative action committee," stated Pallan.[8]

As Pallan pointed out, the affirmative action plan recommended by the Committee on Hispanic Affairs had withered and died on the vine and Latinos' calls for equal treatment by Black officials fell on unsympathetic ears. School trustee John Steward expressed his disdain for Latinos' calls for affirmative action policies, stating that such policies were "reparation" to Black Americans for their years of slavery and not for successfully crossing the "border 10 to 15 times a year."[9]

The struggle over education resources continued unabated, indeed increasing in intensity. Latinos militated against Black teachers who were insensitive to Latino children, while Blacks fretted about having to spend an increasing amount of the school budget on bilingual education, demonstrating little sympathy for Spanish-speaking students. "I have no respect for the language issue. This is America. Because a person does not speak English is not a reason to provide exceptional resources at public expense," said John Steward.[10]

The resignation of Ted Kimbrough, the school superintendent, and the subsequent appointment of another Black superintendent, set off another firestorm of conflict between Latinos and Blacks. After Kimbrough's resignation, Elisa L. Sánchez was named acting superintendent. Sánchez first came to the school district in 1983 as an acting superintendent and was later made a deputy in charge of all instructional and curricula matters. For seven months Sánchez proved her ability to successfully run the school district by steering it through difficult financial waters. Latinos thought that she would be a natural successor to Kimborough. The school board thought otherwise and instead appointed J. L. Handy, a Black educator, as superintendent.[11]

Latinos were outraged and saw Handy's appointment as another example of blatant "systemic discrimination" by African Americans against Latinos. Joseph Ochoa, a Latino activist, went so far as to encourage Latino parents to keep their children at home for several days, which would have the effect of bankrupting the school district. Ochoa made no bones about his feeling, charging that the failure to hire Sánchez was discrimination. "What else is it?"[12]

The Latinos' frustration over their electoral impotence continued into the 1990s. In 1991, Pallan, the sole Latino in the city council races, ran against five Black candidates for the District 1 city council seat. Pallan estimated that although there were about 2400 registered Latino voters he believed would vote for him, they would not necessarily provide him with the more than 50 percent of votes necessary for an outright win, but could potentially catapult him into the runoff election in June. Pallan's prediction turned out to be true, and on April 16 he became the first Latino to secure enough votes to contend in the runoff. Pallan came in second with 21 percent of the vote, and Omar Bradley, a Lynwood High School teacher, secured 31.2 percent of the votes.[13]

A newspaper account reporting the results of Pallan's historic achievement could not help adding the footnote that since 1980 the Latino population in Compton had climbed 131 percent, and that Latinos constituted as much as 44 percent of the total population.

During the runoff campaign, both Pallan and Bradley sought Maxcy

D. Filer's endorsement. Filer had represented District 1 for 15 years, and had chosen not to run for reelection, instead running unsuccessfully for mayor. Given Filer's statements regarding the Latinos in Compton at the time Blacks were seeking to break into the white power structure, it was not surprising that he threw his support behind Bradley's campaign. Pallan, for his part, obtained the endorsement of Assemblyman Willard H. Murray Jr. and councilwoman Patricia A. Moore.

The runoff results confirmed the feeble voting power that Latinos exercised in Compton. Bradley won the runoff election in a landslide, garnering more than 64 percent of the vote. Pallan managed to get only 1,577 votes or only 206 more votes than he got in April. Pallan attempted to put a positive spin on the results by observing, "We are determined to be part of the political mosaic here, and we will be successful. Latinos here in Compton can sway the vote."[14] What the numbers made clear, however, was that Latinos, in spite of their increased population, had a long way to go before they would have the votes to put "one of their own" on the city council.

Meanwhile on the educational front, matters were worsening, approaching near-critical levels. Consistently low educational scores in the Compton School District prompted Assemblyman Willard H. Murray Jr. in 1991 to introduce a bill calling for the California superintendent of schools to take over the district. The Compton school board, outraged by the bill, formally condemned the legislation, and Murray announced that the bill was not active and that in all likelihood he would not introduce it during the next legislative session. Had the bill been successful, it would have been the first time that a school district was taken over because of poor academic scores.

Murray's initial resolve not to introduce the bill in the following legislative session was severely tested by what he witnessed in the schools in Compton: a 29 percent dropout rate (40 percent higher than the statewide average), low test scores (ranked among the lowest in the state), and an overhead that appeared to drain the school budget (23 percent higher than the average for other large school districts). Murray, apparently convinced by what he had witnessed, introduced not one, but four bills that marked Compton for help, including taking it over, because of poor academic performance.

In an attempt to have improvements made to the school system, Murray wanted it examined to determine if Compton exhibited specific elements contributing to its poor performance. Handy responded to this criticism by suggesting that under his administration the school district had begun a recovery. One Compton school employee attempted to place the blame on the exploding Latino population. This argument was based on the fact that the school district witnessed the Latino student population grow from 51 percent in 1990 to 57 percent in the spring of 1992. Only 30 percent of the students had limited English proficiency; 37 percent received welfare; and 65 percent were on some form of subsidized lunch program.[15]

In June 1992, a report prepared by the Department of Education, at the request of Assemblyman Murray, and released by the Los Angeles Office of Education, reported that the Compton school district had not done more with "a multitude of resources." The report noted that Compton students were consistently at the bottom of achievement tests. As an example, in 1989–90, Compton students rated so low on the statewide tests that 99 percent of the students taking the test scored higher.[16] By early December 1992, the Compton school board, still worried about a takeover of the district and unhappy with Handy's administration, fired him, ending his two-year term as superintendent of the school district. The search was on for a new superintendent.

While the search to replace Handy was being conducted, the school board named Harold L. Cebrun as acting superintendent. Cebrun had been working for about a year and half as an area superintendent supervising Dominguez High, a Compton high school, as well as its feeder elementary and middle schools. The school board apparently still refused to recognize the needs of its growing Latino students by naming a Latino school superintendent.

In late February 1993, Latino students at Compton's Whaley Middle School informed school officials that they did not believe they were receiving equitable treatment at the school. The discontent among

Latino students spread to other campuses, and in the spring students, parents, and activists at Walton Middle School charged at a school board meeting that the Black staff discriminated against Latino students. The grievances ranged from insulting remarks made about Latinos to the lack of Spanish-language teachers and materials.

Also in February 1993 Compton school officials revealed that the school district owed the county education office approximately $2 million in back payments for special-education services provided to the district over a period of approximately three years. This revelation was the latest in a series of financial problems the school district had faced. In November 1992, auditors discovered that the district owed approximately $1 million in tax penalties. This audit came on the heels of another that discovered that the school district had wasted millions of dollars on various construction projects and food service. It was concluded that the school district had a total budget shortfall of $4.9 million.[17]

While Kelvin Filer, the school board president, sounded surprisingly optimistic that the matter could be resolved with help from the county, it was disclosed the following month that the school district's debt was greater than the $4.9 million announced and would force the district to request a loan from the state of between $12 million to $16 million just to keep the school in operation through the fall. If such a loan were given to the school district, the state would have the authority to take over the school district and run it. Willard H. Murray, already vigilant of the district's poor academic performance, offered to sponsor legislation to authorize the loan. "I was flabbergasted by this new revelation. I would characterize it as sheer incompetence," he stated upon learning of the financial condition of the school district.[18]

Compton's school district's financial woes were exacerbated by its continuing problem with administration and oversight of the school system. In early May 1993, another report issued by the Los Angeles County Office of Education characterized the Compton school district as one rife with "political cronyism and mismanagement," where leadership was notably absent. The report found problems with almost every aspect of the school system and cited as a glaring example of the fact that the district never "developed consistent philosophy for bilingual education, even though the student population is 57 percent Latino."[19]

In the summer of 1993, the financially strapped district was given a $10.5 million emergency loan, and Stan Oswalt, a state-appointed administrator, was put in place to take over the reins. The school board members were no longer able to vote on school district issues, use their offices, or collect their $1000 monthly stipend.

School board members responded angrily to being relieved of their responsibilities. John Steward, a school board member, wrote to the *Los Angeles Times,* but in expressing his anger he let slip one of the true reasons for his frustration—that school funds were finally being used to address the special needs of the Latino student population. Unable to directly attack this expenditure, Steward charged the state administrator with promoting division between Latinos and Blacks by "focusing district resources on providing additional services to students who speak limited English at the expense of English-speaking students. . . ." Steward did not make clear how meeting the needs of Spanish-speaking Latino students was divisive. He simply stated, "However, the issue here was not overcoming language barriers but divide and conquer."[20]

The battle over representation on the city council raged side by side with the controversy of bias against Latino students in the school district. In 1993 Latinos, in a continuing bid to get some political representation, entered into what they believed was a "coalition" with Omar Bradley, the Black candidate who so soundly defeated Pallan in the city council runoff race for District 1 and who ran for mayor in 1991. Pallan, the longtime Latino activist, supported Bradley during his campaign with the apparent understanding that, if Bradley was elected, he would work to get a Latino appointed to the city council. It was a sentiment that Bradley expressed repeatedly during his campaign and one on which Pallan and the Latino community placed a great deal of faith. After Bradley was elected mayor, an opportunity presented itself for him to made good on his promise when a lame-duck city council voted to install Bradley immediately as mayor, leaving his seat empty. Pallan and other Latino leaders saw this vacancy as a rare opportunity to finally get representation for the growing Latino community. Even if they could not get a city councilman elected on their own, then their "coalition" with Bradley would allow him to appoint a Latino. It was expected that Bradley would work to get Pallan appointed.[21]

Bradley failed to keep his campaign promise, and instead of appointing Pallan, the lame-duck city council appointed Ronald Green, a longtime Bradley supporter and ally—and an African American. Latinos were stunned. Lorraine Cervantes, a Bradley supporter and campaign worker, stated, "I feel betrayed. A few years ago the white man was doing this to the black man and now black men are doing this to brown people."[22] Bradley defended his failure to deliver by stating that Pallan simply did not have the support of the lame-duck council members, and that the lack of support was not because he was a Latino.

The conflict between Blacks and Latinos that manifested itself in the adult world of educational policy makers and political candidates also erupted among youths in the Compton schools. On November 18, 1993, Howard Blume, a reporter for the *Los Angeles Times,* noted that "racial incidents" had occurred in three high schools in Compton—Dominguez High, Compton High, and Centennial High. At Centennial High, what should have been an insignificant incident involving an underclassman and seniors escalated into a fight between Latino and Black students with some forty combatants and onlookers.[23] The Centennial High incident was one in a series of such confrontations. On October 25, fights erupted throughout the Centennial High campus, forcing the school to close early. The following day a fight broke out at Dominguez High, and because students were allowed to congregate in the halls, a large fight developed between Latino and Black students. In early November, a fight between a Latino student and a Black student led to a "brawl" behind the school auditorium during which one student's nose was broken, another student's jaw was fractured, and another suffered cuts. And on November 10, approximately 30 students fought in various fights that took place during the lunch hour.

Blume observed that these clashes were not restricted to Compton, but manifested themselves in Lynwood High, Jordan High in Long Beach, and various schools in the Los Angeles School District. According to Blume's report, these other fights in Compton were directly attributable to a perception that Latinos and Blacks were in competition for limited jobs and community resources and that each group saw such competition as a zero-sum game.

Some Latinos, however, placed the blame on the Black students as well as the school administration. "Most of the problems is blacks attacking Latinos, and that's the way it has always been," opined John Ortega, a Latino activist who was critical of the school district. Black activists saw the problem as one ostensibly created by Oswalt, who was white and who Blacks believed favored Latinos and discriminated against Blacks. Indeed, Amen Rahh, a school board member, repeatedly accused Oswalt of being a racist who instituted neo-Nazi policies targeting Black students and employees.[24] Whatever the cause, it was undeniable that friction between Blacks and Latinos in the adult world had found a parallel manifestation among adolescents.

On February 4, 1994, Jerome Harris, a Black educator, was appointed by the state to replace Oswalt. As former superintendent of the school district in Atlanta, Harris had apparently demonstrated his ability to take on the task of turning the Compton school district around. In the spring of that year he promoted Cebrun from acting superintendent to superintendent of the school district.

This ongoing conflict in the educational, political, and economic arenas was exacerbated when a Latino "Rodney King"–type incident fed fuel to the fire. On July 29, 1994, a videotape was taken of Michael Jackson, a Black Compton police officer, beating Felipe Soltero, a 17-year-old Latino youth who was much smaller than he. The versions of what happened between the Black police officer and the Latino boy were at odds. The *Los Angeles Times* reported that a social worker had gone to Soltero's home where he lived with his mother, his mother's companion, Manuel Shigala, and five other children. The social worker alleged that Soltero interfered with her investigation and called the Compton police for assistance. From that point forward the stories diverge. Jackson alleged that Soltero threatened the social worker and attempted to take the police officer's gun when he was instructed to put his hands behind his back. Soltero alleged that Jackson knocked him to the ground as he was being arrested, and when he stood up the officer struck him in the face with a baton. The videotape, which was shown repeatedly on the local television stations, showed Jackson striking Soltero on the side of the head with his baton, striking him repeatedly with the baton after Soltero had fallen on the ground, jumping on his back, handcuffing him, and dragging him across the ground by his handcuffs.[25]

The incident gave fodder to Latino activists who saw the videotape as yet another manifestation of their struggle against the Black power structure of Compton. Pallan charged that Soltero's beating was an example of racism by Blacks against Latinos, and Arnulfo Alatorre Jr., president of the Latino Chamber of Commerce, stated, with no small amount of hyperbole, that Latinos were treated worse than Blacks were treated by whites in South Africa.

The protest over the beating of Soltero intensified the conflict between Blacks and Latinos. Mayor Omar Bradley appeared to see no reason why Blacks should extend the benefits obtained by Blacks to Latinos. Other Black community leaders saw the situation for what it was. Rev. William R. Johnson Jr., the pastor of Temple Christian Methodist Church, said, "We are today the entrenched group trying to keep out intruders, just as whites were once the entrenched group and we were the intruders."[26]

In the wake of the Soltero beating, Latinos formed a new group, Latinos United Coalition of Compton, which called for the creation of a civil board to review police actions, federal investigation into the Black-Latino conflict, and creation of an affirmative action and job-training program for Latinos.

Bradley, for his part, argued that he was powerless to give political representation to Latinos. "What does the African American do to empower them [Latinos] when it's constitutionally illegal [for noncitizens to vote]?" he told the *Los Angeles Times*.[27] While Bradley could hide behind this argument as it related to elected seats on the city council and the school board, it could not be used for the opening of employment with the city departments or the school district. While city officials reported that Latinos represented over 50 percent of the population, only 10.78 percent of the city's full-time employees were Latinos. Bradley had clearly set forth the only terms under which Latinos would obtain political representation—they would have to wrestle it away by voting Blacks out of power.

Friction between Latinos and the Black city council continued to escalate. In September 1994, the city council agreed to create an Office of Human Relations. Latinos wanted the office to focus exclusively on Latinos and pressed its case by presenting figures from a federal commission that showed that Latinos represented only 10 percent of the city's workforce while Blacks held 78 percent of the jobs. These figures remained constant even though between 1980 and 1990, the Black population dropped 21 percent while that of Latinos rose by 131 percent.[28] Paul Richard, the Black assistant city manager, attempted to deflect the damning nature of these facts by pointing out that Latino employees exceeded the number of Blacks employed by some outside contractors. Latinos, predictably, were outraged at this "apples and oranges" comparison, but it also demonstrated the type of tortured logic that the African American power structure was invoking in order to justify Black overrepresentation on city employee rolls. In another move that further frustrated Latino activists, the city's promise to revise its 20-year-old affirmative action plan to reflect dates by which more Latinos would be employed was delayed.[29]

Meantime, the Black-dominated school board demonstrated its apparent unwillingness to expand Latino representation on the school board even though half of the Compton student population was now Latino. The problem for the school board began when it ousted board member Lynn Dymally in November 1994, because of unexcused absences.[30] The ability to appoint a replacement for Dymally was one of the remaining vestiges of power that the school board still possessed after the school district had been taken over by the state of California.

The board put out a call for applicants, and among the 13 finalists was Martín Chavez, a Latino and a human resources official at the Port of Los Angeles. Chavez had received the top rating from a screening committee, and the Latino leadership in Compton expected that he would be appointed. The school board, however, had other plans. Instead of selecting Chavez, the school board appointed Black candidate Saul E. Lankster to the vacant position. Lankster's selection was immediately mired in controversy. He had served on the Compton school board from 1977 to 1981, but he had also been convicted of felony charges for selling "false traffic school diplomas" to state investigators. His conviction resulted in a sentence of 120 days in jail and he was given three years' probation.[31]

In addition to concerns over his criminal conviction, Lankster's appointment was challenged by Jerome Harris, the administrator appointed by the state of California to run the school district and who succeeded Oswalt, because the decision appointing Lankster was conducted in secret and thus in violation of California's public meeting laws. The school board acknowledged the procedural defect involved in appointing Lankster and scheduled another vote, to be taken on the following Friday.[32]

Latinos, as might be expected, were outraged at what they considered another clear act of disenfranchisement by Blacks and further confirmation that Blacks would not voluntarily share power. "It's time the board stops playing these racist games and hires the best-qualified candidate," Pallan told the *Los Angeles Times*.[33]

The school board had made it amply clear that it would correct the procedural errors it had previously committed and would reappoint Lankster to the school board at its November 18, 1994, meeting. The school board was not given that opportunity, however. The meeting was canceled by William Dawson, the acting state superintendent of public instruction, after he informed the board that he would make the final determination about the secret vote.[34]

The controversy over Lankster's appointment spilled over into the new year, and in February 1995, the California state school superintendent, Delaine Eastin, declared that Lankster could not serve on the school board because of his 1985 conviction. Eastin also found that Lankster's teaching credentials had been revoked and that he had refused to provide an explanation to state officials as to why they had been revoked. Eastin also scolded the school board for initially appointing Lankster through a secret ballot.[35] Several of the school board members reacted with anger and indignation, frustrated at their inability to exercise the little power that they still possessed. However, Gorgonio Sánchez Jr., the only Latino school board member, agreed with Eastin's decision, stating, "If you don't have anything to hide, you should not be afraid to provide the information they ask you to. You should be trustworthy."[36]

In 1995, three Latinos ran for city council seats: Gorgonio Sánchez Jr., Alfonso Cabrera, a five-time candidate, and Lorraine Cervantes, a longtime activist. The Latino Coalition cast its support behind Sánchez and Cervantes because it was believed that of the three Latino candidates, they had the best chance at winning a seat.

In April all three candidates lost, victims of the lack of Latino voters and an absence of Black support. Of the three candidates Lorraine Cervantes garnered the most votes, with 18.6 percent. Sánchez and Cabrera received 12.5 percent and 5.1 percent, respectively. Pallan, for his part, promised to mobilize the community and raise funds for the next attempt at placing a Latino on the city council.[37]

The school board welcomed 1996 with a renewed attack on Jerome Harris, accusing him of failing to improve educational standards and overloading the school district with administrators. Harris countered by referring to his record, which reflected an improvement on the California Achievement Test each year that he oversaw the school district. Harris, however, had already announced that he would be leaving his post at the end of the school year. Under pressure from parents and school board members, Harris announced that he would resign early, at the end of March. He was replaced by Randolph E. Ward, a Black educator who came to the district from Long Beach.

Latinos' struggle to get representation on the city council dragged on into 1998. By then, Mayor Omar Bradley had made it absolutely clear that the only way that Latinos would get a seat on the council was if they were able to vote someone on board. There was no olive branch extended to the Latinos, no prospect of forming a coalition. After all, why did Blacks need a coalition when they held all the power? The *Los Angeles Times* reported Bradley as saying that he would "not give them [Latinos] a hand into government" and that if Pallan and other Latino leaders wanted to get Latinos elected to office, they should "get some votes, then they'll get some elected officials."[38]

In 1998, the *Los Angeles Times* reported that academics who have studied race relations concluded that Compton's Black power struc- ture bordered on xenophobic behavior.[39] The *Times* further observed that Compton, in time, could share the fate of its neighbor city Lyn- wood, where Latinos had finally gained the political strength to sweep Blacks out of office and bulldoze the Black power structure. Indeed, within weeks of being voted into office, Latino mayor Armando Rea used his voting block on the city council to relieve various Black gov- ernment executives of their titles if not their jobs.

The *Los Angeles Times* article stung Compton officials and prompted Legrand H. Clegg II, the Compton city attorney, to accuse the newspaper of being "racist." Clegg wrote, "To select Compton, one of only two black-run municipalities in this county, as a case study in Latino political underrepresentation is blatantly racist and mean- spirited."[40]

Have things changed since 1986, when Latinos first started to strive for political representation? The answer is no. According to Claritas, a marketing company that provides data on demographic changes, Lati- nos grew from 44 percent in 1990 to 59 percent in 2001 as a percent of Compton's total population. However, according to the Southwest Voter Registration Education Project, Latinos represent only about 15 percent of the voters in Compton. This feeble voting power has allowed African Americans to retain control of the city council and school board. As of 2002, the city council was all Black and the school district had only one Latina out of five school board members.

Compton's entrenched Black power structure is an object lesson for Latinos who hold the idealized notion that African Americans not only sympathize with Latinos' history of struggle and oppression but will also voluntarily share with them the power that they have earned. What Latinos have learned is what their counterparts learned in the city of Lynwood—wait, increase the voter rolls, and when they reach critical mass, seize the power.

Houston, We Have a Problem

Latinos Abandon Party Loyalty
to Vote for One of Their Own

We're on the cusp of assuming what everybody said was in our cards. There's Republican vs. Democratic in the mayoral runoff, Hispanic vs. black, conservative vs. liberal and emerging power taking on established power. [Orlando] Sanchez has already wrapped himself in the flag, and patriotism is very big in our community. Even if Sanchez doesn't win, it's a dramatic step forward. . . .

District I tells us that party loyalty doesn't mean a damn thing when you get to vote for one of your own. It tells us we don't care what our leadership is doing, we're going to vote for a cousin.

TATCHO MINDIOLA
Director of the University of Houston's Center for
Mexican-American Studies

In the Houston election of 2001, Orlando Sánchez, a Latino, challenged incumbent Lee P. Brown, an African American, for the highest and most powerful position in city government. This was a historic moment—the first time such a challenge had occurred in Houston's history and one of the few times in any major city. What further distinguished this race was that Sánchez, albeit Latino, was a fair-skinned, blue-eyed Cuban American, not a Mexican American like the majority of the Latino population in Houston. Sánchez was a Republican, and by all accounts a conservative Republican, in a city where most of the Latino voters are Democrats. Sánchez was so out of sync with the traditional Latino leadership in Houston that when he ran for city council in 1995 he was branded as anti-Hispanic. Sánchez ran hot and cold on affirmative action, as that policy was formulated in Houston's Minority, Women and Disadvantaged Business Enterprise Program, whereas most Latinos favored affirmative action in almost all of its incarnations.[1]

Brown's political profile was impressive. He received a Ph.D. in criminology from the University of California at Berkeley, was a former Houston police chief before taking a similar position in New York City, and then became drug policy chief in the Clinton administration. Not only did Brown have a solid academic and professional background, he had a positive and proven track record with the Latino community. During his two terms in office he appointed a Latino liaison to his office, created a Latino advisory committee (with whom he met on a daily basis), promoted Latinos to key administration posts, and ensured that Latinos benefited from city spending as a result of the very affirmative action policy that Sánchez railed against. One of his closest political consultants was Marc Campos, a second-generation Mexican American,[2] and traditional Latino leaders had gone on the record stating that they have enjoyed tremendous inclusion during Brown's tenure.[3]

So what happened? How was it that an Anglo-looking Cuban American with conservative Republican politics—a man who opposed an affirmative action program that clearly benefited Latinos, who was outside the circle of the traditional Latino leadership—almost defeated a two-term African American incumbent by pulling in 72 percent of the Latino (largely Mexican American) vote, which represented 18 percent of the general electorate?[4] Why did Latinos align themselves with conservative white Republicans to support Sánchez? The answer, I believe, is found in Tatcho Mindiola's statement: "There's a hunger, a starvation, for one of our own to score a major victory; for our community to begin asserting ourselves at the polls and finally dispel the old stereotype that we don't vote. . . . This is an ethnic pride thing."[5]

The "ethnic pride thing" had been building over the years in Houston. It was rooted in a history of failed cooperation between the two groups, early and sustained Black political success, and the recent explosion of the Latino population. While the current population of Houston is approximately 31 percent Anglo, 38 percent Latino, and 24 percent African American, this almost equal balancing of numbers is a recent phenomenon. As recently as 1970 Anglos were still the majority population and the Latino population was still comparatively small. However, a mere 30 years later the numbers had shifted dramatically: Latinos now were in the majority, Anglos made up less than a third of the population, while the proportion of Blacks remained largely unchanged.[6]

These demographic changes were reflected in Houston's political landscape. Between 1955 and 1979 Houston's elected officials—mayor, controller, and eight city council members—were elected at-large rather than by district. The net effect of such an electoral scheme was to water down any minority representation in city politics at a time when Anglos were a majority of the population and approximately 70 percent of the registered voters. However, this ended in 1979 when the U.S. Justice Department compelled Houston to enlarge its city council to 14 members, with 9 members elected from districts and 5 in at-large elections. This reduced the control of white officeholders such that in 2002 the white elected officials were joined by an African American mayor and a Mexican American controller. The city council also included two Latinos, three African Americans, and one Asian American.

And in 1993, term limits were imposed so that the mayor, controller, and council members could not serve more than three terms in their lifetime. Term limits began to move members off the city council in 1995.

BLACK-LATINO HISTORY IN HOUSTON

Blacks and Latinos in Houston have a long shared history. Black slaves, along with Mexicans taken from Santa Ana's army, helped clear the swampland on which the city was constructed in 1836.[7] On June 19, 1865—"Juneteenth"—the day on which word reached Texas that the Civil War was over and the slaves were free, Houston counted 1000 Blacks among its residents. By the 1900 Census, Blacks numbered 14,608, representing approximately one-third of the city's population. Latinos were a mere 1000.

Houston's Black population continued to grow as the result of migration from the outlying areas. By 1910 Houston's political wards began to assume a distinct racial and ethnic flavor. The third, fourth, and fifth wards were where Blacks were concentrated, while Mexicans, who had grown in number as a result of immigration, were concentrated in the second ward.

This political segregation was due to several factors. Tatcho Mindiola Jr., Yolanda Flores Nieman, and Nestor Rodriguez, scholars who have studied Latino-Black relations in Houston, and colleagues argue that Jim Crow policies of segregation created boundaries that separated all ethnic groups. There were Anglo, Black, and Mexican schools, churches, and restaurants. It was a division that would continue into the future, even as immigration from Mexico and other Latin American countries increased.

Mindiola notes that it was not just whites who imposed Jim Crow on Blacks: Mexicans also barred Blacks even though they themselves were prohibited from entering many white-owned establishments. One Houston Mexican-owned restaurant chain refused service to African Americans right up until the enactment of the 1964 Civil Rights Act.[8] Mindiola further points out that Latino leaders in Houston worked against attempts to have Latino students lumped with Black students. The leaders argued, curiously enough, that Latinos were "white" and therefore did not fall under the penumbra of Texas segregation laws. These acts most certainly alienated Blacks from Latinos.

Divisions between Blacks and Latinos also appeared when Latino leaders found themselves at odds among themselves on how Latinos should react to Black action aimed at ending segregation. Mindiola notes that "some favored working with the NAACP, while other leaders felt this alliance would only serve to antagonize Whites and further distance them from Hispanics."[9] One camp argued that Latinos and Blacks should form a united front. Another camp believed that to do so was tantamount to admitting that Latinos were less than white. These conflicting views "divided two prominent figures in the League of United Latin American Citizens, a national Hispanic organization."[10]

For a brief period, during the Black and Chicano social movements of the 1960s and 1970s, Blacks and Latinos worked on common issues and goals—some meaningful, some symbolic. During this time, Mindiola observes, "Members of both groups supported each other ideologically and sometimes cooperated in political work."[11] Perhaps the most common manifestation of such cooperation was the joining together of Latino and Black students for demonstrations and protests. During this time, Mindiola writes, the accepted doctrine regarding Latino-Black relations was "that people of color in the United States had a common enemy and thus a common stake in struggles to transform U.S. society."[12]

The 1980s brought significant changes to Black-Latino relations, including significant growth in the Latino population as a result of immigration. In 1980, 40 percent of the 116,084 Latino immigrants in the Houston metropolitan area had immigrated within the prior five years. Houston's Latino population now ballooned to 281,000. By 1990 the number of Latino immigrants in the Houston metropolitan area had grown to 274,000 while the total Latino population of the city of Houston had increased to 450,000. Mindiola observed that by the year 2000 "approximately half of all Hispanics in the city were foreign born, while the proportion of foreign born remained low among Blacks."[13]

The crush of Latino immigrants created a new political climate in the city of Houston and its environs. Latinos, equal in numbers to African Americans, began to demand parity in appointed positions in public and private institutions. Latinos also expected—perhaps naively, based on the immigrant status of the new arrivals—to match the political power of African Americans. As in Compton, Latinos in Houston looked around and saw their numbers growing but not their political power. This disparity no doubt frustrated many of Houston's Latino leaders.

BLACK POLITICS IN HOUSTON

Though the percentage of African Americans in the total population of Houston has remained almost constant over the last 60 years, several factors have combined to give Black voters in Houston significant political power: relatively high voter registration rates (70 percent), high turnout in city elections, and an ability to unite behind a favored candidate in municipal contests. This is confirmed by the fact that between 1973 and 2003, 14 of the 15 winning mayoral candidates were swept into office with strong Black support. Not only were Black voters the invisible force behind mayoral elections beginning in 1973 but they also managed to elect an African American to the city council in 1979.

However, it was not until 1997 that African Americans were able to elect one of their own as mayor. This late success was the result of the voters casting their votes strictly along racial lines—whites for the white candidate and Blacks for the Black candidate. With only 25 to 30 percent of the voting population, Blacks were unable to elect their candidate as mayor on their own. Things might have been different if they had been able to form a coalition with Latinos, but this never happened.

This political weakness was exemplified in the 1991 mayoral race. Sylvester Turner, a Black state representative, appeared to have a decent chance of becoming mayor. His academic and professional credentials (Harvard Law School, a successful lawyer and state representative) made him a likely candidate to draw significant white votes as a crossover candidate. In addition, by 1991, African Americans represented 35 percent of the electorate, increasing their political muscle. Finally, Houston's voters appeared ready for a change from the 10-year reign of mayor Kathryn Whitmire.

In the general election Turner faced Bob Lanier, a wealthy land developer, and incumbent Whitmire. When the voting booths closed,
Turner came away with 36 percent of the votes, Lanier 43 percent, and
Whitmire with just 20 percent. Just weeks before the December runoff,
polls had Turner even or slightly ahead of Lanier. Turner had indeed
succeeded in becoming a crossover candidate for the moment at least.

But in the last days of the race, his campaign was marred by negative media coverage. The *Houston Chronicle* reported that "he failed to
repay Harvard Law School loans, misrepresented a client's fire insurance claim, failed to renew his bar dues, and wrote a $22 'hot check' in
1984." [14] The negative publicity was a sufficient blow that he lost some
of his white support. When all was said and done, Turner received 97
percent of the Black vote, less than 30 percent of the Latino vote, and
only 20 percent of the white vote. He lost to Lanier by a margin of 47
percent to 53 percent. Latinos, clearly, had no inclination to join with
Black voters in putting the first African American mayor in office.

Even though he lost, Turner's strong showing heralded the arrival of
Black political power in Houston. It now appeared that with the right
combination of factors and the right individual, it was possible for a
Black candidate to become mayor. Indeed, it was Turner's strong showing that played a role in convincing former Houston police chief Lee P.
Brown to move back to Houston in 1995. Brown had served as New
York City police chief from 1990 to 1993, and he was President Clinton's
first "czar" in the war on drugs. Upon his return to Houston, Brown
took a position at Rice University and began to prepare to run for
mayor in 1997, when Bob Lanier could not run again because of term
limits.

In the November 1997 general election, Brown came out ahead of
five other major candidates, owing principally to the overwhelming
support of Black voters. In the December runoff election he defeated
Republican businessman Rob Mosbacher by a 53 percent to 47 percent
margin—the exact percentages by which Turner lost to Lanier six years
earlier. Brown managed to get 26 percent of the white vote and 95 per-

cent of the Black vote. Latinos chose to split their vote (small as it was) almost evenly between Mosbacher and Brown.[15]

Finally, an African American had succeeded in becoming mayor of Houston. The significance of this achievement can be measured by the power of the mayor's position, which combines the role of a city manager with that of city chief. The mayor develops the "city budget, hires and fires all department heads, oversees the municipal judiciary, and votes on council decisions."[16] The mayor also has the authority to appoint members to regional boards such as the Houston Port Authority and the Metropolitan Transit Authority. The mayor's office in Houston, therefore, is not merely a symbolic position but one with significant power and control.

African American voters continue to wield their power in Houston politics through their electoral numbers, their ability to unify behind a single candidate, and their ability to turn out in large numbers when issues they regard as significant are on the ballot.

LATINO POLITICS IN HOUSTON

Even though Houston's Latino population is the fastest-growing segment in Houston, its population explosion has not been mirrored by an equal growth in its voting power. In 2000 Latinos represented 38 percent of Houston's population but only 7 to 9 percent of the voters in the runoff between Brown and Mosbacher. Richard Murray and Bob Stein argue that the disparity between population numbers and voting power has four causes:

1. The Latino population is younger than other groups, which means that the voting-age population is a lower percentage than the total population.
2. Approximately 30 to 40 percent of Latino adults are not citizens and thus cannot vote.

3. Of those Latinos who are eligible to vote, only half of them register.

4. Even those who are registered do not turn out to vote in the same numbers as whites and Blacks.[17]

The fact that Latinos do not coalesce behind a candidate has also been one of the major reasons why they have failed to exercise political power commensurate with their numbers. Unlike their African American counterparts, they have even turned on their own on occasion. For example, Ben T. Reyes was the most highly recognizable Latino in Houston in the 1980s and 1990s. However, in 1992 and 1994 he lost Democratic primaries in the Latino 29th Congressional District because enough Mexican American leaders and voters supported an Anglo, former State Senator Gene Green, rather than Reyes.

Unless they were willing to form a coalition with other groups, they could not win the mayoralty. Indeed, their only political power appeared to be the ability to tip a close election in favor of one or another candidate. Latinos have successfully elected other officials, but they have been unable to "capture the flag," the true symbol of power and success in Houston politics—the mayor's office.

THE LATINO CANDIDATE:
ORLANDO SÁNCHEZ

From his first appearance on Houston's political landscape, Sánchez has been a different kind of Latino. That Sánchez found himself in Houston at all was truly serendipitous. He was born in Cuba of middle-class parents. The family left Cuba after Castro assumed power, eventually ending up in Venezuela, where Sánchez's father, Orlando Sánchez-Diego, was a baseball broadcaster. That was where the owner of the Houston Colt .45's found Orlando Sr. in 1962 and brought him to Houston to be the Spanish-language voice of the Colt .45s. Orlando Sr.'s facility with the Spanish language was passed on to Orlando Jr., who by all accounts speaks it flawlessly. Orlando attended the University of Houston and graduated cum laude. He then served in the U.S. Air Force and the Texas Air National Guard and eventually took a job as a probation officer in Harris County. It was while holding this position that he launched his political career.

While it is difficult to state what factors led to Sánchez's decision to affiliate himself with the Republican party, it was a choice he made early on in his political career and he has never strayed. In 1992 he ran as a Republican candidate for state representative from District 132 against Democrat Scott Hochburg. His platform included such traditional conservative views as opposing any state income tax and trimming bureaucracy. His extreme conservatism, and some would argue his anti-Latino stance, was reflected in his proposal that all "illegal" aliens who were charged with murder be required to post a $100,000 bond. This radical idea was apparently inspired by an event where a young undocumented immigrant from Colombia was charged with the murder of a 12-year-old girl. The teenager was released on a $25,000 bond but failed to appear at the next court hearing. It was assumed, perhaps correctly, that the accused had fled the country.[18]

The fact that this proposal was directed at undocumented immigrants (many of them from Latin American countries) and smacked of unequal treatment under the Constitution did not appear to dampen Sánchez's enthusiasm for the idea.

Even though Sánchez was endorsed by the Baptist Ministers Association, a group of Black ministers representing churches who claimed as many as 650,000 members and which traditionally backed Democrats, he lost the November election to Hochburg by a margin of 44 to 56 percent.

Without much of a respite, in March 1993, Sánchez declared himself a candidate for the Houston city council in District C. His platform, no doubt based on his experience as a probation officer, included expulsion of students caught putting gang graffiti on public schools and strict enforcement of teen curfews. Sánchez also reaffirmed his position for structuring the criminal bond system to prevent undocumented immigrants from fleeing the country, and for good measure he called for Houston to take the lead in forcing the federal government to deport illegal aliens. He was moved to this latter position by his experience as a probation officer where he was told that at least half of the gang members in the southwest part of Houston were in the country illegally. Sánchez could openly and freely argue for the quick deportation of illegal immigrants, he stated, because he himself was an immigrant and thus, ostensibly, immune to being labeled an immigrant basher.[19]

Though Sánchez stated that he had the support of nonpartisan Latino organizations, he did not campaign as a candidate who represented the Latino community. Unlike his run for the mayor's position later in 2001, when he was strident about his "Latinoism," in 1993 Sánchez did not refrain from being identified as Latino, but he also did not overemphasize it. However, the demographic backdrop to Houston politics was changing, and in time Sánchez would tumble to this fact.

Once again, Sánchez was unsuccessful in his electoral bid. When the electorate went to the polls on November 2, 1993, Sánchez came in fifth in a field of seven candidates, pulling in only 10.4 percent of the voters.[20]

Two years later, in 1995, Sánchez once again declared himself a candidate for an at-large seat on the city council. By now Sánchez no longer listed himself as a probation officer, having left that position in 1994, but instead identified himself as business consultant. Apparently, he had been "dressed up" by his supporters, such that the *Houston Chronicle* reported that Sánchez was "a consultant for a number of homebuilders and construction companies. Sánchez has represented builders in disputes with federal regulatory agencies, including the Department of Labor and the Occupational Safety and Health Administration."[21] How being a probation officer prepared him for such a role is unclear, but what was clear was that he was now elevated in both profession and status.

By now Sánchez was also being recognized nationally as a darling of the Republican camp, which was eager to attract Latino voters. As a consequence, Sánchez was endorsed by Harris County GOP chair Betsy

Lake and no less a figure than Tom DeLay, who at that time was the House majority whip.[22]

In the November 7, 1995, general election, Sánchez and David Ballard, a real estate broker, found themselves as the front-runners of a nine-candidate pack and headed for a December runoff election. In announcing the runoff candidates, the *Houston Chronicle* stated, "Sánchez supports the city's affirmative-action 'goals' for awarding at least a minimum number of contracts to firms owned by women or minorities. But he says a substantial amount of the $1.6 million spent annually to administer affirmative action should be used for other purposes."[23] There was no explanation of how contracts could be awarded to minority and women-owned firms without an infrastructure to assure that such was the case.

Weeks before the runoff, Sánchez was attacked by the traditional Latino political leadership of Houston because of his Republican ties. Frumencio Reyes, the vice chairman of the Harris County Mexican-American Democrats, as well as Diane Olmos, a Latino Democratic activist, accused the Republican party of using Sánchez to advance its "anti-education, anti-affirmative action and anti-Hispanic" policies.[24] They added, for good measure, that he was "no friend of Hispanics."

Sánchez responded by stating that his supporters included approximately 25 Hispanic Democratic precinct chairs and that a Latino "unity rally" held for him was attended by Democratic state representative Gerard Torres and Latino council members Gracie Saenz and Felix Fraga. Sánchez emphasized that he was a candidate for all Houstonians. He did well in the November 7 general election in Latino neighborhoods, which was attributed to the fact that his was the only Latino name on the list. While that may have been the case, credit also had to be given to his campaign style and to what was widely acknowledged as tremendous charisma based in some part on what has been described as his "movie star" good looks. Sánchez, with appeal to Latinos and his espousal of conservative views, was beginning to reap the benefits of the unlikely coming together of voters—Latinos and conservative Republicans.

Victory finally graced Sánchez when he won the city council seat. It was a real squeaker, with Sánchez winning by only 115 votes. But the margin was immaterial—he now joined the political power elite of Houston. The day after his victory, Sánchez stated, "The voters of the city are mature—people don't look at race or ethnicity. They look at the issues."[25] In 2001, he would again use this statement, but would also add an exaggerated wink and a nod to his ethnic background.

Days after his election, Sánchez came out swinging against the affirmative action program administered by the city of Houston by opposing the mayor's approval of the program. Sánchez once again argued that Houston should use the state certification records for the local program and spend the money used to administer the program to pay off some debt.

Sánchez would hold on to his city council seat for six years, winning reelection in 1997 and 1999. By the time he challenged Brown for mayor he was termed out of office. Term limits demanded that he seek either another or a higher position in order to remain in Houston politics.

THE BLACK CANDIDATE: LEE P. BROWN

If central casting wanted to pick a Black candidate to contrast Sánchez's political qualities, they could have done no better than Lee Brown. Against Sánchez's movie-star good looks, charisma, and natural knack for politics stood Brown's low-keyed personality, discomfort with the world of politics, and intense sense of privacy. Brown's lack of "style" moved the *Houston Chronicle* to editorialize: "Brown has the personality of the complete and unabridged audio version of *War and Peace*."[26]

However, in the world of politics, as in so many things in life, success is sometimes nothing more than a matter of timing. And Brown's candidacy in 1997 came about at the right time. In the prior two decades Black voters had tilled the electoral soil for a Black mayoral candidate by consistently representing about 30 percent of the vote, a percentage that they had proven could be coalesced behind a single candidate. However, it was believed that if a charismatic candidate appeared on the scene, then the Black voting percentage could increase. Clearly, Brown did not have this type of magnetism. As it turned out he did not need it. The spark that would draw in Black voters behind Brown was Proposition A, a controversial proposition that sought to eliminate the affirmative action program in Houston. Of course, Brown would also have to get white crossover votes and convince some of the Latino voters that he was their candidate. If he did all this, then he could be the first Black mayor in Houston.

The general election fielded candidates of various backgrounds, political persuasions, and ethnicity. In addition to Lee Brown, there was city controller George Greanias, businessman Robert Mosbacher, Anglo councilwoman Helen Huey, and Latina councilwoman Gracie Saenz.

Saenz was not the first Latino to seek the Houston mayor's office. Leonel Castillo ran for mayor in 1979 after completing his tenure as director of the U.S. Immigration and Naturalization Service. Castillo placed third among the candidates, with 23 percent of the vote.[27] At the time Latinos represented only about 18 percent of the Houston population. Saenz was running in a new era, when the Latino population had almost doubled its population numbers and increased its voting percentage to 8 to 10 percent.

Proposition A drew national attention. Jesse Jackson spoke against its passage at Texas Southern University, and when NAACP President Kweisi Mfume came to Houston to speak at an NAACP dinner, he too urged Houston voters to defeat Proposition A.[28] Later, Mfume, speaking only for himself, since the NAACP did not officially endorse candidates, urged the voters to support Brown.[29] The spark that Brown needed to increase the number of African American voters had lit the fire of enthusiasm in the Black community.

While Brown did not win the general election on November 4, he was the top vote-getter, with 42 percent, followed by Mosbacher with 29 percent.[30] Saenz finished fourth, managing to get only 7 percent of the vote, running most strongly in Latino neighborhoods.[31]

Proposition A did its job, helping to turn out 47 percent of the registered voters in middle-class Black precincts and 41 percent in selected middle-class white precincts and increasing the total Black vote by 5 percent to 35 percent. However, while voters in the white precincts voted in favor of Proposition A to abolish affirmative action by an average ration of 2 to 1, voters in Black precincts voted to keep affirmative action by a ratio of 9 to 1.[32] The impact of Proposition A was best described by Sanders Anderson, a political scientist at Texas Southern University: Black voters "were concerned about Lee Brown, yes, but the affirmative-action vote was the emotional vote that caused people to react."[33]

No sooner had the dust settled than Brown and Mosbacher set about campaigning for the December runoff vote. Mosbacher, apparently oblivious to the impact that Proposition A had in turning out Black voters, immediately announced that he favored eliminating the city's affirmative action program even though he had originally opposed passage of Proposition A. Mosbacher's change of mind may have been inspired by the ruling of a federal judge about a week before that struck down the Houston Metropolitan Transit Authority's affirmative action program. By making such a pronouncement, Mosbacher effectively ensured that Black voters would once again come out in large numbers to support Brown.

Mindful that it was the Latino vote that was pivotal in white candidate Bob Lanier's win over Black candidate Sylvester Turner in 1991, Brown and Mosbacher set out to galvanize the support of the approximately 30,000 Latino voters. Clearly, one of the keys to getting this support was getting Saenz's endorsement. Tradition would have suggested that Saenz, the lone Latino mayoral candidate, would have thrown her support behind Brown. He was a Democrat, as was she; he was a person of "color," as was she; and he was a strong supporter of the city's affirmative action program, as was she. Saenz, however, ignored all of these compelling reasons and threw her support behind Mosbacher.[34]

Mosbacher also won the support of the Houston Hispanic Chamber of Commerce political action committee and Comerciantes Latinos

Unidos de Houston—two Latino business groups that were impressed with Mosbacher's experience with his family's energy company.[35]

Brown, for his part, received the endorsement of state senator Mario Gallegos, as well as other leaders and Latino groups, including the Harris County Tejano Democrats.

Brown was also busy lining up the necessary support to attract the elusive 30 percent crossover white vote. Former mayors Whitmire and Lanier and former mayoral candidate Greanias all supported Brown. The Democratic Party also demonstrated its support for Brown: Al Gore came to Houston to campaign for him, and Clinton taped a political commercial supporting him.

When the ballots were tallied after the December runoff, Brown became the first Black mayor of Houston. He not only carried the African American vote (which once again rose to the occasion and increased its representation to 35 percent), but he came within 3 percentage points of capturing the necessary 30 percent white vote. And in spite of Saenz's support of Mosbacher, Brown managed to split the Latino vote.

From the onset of his mayoral term, it appeared that Brown understood that one of his principal jobs was to reach out to the Latino population of Houston. Indeed, it appeared imperative for him to do so in order to combat the high visibility of Blacks in power in city government. A survey of Houston's city hall revealed a dominance of African Americans in positions of power, including the positions of city attorney, police chief, and the heads of personnel, solid waste, housing and community development, health and human resources, and the Housing Authority.[36] The fear among Latinos was that if such dominance existed without a Black mayor, what would the power landscape look like with one.

The Thursday following his victory, Brown appeared at the annual meeting of the 1000-member Houston Hispanic Chamber of Commerce even though its political action committee had endorsed Mosbacher. This appearance was followed by a Saturday morning meeting with a group of Latinos who put hard questions to him: "The venue was standing room only; the format, question and answer. Of those questions, three of the first four dealt with race and the historically competitive, sometimes acrimonious, relationship between Hispanics and African-Americans."[37] These were questions rooted in a feeling that "Many Hispanics feel that African-Americans have dominated race relations and the civil rights agenda; that it is always a black and white thing. Many African-Americans feel Hispanics have coattailed on the black fight for civil rights; many say they are anti-Spanish and feel economically threatened by new immigrants."[38]

There were no real challengers to Brown's reelection as mayor in 1999. In the end he captured 67 percent of the votes but was opposed by two relatively unknown and underfunded candidates, one of whom spent only $50 on the race. His poor showing against these political straw dogs reflected strong criticism of his two years in office and revealed that he could be vulnerable in 2001. During his first two years many citizens began to question his fiscal and managerial abilities. He also appeared unable to sway the hearts and minds of progressive white voters, which, by all rights, should have been solidly in his camp given the support he received from former mayoral candidate George Greanias. Added to these material deficiencies were less critical but nevertheless meaningful observations that Brown was not a "compelling communicator" or an inspiring leader.[39] The message was clear—unless Brown could right the wrongs that existed within his administration, he would be susceptible to a serious challenge from a well-funded candidate of whatever ethnicity or political stripe.

THE FACE·OFF

As a consequence of not having to expend any substantial amounts of funds in his 1999 reelection campaign, Brown entered 2001 with a considerable war chest. In March 2001, it was estimated that Brown had about $2 million at his disposal. Sensing that both Sánchez and city controller Sylvia Garcia would make a run at him, Brown continued to raise funds.

Brown also continued to woo Latino voters, and in April 2001, the *Houston Chronicle* noted that he was endorsed by about 75 Latino business and political and community leaders.[40] The group, which consisted mostly of Democrats, included state senator Mario Gallegos, city councilman Jon Castillo, former councilman Felix Fraga, school district board member Esther Campos, and state representative Jessica Farra. The article ended with the seemingly innocent sentence that "Councilman Orlando Sánchez appears poised to announce as the first Hispanic Republic to run for mayor."[41] Brown, clearly anticipating Sánchez's candidacy, was already lining up his Latino political backers.

Even before Sánchez formally announced his bid to become mayor of Houston his candidacy was analyzed in the context of his Latinoism. A political columnist for the *Houston Chronicle* correctly observed that Orlando had to get almost the same level of support in white west Houston as did white Republican Mosbacher. The analyst observed that Sánchez could potentially succeed in doing this because "Anglos appreciative of Hispanic politics are appreciative that Cubans are more conservative than Mexican-Americans."[42]

Almost from the inception of his run for the mayor's office, Sánchez was embraced by the Republican Party as a Latino whom they could support because of his ideology and one with the potential to win. Gary Polland, the Harris County Republican Party chairman, committed himself to help Sánchez raise at least $1 million and added, "I think the money will be there for him because he is an attractive candidate for Republicans at this time."[43] The outstanding question was, of course, could he pull in the Mexican American vote, which had historically gone to the Democratic Party.

In late April Sánchez formally announced his candidacy, joining City Councilman Chris Bell in what was now a three-man race. His kickoff speech was the blueprint for how he would combine his Latinoism and his conservative agenda throughout his campaign. In that speech he highlighted his Latino heritage by peppering it with Spanish phrases, stating, for example, *Podemos hacer mejor. Podemos ser mejor,* "We can do better. We can be better."[44] As for his goals, they included public safety, the city's infrastructure, traffic, the city budget, and taxes. It was a pattern he would repeat throughout his campaign. He would appeal to the Latino voter on the simple basis that he was a Latino and not because of any apparent program or plans specifically aimed at benefiting them. He would appeal to conservative white voters with fiscal conservatism and a program for civic improvements without details as to how they would be accomplished.

This approach was demonstrated when he, Brown, and Bell appeared at a Hispanic Chamber of Commerce luncheon four months before the November election. Brown detailed his inclusion of Latinos in his administration by noting that he had created a full-time Latino liaison to his administration, appointed Latinos to top municipal boards, and increased city contracts to Latino-owned businesses. When it was Sánchez's turn, he flashed his naturalization certificate and announced that when he became a U.S. citizen it was "one of the proudest moments" of his life.[45] He then segued into a request that the Latinos in the audience support him in accomplishing something that had never been done before by electing him mayor of Houston. He concluded with "Our time has definitely come."[46] No plan, no program, no proposal, and certainly no detail as to why he should be elected mayor other than that he was Latino and it was time for a Latino, no matter his political leaning, to become mayor of Houston. Not only did he fail to provide any detail on how his election would benefit Latinos. He also omitted his prior stance of strict enforcement of immigration laws and deportation of illegal immigrants. A stance, no doubt, with which many in the audience that day would disagree.

An example of this fiscal conservatism was his opposition to Brown's call for a 1 percent tax increase on property taxes. Brown intended to use the revenues to increase firefighters on fire trucks from three to four. It would also reverse the 1 percent tax decrease passed by the city council (while Sánchez was on the council) over Brown's objection. On the same day that Brown made the tax increase proposal, Sánchez, true to his fiscal conservatism, called for a tax cut. Sánchez offered no specifics on how the tax cut would be implemented, simply offering that "the City should determine what it needs to spend, then give the rest back to taxpayers."[47]

Because Sánchez was running as both a Latino and a conservative, on occasion he was forced to contradict himself. Such was the case regarding the city's affirmative action program. The program, which asked that city contractors make a "good-faith effort" to send about 20 percent of their work to businesses owned by minorities or women, was started in 1984 and had survived a citywide referendum (Proposition A) and several court challenges, and had substantially benefited Latino businessmen. It was estimated that Latinos had received approximately $212 million in minority contracts while Blacks got approximately $140 million since Brown took office.[48]

Sánchez, now sensitive to his potential Latino constituents, tried to finesse the issue. In an interview with the *Houston Chronicle* he dismissed the contracts awarded to Latino businessmen and focused instead on the fact that the program cost $1.8 million to administer. "It's a sham," he harangued. "It's a joke."[49] However, in a prior meeting with the Hispanic Chamber of Commerce, Sánchez announced, without reservation, "I've told the mayor a number of times, every time on the City Council agenda when we have goals that are set by the affirmative action department, I've congratulated him publicly for exceeding them. I support minority participation in the contracts department."[50]

Along with finessing his Latino constituents, Sánchez hammered away at his platform, which he had now honed into an appealing amalgam of talking points that included a well-funded fire department, better-coordinated construction project, citywide childhood immunization, and improvement of roads, sewers, and neighborhoods. That he could not provide any real details as to how he would accomplish these goals did not seem to matter to his targeted constituencies.

Sánchez's approach to winning the hearts and minds of the Latinos began to succeed leading one Latina to observe, a month before the general election, that Sánchez "is the first serious Hispanic candidate for mayor since the new demographics became a reality. He's the first one out of the chute for the whole Hispanic community, and a lot of folks are thinking, 'Is this the time? Is he the one? Is it our turn at the helm?' "[51] The ethnic thing was beginning to burn hot among Latinos regardless of Brown's umbrella, under which many Latinos also stood huddled.

Something else was happening in the Latino community that would have an eventual impact on the outcome of the race but which was not inspired by any of the three mayoral candidates. Several weeks before the general election, the National Association of Latino Elected and Appointed Officials (NALEAO) launched a campaign to increase the number of Latino voters and increase turnout on Election Day. The nonpartisan efforts included three community forums that would be televised on the local Spanish-language Univision channel, as well as 20 bilingual billboards placed in heavily dominated Latino communities. There were two successive mailers urging 50,000 registered Latino voters to get themselves to the voting booths. Finally, on Election Day Univision and several Spanish-language radio stations aired public service announcements and provided continuous coverage.[52] In the end, these efforts resulted in an increased turnout of Latino voters, many of whom would vote for Sánchez.

The November 6 general election provided no clear winner. It had already been generally accepted that Brown's poor approval ratings based on his two-year term record, and Sánchez's momentum, would force them into a runoff. Brown got 43.5 percent of the vote, Sánchez received 40.3 percent, and Bell 15.8 percent.[53] Once again Black voters voted overwhelmingly for Brown, giving him 88 percent of their vote. Latinos, in contrast, voted 62 percent for Sánchez and 25 percent for Brown. Among white voters, Brown received 27 percent, and Sánchez 60 percent.

The numbers clearly showed that Brown needed the Black block vote and a significant percentage of the white crossover vote. Sánchez, on the other hand, would have to continue to energize the Latino voters while sustaining his appeal to white conservative Republicans.

With his tremendous showing in the general election, Sánchez was now fully embraced by the Republican Party. Jack Rains, a Republican former Texas secretary of state stated, "This is the first time in history a Hispanic has been at the top of a ticket in Houston. . . . From now until the runoff election we expect to continue to build excitement and gain a larger percentage of the growing Hispanic vote."[54]

If Latinos had caught the scent of success because of Sánchez's candidacy, African American voters were equally adamant about "one of their own." Sanders Anderson, the Texas Southern University political science professor, observed that many Blacks believe "Brown deserves a third term because it might be the last chance for a Black candidate to be elected mayor, especially with the growing Mexican-American population."[55] Black voters, like their Latino counterparts, saw it as a slugfest between two ethnic groups. One Black pastor stated: "This race is going to boil down to race. It's just a natural thing. We all want to be able to claim our person as the mayor of the city. They are already saying it's time for a Hispanic mayor and they should feel that way."[56]

Days before the election, Sánchez received a boost when President Bush endorsed him over Brown and New York City Mayor Rudy Giuliani taped both radio and television spots for him. Sánchez also received the endorsement of Bush Sr. and the former first lady, who recorded television commercials for him. Brown countered with an endorsement from Clinton, who taped an ad for him.

There was no doubt that the runoff would be close, that perhaps only hundreds of votes would decide the victor. Perhaps it was this knowledge that inspired the Brown campaign to send out a telephone message that featured Lavon Harris, the sister of James Byrd Jr. In 1998, three white men dragged Byrd, a Black man, to his death in Jasper, Texas. In the recording, Ms. Harris accuses "some of Mr. Sánchez's supporters" of sending out "flyers calling Mr. Brown racist names." Harris continues in the recorded call to state that the election for mayor was important to her because "Sánchez . . . helped lead the fight against the James Byrd Jr. hate-crimes law."[57] The phone message ended with Harris saying, "Please make sure to vote for Mayor Brown, because if hate wins, Houston loses." However, according to a report by the UPI, "Sánchez voted against a resolution concerning the Byrd hate crimes bill in the City Council. But all the resolution would have done is make passage of that specific bill an identified goal of the council's legislative agenda in Austin."[58] Gary Polland, the Harris County Republican chairman, stated that "the Sánchez campaign never sent out anything of the sort. . . ."[59]

If Proposition A was the lightning rod in the 1997 mayoral election, the Harris call served a similar role in the 2001 election. At the runoff election Brown defeated Sánchez by a margin of 52 percent to 48 percent. Blacks once again closed ranks behind Brown, voted in increased numbers, and gave over 90 percent of their vote to him.

Latinos had increased their voting power, thanks in part to the Sánchez candidacy and NALEAO's efforts, to 18 percent of the electorate—almost doubling their numbers from when Mosbacher ran against Brown four years earlier. Of those Latinos voting, 72 percent voted for Sánchez, while 28 percent voted for Brown. The numbers made it clear that if Latinos had voted as a block in support of Sánchez, they would have had their wish—the first Latino mayor in the history of Houston.

The "ethnic pride thing" swelled the ranks of Latino voters during the heated race, increasing the future political power of Latinos in Houston. Unfortunately, it also blinded Latinos to the fact that it was the Black candidate who had demonstrated that his administration was inclusive and most likely to benefit Latinos. Brown had extended a hand to Latinos and brought them into the mayoral circle of power, just as advocates of the overarching alliance of peoples of color insist will occur. But Sánchez, regardless of his country of origin and his stance against illegal immigrants and the city's affirmative action program, was "one of their own." In the end that was enough to convince a majority of Latinos to abandon their traditional political party to vote for him, and in so doing almost bring to fruition their dream of winning the highest political office in Houston.

The Big *Manzana*

The Troubled Road to a Latino-Black Coalition and the Latino Mosaic of New York City

The 30-second TV spot is titled "Oficiales," but an even better name would be "The Rainbow Coalition." Against a rapid montage of black and brown faces, a parade of Latino elected officials appear before the camera speaking in Spanish and endorsing Carl McCall. "He's *our* candidate. . . . He understands *our* problems. . . . He deserves *our* vote," they say one after another. The underlying assumption is as obvious as the droning pronoun: blacks and browns have the same issues politically, and this year, as in years past, whites should expect them to vote as one.

In fact, that's highly unlikely—the truth is there is no meaningful rainbow coalition in New York. A few black and Latino leaders have been acting in concert in recent years, and many of the city's Latino elected officials have lined up behind Mr. McCall. But black and brown voters are not automatically in sync—far from it.

TAMAR JACOBY
Senior fellow at the Manhattan Institute for Policy Research

I n 2001 Fernando Ferrer, the Bronx borough president, concluded that conditions were ripe for the first Latino mayor of New York to be elected. True he had run for that office in 1997 and had dropped out a few months into the campaign after he concluded that he could not mount a successful campaign, but he saw things differently in 2001. There was no Black candidate who was scheduled to run, so he be-

lieved he would be the beneficiary of the Black vote. The Latino population of New York City had grown dramatically and was now 27 percent
of the total population. He recalled that a Black-Latino coalition had
been instrumental in electing David Dinkins mayor in 1989, so such a
coalition proved, ostensibly, that it could put its candidate of choice in
the mayor's office. Freddy (his common nickname) felt a special kin-
ship and bond with Al Sharpton, the quasi-official spokesman for New
York City's African American voters, and was convinced—nay, certain—that Sharpton would easily throw his support behind Ferrer's
campaign. Bolstering this conviction was the perception that termed-
out mayor Rudy Giuliani was no friend of minorities. It was widely believed that Giuliani excluded minorities from his inner circle of
confidants, did not consult with them about their communities, and at
times was considered outright hostile to peoples of color. In Ferrer's
estimation, Giuliani himself had helped prepare the ground for a successful run by a Latino for the highly coveted office. Ferrer, with his
mélange of disenfranchised supporters, was convinced that he could
represent "the other New York"—that constituency that felt shut out
by the power elite, wealthy, glittery New York.[1] He envisioned, perhaps,
that he and his supporters would take Gracie Mansion and, using
Andrew Jackson as their model, party like it was 1831—fling the doors
wide open and welcome one and all, regardless of race, class, or status,
to one hell of a *pachanga*.

This perfect plan was, unfortunately, flawed from the onset. Either
Ferrer did not see the weak stitching of his political coat of many colors, or he chose to ignore it. The first defect was Ferrer's infatuation
with the growth in New York City's Latino population. The raw numbers were dazzling because they approached almost a third of the total
population. But if he had dug deeper, he would have uncovered two
alarming facts, facts that had contributed to the defeat of Antonio
Villaraigosa in Los Angeles and Orlando Sanchez in Houston. First, he
would have realized that raw population numbers do not necessarily
translate into equally large voting numbers. Ferrer is Puerto Rican. All
Puerto Ricans are U.S. citizens and entitled to vote once they reach the

requisite age. If the tremendous growth in the Latino population of New York City had been driven by an influx of Puerto Ricans, then Ferrer would have had cause to salsa. But that was not the case. In fact, the opposite is true. Between 1990 and 2000, the Puerto Rican population dropped from half of the city's Latino population to just over a third. It was the "new Latinos" who were inflating the numbers. In the past 10 years Dominicans had poured into the boroughs and increased their numbers to 222,287. Mexicans almost doubled their numbers, and Latinos from Costa Rica, Guatemala, Honduras, Nicaragua, Panama, and El Salvador, and from countries throughout South America, added their numbers to the Latino mosaic of New York City.

These "new Latinos" were not like their Puerto Rican counterparts. Not only did each group add its own unique flavor to the Latino populace, but many of them were not U.S. citizens. Without this qualifying badge the best they could do was give emotional and psychological support to Ferrer. They could not give him what he really needed— votes in the bank. It is hard to believe that Ferrer was blind to this fact, but his constant exultation in the growth of the city's Latino population suggests that his vision was, at the very least, impaired.

The second lesson that Ferrer failed to grasp was that Latinos do not always turn out in large numbers for their candidate of choice. Villaraigosa and Sánchez would have won if the registered Latino voters had come out in force and coalesced behind them. Unlike Black candidates, who can often rely on an almost unanimous vote from Black voters, Latino candidates cannot rely on Latinos to vote as a block. Frequently, they split their vote based on the candidate or the issues. Ferrer did not seem aware of this. "David Dinkins got 70 percent of the Latino vote in 1989. Does anyone seriously believe I'd receive less than that," he told the *New York Times*.[2] Did he forget that in the general election Herman Badillo, the Democrat-turned-Republican, was also running? Yes, Latinos overwhelmingly vote Democrat, but did he seriously not believe that some Latinos might switch party loyalty and vote for Badillo?

The Latino voter aside, Ferrer also made a serious error in presuming that a Latino-Black coalition was a given. Politicians, no matter their ethnicity or political persuasion, are not unlike thin-skinned elephants. Once pricked, they do not easily forget the wound or the person who injured them. Ferrer neglected to take into consideration that in his long and varied political career he himself had not always rallied to the call when the candidate was Black. It was as if Ferrer were saying, "Hey, let's start a Latino-Black coalition and forget about what I did in the past." In the world of New York City politics, nothing is automatic. Relationship, mutual support, and histories are what matter, and they are not necessarily tied to the black and brown thing. A scratched back here requires a scratched back there, and ethnicity be damned.

Finally, Ferrer did not take into consideration that his call for a Black-Latino coalition might frighten, or at least alienate, the "white folk." And frightened whites who vote are among the worst kind of political enemy to have. It was frightened whites, in partnership with equally distraught Blacks, who voted against the racialized and radicalized image of Villaraigosa in Los Angeles. It was conservative whites who almost elected Sánchez to the mayor's office in Houston. It should not have escaped Ferrer that when all is said and done, minority candidates need white voters. In fact, if Ferrer had done some homework before formulating his strategy, he would have discovered that with the single exception of David Dinkins in 1989, every candidate who become mayor of New York City during a racially polarized contest did so primarily on votes cast by conservative white voters. Ferrer should have understood from the very beginning that he would need a certain percentage of white voters to become New York's first Latino mayor. Perhaps he believed that conservative white voters were lost to him anyway, and that liberal white voters would appreciate his strategy and support his coalition. This, at least, was the very conclusion that Angelo Falcon, a staff member of the Puerto Rican Legal Defense and Education Fund, reached when he observed that Ferrer needed at least 80 percent of both the Latino and the Black vote and at least 20 percent of the white vote to win.[3] But Ferrer did not perceive these flaws in his approach, so his campaign began on the wrong foot almost from the get-go. Not surprisingly, he was defeated in the New York City primary on September 23, 2001.

Early in his campaign, Ferrer had stood on the steps of city hall and exchanged endorsements with H. Carl McCall, the Black state comptroller who was running for governor of New York State. This mutual endorsement sealed Ferrer's commitment to a nascent Black-Latino coalition that, he believed, would blossom as the months passed. Things looked oh so good that day.

However, behind the scene was the political carnage left over from Ferrer's previous short-lived mayoral bid. At that time he had assembled considerable support from Black politicians throughout the city only to abruptly pull out before the primary. These supporters were left with a bitter taste in their mouths. Now they wanted to wait and see if he was for real this time.

The more serious ghost hovering over the Ferrer-McCall photo-op was a whole history of failed Latino-Black coalitions in New York City, especially the one involving Herman Badillo's mayoral bid in 1985. Badillo had served as the city's first Puerto Rican congressman, Bronx borough president, and deputy mayor. It appeared that Badillo had a decent shot at the election except that Black leaders inexplicably threw their support behind Herman "Denny" Farrell, a weak and little-known candidate. This Black failure to support the Puerto Rican candidate caused bitterness between the two groups for years after.

The one bright spot in the otherwise troubled history of Black-Latino coalitions was the election of David Dinkins in 1989, a Black candidate who garnered 56 percent of the Puerto Rican vote. But once he was in office, Latinos and Blacks alike accused him of ignoring them, so they "stayed home" during the next election, and Dinkins lost to Giuliani.[4]

Ferrer soon discovered that Sharpton was not responding to his call for a Black-Latino coalition. He should have known that making political alliance with Sharpton was not unlike making love to a porcupine—it had to be approached with caution and executed with extreme care. Ferrer, it turned out, knew little about porcupines.

Sharpton, the media-savvy and media-gluttonous politico, under-stood that in the year 2001 the Black vote would be pivotal. In the words of Mark Green, one of the other Democratic candidates, New York City had become such an assemblage of ethnic, religious, and racial groups that *all* of its residents were now essentially minorities. Every minority was important, and Sharpton, as the acknowledged leader of the African American community, was being courted by all the candidates. His support was a valuable commodity, and his street smarts prevented him from giving his support away for nothing. Far from it—he would demand a high price in exchange for his support. So when Ferrer came a-courtin' with his Rainbow Coalition bouquet in hand, Sharpton demurred and said, "Yes, but if I do that for you, I want you do something for me." The "something" was a promise by Ferrer to endorse Black candidates running for Bronx borough president and city comptroller.[5] William C. Thompson Jr., an African American, was one of the people running for city comptroller, but there was no Black candidate running to replace Ferrer as Bronx borough president. In essence, Sharpton was demanding that Ferrer give him a blank check on which Sharpton could write the name of any Black candidate he wanted, regardless of background, qualifications, or platform. Truly a pig in a poke.

As political haggling goes, Sharpton's demand was not unusual and perhaps not even unrealistic. The concept of quid pro quo has a long and honored tradition in political negotiations. But Sharpton vio-lated one of the cardinal rules: Instead of making his proposal in a back room somewhere, he did it out in the open in the glaring light of the media.

In making his demands publicly, Sharpton not so obliquely referred to the long history of political tensions between Blacks and Latinos in New York. And how could Ferrer help to heal these wounds? Well, for starters he could agree to Sharpton's demands. "If there's going to be a real coalition, we want a real coalition. I am telling you on the record that without those two issues resolved, there will be no endorsement. I do want to heal the rift, but healing means that everybody must be a part. They're talking about a black-latino coalition. I mean where is it?" Sharpton told the *New York Times.*[6] In another interview Sharpton was no less blunt about the meaning and impact of a Black-Latino coalition. Sharpton converted Ferrer's appeal into a demand to which Black leaders, no matter their ilk, had to accede. "He cannot go to the black leadership trying to blackmail us into a black-latino coalition, and then—when we say, 'Well, where's the black side of this?'—turn around and say: 'Oh no, no, no. You can't talk about race.' "[7]

Sharpton had turned Ferrer's request on its head by recasting it as a nonnegotiable demand. He twisted Ferrer's request to look something like this: Ferrer insisted that Sharpton could support only Ferrer; Sharpton could support only Ferrer because Ferrer, as a Latino, was entitled to Sharpton's support. Sharpton stated as such when he advised the *Daily News* that if Ferrer had come to him and requested his support based solely on his merits then he would not have made the demand that in exchange for his support, Ferrer had to support the two Black candidates identified by Sharpton.[8]

By taking the matter public, Sharpton succeeded in putting Ferrer in a real bind. Sure, Ferrer wanted Sharpton's support, but if he agreed to the demands, then he would be seen as a Sharpton puppet—someone being told what to do by one of the most controversial and, in certain quarters, most disliked figures in New York City politics. It could even be seen, by some people, as putting a Sharpton surrogate in office. However, Sharpton, at least in the spring of 2001, made it amply clear that he would not rally Black voters behind Ferrer unless Ferrer capitulated to the stated demands.

In an attempt to find a way around this dilemma Roberto Ramirez, the Bronx Democratic leader and one of Ferrer's political advisers, proposed that the Democratic party leaders put together a ticket that supported Ferrer for mayor and Thompson for city comptroller. Thompson, no fool he, immediately announced that he did not want to become embroiled in the ethnic/racial battle by stating that he was not seeking any endorsement by a mayoral candidate.

Ferrer did not hesitate in rejecting Sharpton's demand. Could he do otherwise? He made decisions on merits, not on race, Ferrer announced boldly to a reporter from the *New York Times*.[9] Of course, it helped that all three other Democratic candidates announced that they too would reject such a demand from Sharpton in exchange for his support. However, the other three candidates had not predicated their candidacy on a direct appeal to a Black-Latino coalition. Without Sharpton's support, Ferrer could once again forget about his race to become mayor.

Why had Sharpton hoisted Ferrer on his own petard? Well, when Ferrer dropped out of the mayor's race in 1997, he did not throw his support behind Sharpton. Instead he backed white candidate Ruth Messinger. Four years later Sharpton, still feeling the sting of this betrayal, said, "If it's all about black-Latino unity, how come he endorsed Ruth Messinger instead of me when he dropped out of the race in 1997?" Sharpton told advisers to Lenora Fulani, chair of the Committee for a Unified Independent Party, a think tank in Manhattan.[10]

Sharpton continued his attack on Ferrer in the days following. He publicly pointed out that Ferrer was having trouble lining up other Black supporters, such as Dinkins, Congressman Charles Rangel, and Dennis Rivera. How, Sharpton insisted, could Ferrer be talking about a Black-Latino coalition when he had failed to get these important leaders behind him?

Ferrer's struggle with Sharpton was having the intended effect among Black voters. A poll conducted by Quinnipiac University released in the spring of 2001 showed that Mark Green was doing twice as well among Black voters as Ferrer. Among Black registered Democrats, 40 percent supported Green, while Ferrer was getting 20 percent. Not bad for a Jewish guy who was not running on any kind of coalition platform. The survey held further bad news for Ferrer. It appeared that his clarion call for a Black-Latino campaign was indeed alienating the "white folk." The same survey showed that he was getting a dismal 6 percent of the Jewish voters. "How does a New York politician court Jewish voters while he's chasing Al Sharpton for his endorsement?"

asked *New York Times* columnist Bob Herbert.[11] Certainly, a portion of the liberal white vote had slipped out of Ferrer's grasp.

Ferrer had also publicly pursued David Dinkins. After all, Dinkins, the only Black mayor of New York City, had been carried into office on the shoulders of Black and Latino voters, so it seemed only appropriate that Dinkins should throw his support behind the Latino candidate. But while Ferrer was focused on soliciting Sharpton, Dinkins dropped the equivalent of an atomic bomb on Ferrer and his dream of a Black-Latino coalition: he announced that he was supporting Mark Green. Ferrer tried to spin the decision by noting that Green had served as consumer affairs commissioner under Dinkins. The real reason why Dinkins refused to support Ferrer was a faux pas that Ferrer committed during a televised debate. Ferrer was asked who he would vote for in a hypothetical mayoral run that included Dinkins, Ed Koch, and Rudy Giuliani. Instead of immediately blurting out Dinkins's name, Ferrer hesitated. Later Ferrer weakly explained that he had been cut off by a questioner before he had a chance to answer.[12] But Dinkins was reportedly "agitated" by Ferrer's hesitation, and this was apparently what pushed Dinkins into Green's camp.

Ferrer's dream of a Black-Latino coalition had become a nightmare. Sharpton had whipsawed him with his demands and Dinkins had thrashed him with his support for Green. These public setbacks not only affected Ferrer's ability to attract Black voters; they also affected his standing in the Latino community. The same poll that showed him pulling in only 20 percent of the Black vote revealed that he was receiving only 38 percent of the Latino vote, with 18 percent undecided and the remaining voters split among the other three Democratic candidates.[13]

Outside events also affected Ferrer's mayoral candidacy. One of these developed as a result of the protests against the U.S. Navy military exercises on Vieques, an island to the east of Puerto Rico with an approximate population of 9,400. In 1941, the U.S. Navy obtained two-thirds of the island for storage of weapons and as a site for bombing exercises. While the U.S. naval presence had sparked protests by both residents and outsiders as early as the 1970s, it was the killing of David Sanes and the wounding of four other Vieques residents on April 19, 1999, during a bombing exercise that inspired renewed and more vigorous protests on the island. Joining this legion of demonstrators were Sharpton, city councilman Adolfo Carrion Jr., State Assemblyman José Rivera, and Ferrer's political consultant, Roberto Ramirez.

While the first wave of demonstrators were given relatively light sentences ranging from fines of up to $1000 or time served during their initial arrests, the late-arriving group was given harsher sentences—among this group were the New York political contingent. A federal judge in San Juan, Puerto Rico, imposed extended jail sentences on Sharpton, City Councilman Carrion, State Assemblyman Rivera, and Ramirez, for protesting the U.S. Navy bombing of Vieques. The judge sentenced Sharpton to 90 days in jail, and everyone else to 40 days.[14] The four men served their sentences at the Metropolitan Detention Center in Brooklyn, a maximum-security federal prison.

In early June another poll put out numbers that must have heartened Ferrer. The Hispanic Federation found that Ferrer was the overwhelming favorite of Latino voters, with 63 percent support; Green got 7 percent, City Council Speaker Peter Vallone got 7 percent, Controller Alan Hevesi got 3 percent, and 17 percent were undecided.[15] The same pool showed that 52 percent of the Latinos gave Giuliani a positive rating.

About a week after the poll numbers were released, Michael Bloomberg announced his candidacy in an explosion of publicity and expectation. With $4 billion at his disposal, Bloomberg promised to be a formidable opponent. Not only did he have the funds to run an effective campaign, but he was also a candidate that white voters were comfortable with. He was, after all, one of their own. Bloomberg, however, made it clear from the start of his campaign that he was not going to concede the Latino vote (or the Black vote, for that matter) to any candidate—not to Badillo, his Republican challenger, and certainly not to Ferrer.

Indeed, Bloomberg must have anticipated his run for some public office as well as the importance of the Latino vote because about a year prior to entering the mayoral race he began learning Spanish. When he launched his campaign, he ran a series of bilingual television ads where he asks that his audience forgive his terrible accent and then, in Spanish, asks Latino voters to stop him in the streets and talk to him.[16]

While Sharpton cooled his heels in prison, the fight for the Latino vote was in full swing. Green courted and received the support of 80 Latino Pentecostal ministers, mainly from the Bronx. About a week later Ferrer was endorsed by a group of Latino evangelical leaders who avowed that they represented about 350,000 New Yorkers. Their members were mostly immigrant "new Latinos" from Central and South America.

Entering the start of summer Ferrer stepped up his "other New York" campaign in order to distinguish himself from the other candidates. By now he had also downplayed his prior strong and direct appeal to Latino voters as well as his goal of creating a Latino-Black coalition. Sharpton's demand still hung in the air. When Carrion, Ramirez, and Rivera were released from prison in late June, Ramirez was asked if he had succeeded in persuading Sharpton to endorse Ferrer. Ramirez refused to answer the question.[17]

Ferrer, feeling the need to bring an end to the Sharpton thing, visited him in prison on August 11. While Ferrer would not reveal what he and Sharpton discussed, there was little doubt that Sharpton's support for Ferrer's candidacy was at least one of the topics. It appeared, at least for the moment, that Ferrer's persistence was meeting with some success. That day, a gathering of Black Democrats, including Charles Rangel, were contemplating backing him.

On August 17, 2001, a day later, a group of Black and Latino politicians announced their support for Ferrer and Sharpton was finally released from prison. Among the supporters was Rangel, who attempted to make it clear that the group endorsing Ferrer did not do so on the basis of race or ethnicity. And Ferrer, wiser for his experience, did not talk about a Black-Latino coalition but instead cast his support from the Black and Latino politicians as one in which the "other New York" would be represented. Conspicuously missing from the event was the recently released Sharpton.

About 10 days later and approximately two weeks before the original primary date of September 11, 2001, the union that Ferrer had been seeking since the commencement of his campaign was finally consummated. In the basement of Mount Sinai United Christian Church on Staten Island, Sharpton finally relented and announced his support for Ferrer. While the endorsement came at the eleventh hour, Ferrer could not have been happier. Maybe the change came because of the many days that Ramirez had spent next to Sharpton in prison, or because other prominent Black leaders had thrown their support behind Ferrer. Whatever the reason, Ferrer was delighted with the endorsement. Ramirez was quoted as saying, "I would say that Reverend Sharpton's endorsement today—the timing of it, the weight of it and the tone of it—it's a big event." [18] Sharpton had apparently dropped his earlier demand, suggesting that he himself was cornered: he could abstain from supporting any candidate; he could support Ferrer; or he could support one of the three other Democratic candidates.

A less emotional analysis of the endorsement suggests that it came too late in the campaign. If Sharpton had endorsed him earlier, Ferrer's campaign might have taken on a different aura. Other Black leaders, including Dinkins, might then have united behind Ferrer. With an early endorsement, Ferrer could have presented a strong face to the Latino voters and perhaps received even greater approval in the early polls, where they showed that, among Latinos, Ferrer was always the largest vote-getter. Who knows what might have happened. What did happen was that Sharpton waited until two weeks before the election to bless Ferrer with his support.

By this time, pundits were doubting that Ferrer had succeeded in pulling off a true Black-Latino coalition. Could a coalition that did not include Dinkins—the city's only Black mayor, the person who coined the phrase "a gorgeous mosaic" to describe New Yorkers—truly be called a Latino-Black coalition? The short answer is no. By this time in the race, Green also had an impressive list of Black and Latino support-ers. Perhaps sensing the weakness of his position, Ferrer vacillated be-tween crowing about his Black-Latino coalition, calling it a "coalition of consciousness," and calling it a coalition for the "other New York." Also, by this time in the race, Ferrer had realized that he needed white voters. Ramirez went to great lengths to emphasize that, even as he was appealing to Latino and Black voters, he did not want to exclude any other groups.

The world knows what happened on September 11, 2001. The day on which the New York City primary was to take place, New York City became the victim of the most horrific terrorist attack in American history. The Twin Towers, symbols of American wealth and power, were reduced to rubble as two commercial airline planes tore into them. The rising smoke and dust covered the city, striking fear and awe in the hearts of most residents. Giuliani, for all of his critics and detractors, rose to the occasion and demonstrated a strong and powerful leader-ship. He took the helm of a New York City that was listing from a griev-ous blow, and in the weeks that followed he managed, through perseverance and strength of character, to help right the mighty vessel and put it back on course. The mayoral primary election that was to take place on September 11 would wait until September 25.

On September 27, 2001, newspapers were reporting that Ferrer and Green were headed for a runoff contest. Ferrer had managed to pull in 35 percent of the vote, followed by Green with 31 percent. Vallone re-ceived 20 percent, and Hevesi was last, with 12 percent. Among Black voters Ferrer pulled in 52 percent. Hardly the overwhelming numbers that he expected, given his concerted efforts to build a Black-Latino coalition, but respectable numbers nevertheless. Surprisingly, Green managed to get 34 percent of the Latino vote, while Vallone and Hevesi received an insignificant 4 percent and 9 percent, respectively. As it turned out, the Hispanic Federation poll, which gave Ferrer 63 percent of the Latino vote, was closer than the earlier Quinnipiac poll, which showed Ferrer receiving 72 percent of the Latino vote. Ferrer's repeated call for a Black-Latino coalition did manage to alienate the white voters. He received only 7 percent of that vote, while Green got 40 percent, Vallone 31 percent, and Hevesi 20 percent.[19] Ferrer, if he was going to win the runoff, needed to improve his white voter numbers. Finally, the same poll found that Giuliani had an overall 67 percent approval rating. None of the other candidates even approached that number.[20]

Things got somewhat complicated for the Democrats after these numbers were released. Giuliani had been termed out of office, but the tragedy that had struck New York and his performance under pressure had people talking about the possibility of extending his tenure as mayor by an extra three months or placing his name on the November runoff ballot for a third term. The Black and Puerto Rican Legislative Caucus in Albany, which included a number of Green supporters, did not want an extension of any kind for Giuliani. Green, who ran surprisingly well among Black voters, did not want to cross such a group and expose himself to the potential of losing any percentage of his Black voters.

Green also feared that with Giuliani on the ballot he could lose some of his white voters—the largest group supporting his mayoral run. As one state legislator stated, "Ferrer wins if we don't get the white vote out. If whites think Mr. Giuliani is running in November, they are not going to vote in great numbers."[21]

Ferrer had his own concerns about Giuliani. His dismal performance among white voters forced him to concentrate on what he could do to improve his performance with this group. If Ferrer was viewed as a roadblock to extending Giuliani's term, then he could be a victim of a backlash.

The endorsements flew fast and furious after Ferrer and Green found themselves in a runoff. Koch lent his support to Ferrer, spurred by Ferrer's outspoken opposition to Giuliani's plans for a three-month extension or an opportunity to seek an additional term in office. Koch, it was hoped, would at last be the magnet to attract the much-needed white voters. Also, by now, Ferrer was trying to distance himself from the "Black-Latino coalition" and "other New York" approach since he understood that he now needed white voters. However, this was no easy matter. In a debate with Green in early October, Green dangled the "other New York" statements before Ferrer like some roadkill that Ferrer had recklessly flattened but long since forgotten.[22] The best Ferrer could do was hold his nose.

On October 11 the drama finally came to an end for Ferrer. At 10:40 P.M. Ferrer called Green and conceded the race to him. When the votes were tallied, Green got 52 percent of the vote to Ferrer's 48 percent. Most pundits argued that Green was helped by Ferrer's outreach to Sharpton and the call for the creation of a Black-Latino coalition. Indeed, one cartoon from the *New York Post* depicted a diminutive Ferrer as a puppet to the inflated Sharpton. This perception, right or wrong, was no doubt aided by Sharpton's early demands on Ferrer, and it succeeded in scaring off the white voters. This was confirmed by an Edison Media Research exit poll that showed Green receiving 83 percent of the white vote and Ferrer 17 percent. The Black-Latino coalition that Ferrer so desperately wanted did, however, prove out. Black voters gave him 71 percent of their vote and Latinos gave him 84 percent of their vote.[23] It was just that even with this overwhelming vote, he still needed a larger number of voters than he eventually got.

Was this a successful coalition between Latinos and Blacks? There are arguments for both sides. Sharpton finally came around and threw his support behind Ferrer, but his initial public responses appeared more like deliberate acts to sabotage than assistance in its creation. His torturing of Ferrer might have continued indefinitely if Sharpton had not decided to protest the bombing in Vieques. For approximately 90 days, his imprisonment effectively hog-tied him.

The other argument against the validity of this as a Black-Latino coalition is that support from other significant Black politicians went to Green. Dinkins is the premier example. His support of Green swung a significant number of Black voters toward Green in the general election. Had Dinkins rallied behind Ferrer, and Sharpton not bedeviled Ferrer with his demands, it is arguable that Ferrer would have avoided a runoff and faced Bloomberg invigorated by his win and with a well-oiled Black-Latino coalition.

Earlier this year Sharpton filed papers seeking the Democratic Party's nomination for the 2004 presidential race. What was his incipient platform? Besides being against the war, the death penalty, and the tax cuts across the board, he also announced that as a Black candidate he would reach out to disaffected voters, including Latinos, Blacks, and young people. If this sounds strangely familiar, it is. It is not at all unlike Ferrer's campaign based on the "other New York." Sharpton better hope for two things in his presidential campaign. First, he better hope that a Latino group does not come to him and publicly say, "Yes, we will support you if you do this thing for us." And that the thing they publicly ask for is not as unreasonable as what he asked of Ferrer. Second, he also better hope that by campaigning on his "other America" platform, he does not scare off the "white folk" because, after all, he now knows that he needs them if he is ever going to win.

Visions of the Future

Well, it's official. Hispanics now are the largest minority in the United States—37 million people, the Census Bureau announced. . . .

The nation has crossed a significant demographic threshold. There is likely to be political, social, and economic fallout. Changes are likely to be felt for many years. . . .

MARIA PADILLA
Reporter, Orlando Sentinel

There will be those who will respond to what has been presented in the foregoing chapters with examples of "alliances" or "coalitions" between Latinos and Blacks in order to contradict the fact that conflict between Latinos and Blacks exists. Even Yzaguirre and Kamasaki, in the postscript to their article published in 1995, pointed to actions taken by certain Black leaders that gave them hope that relations between Latinos and Blacks had improved since their initial presentation. They cited the efforts of Myrlie Evers Williams, a past chairwoman of the NAACP, as someone who demonstrated an attitude of inclusion toward Latinos in the organization's civil rights efforts.

That some Black-Latino alliances exist, that there are certain circumstances where Latinos and Blacks have come together to support one another in the economic, political, and educational arenas, is not disputed. What is disputed is the presumption that simply because Latinos and Blacks are "peoples of color" (a term fraught with problems when applied to the spectrum of people that comprise the Latino population of the United States), any and all differences that may exist are put aside and mutual support in all endeavors is the natural order of things.

The reality is that a divide exists between Blacks and Latinos that no amount of camouflage can hide. For each analysis that finds that Latinos and Blacks have a "natural" basis for mutual support because of a common history of suffering and oppression, there are others that find great antipathy between the two groups. There is no better example of the latter than the findings reported by David O. Sears, a professor of political science and social psychology at the University of California at Los Angeles.[1] Sears asked Latinos and Blacks, "Are ethnic groups in Los Angeles in conflict or are ethnic groups getting along these days?" Close to half of the Latinos and Blacks responded that ethnic groups were in conflict. And when Latinos and Blacks were asked what group was in most conflict with their own, more than half of the Latinos identified Blacks as the group with whom they are in conflict. Two-thirds of Blacks pointed at Latinos as the group with whom they were most in conflict.[2]

Other academics, including Black and Latino scholars, find agreement with Sears's work. They cannot be accused of some nefarious plot to instigate animus between the two groups. Such conspiracy theories are outdated baggage from the 1960s and 1970s that have no place in the contemporary analysis. The truth is that some animus does exist between the two groups, and the source of those feelings is not imposed from without but is homegrown.

Examples of this antipathy are found throughout the various chapters of this book—in the political arena, in the employment sector, and certainly in the struggle for educational resources. I give you another example—California's Proposition 187. Proposition 187 was a patchwork of different policies that had as their ultimate goal stopping illegal immigration into California and punishing undocumented immigrants already living in California. The most controversial parts of the proposition barred anyone who was not a citizen, a legal permanent resident, or a legal temporary visitor from obtaining public social services, health care, and education. Each section of the proposition was slightly different, but generally they all required that service providers verify the immigration status of anyone seeking services. If the service provider found that an applicant was violating—or was reasonably suspected of violating—immigration laws, he or she was obligated to notify state officials and the INS. The service provider also had to inform such immigrants that they were out of status.

The majority of Latinos opposed Proposition 187 not only because they viewed it as callous and inhumane, particularly as it applied to children, but also, no doubt, because there was a sense of "There but for the grace of God go I." Miguel A. Pulido, a Santa Ana city councilman, expressed his opposition by stating that he did not "want to see kids thrown out of school. That's wrong. I don't want to see hospitals act as INS agents."[3]

The majority of Blacks, however, favored passage of Proposition 187. Feeling the heat of competition from undocumented laborers in the workforce, Blacks supported Proposition 187 because it appeared to present a solution to this problem. And while John W. Mack, president of the Los Angeles Urban League, publicly condemned Proposition 187 as an "attack on all Californians" in an editorial in the *Los Angeles Times,*[4] Kevin Ross, chairman of the Los Angeles chapter of the NAACP, gave voice to an opposite view. Even though Ross declared that he would not vote for Proposition 187, he assured readers that "large numbers of African Americans" would support its passage. Why?

> Because the opponents of the ballot measure, including the 70,000 protesters who marched a week ago down streets named after Mexicans prominent in Los Angeles history, have ignored long-running tensions between the black and Latino communities. There is fighting in the high schools and prisons, a tenuous gang truce in Venice, a power struggle in Compton. . . . Many black people don't care that Proposition 187 is being financed by racist organizations. . . . If the initiative creates a McCarthyite police state, the attitude is, "So be it."[5]

The passion that Ross felt about the Latino-Black friction was palpable in the editorial. It seethed with emotion, and when he wrote about Gloria Molina, the Latina Los Angeles County supervisor, and her accusation that Yvonne Brathwaite, a Black Los Angeles County supervisor, was a racist for her views on the solution to the problem of day laborers (mostly Latinos), the words smoldered on the page. "The $15 billion in federal aid this state receives due to the presence of illegal immigrants is still taxpayer money. And for those who insist on comparing African Americans with illegal immigrants, that only serves to further alienate potential allies."[6] On Election Day, Ross's prediction that Blacks would vote in favor of Proposition 187 proved true. The majority of Blacks (55 percent) along with a majority of whites (83 percent) combined to pass the proposition. Indeed, in case after case it was clear that African Americans, in pursuing their own goals, are more likely to form coalitions, alliances, and support groups with whites than they are with Latinos. What does all this mean for the United States? What is the future of the relationship between Blacks and Latinos now that Latinos are the country's largest minority group? Do they now get a turn at the helm of the civil rights ship? Can Latinos now turn the sails in the direction that they choose? And if they do, how considerate should they be of African Americans?

In the foregoing chapters we have seen that in the real world the ostensible moral and philosophical bases for coalition politics have largely fallen apart because of competing self-interests. In particular, we saw that when confronted with a zero-sum game, self-interest drives a wedge between the groups. Houston taught us that Latinos, in a fervent desire to elect one of their own, were willing to forsake their political party as well as a Black candidate who had proven that he was inclusive. Compton taught Latinos that Blacks, once in power, looked out for themselves, forcing Latinos to keep knocking on opportunity's door. And Miami taught Blacks that the same held for Latinos. What will happen between Latinos and Blacks from this point forward may not be predictable with any degree of certainty, but there are certain predicates—axioms, if you will—that change the mathematical equation of race relations in the United States and in particular the relations between Latinos and Blacks.

AXIOM 1

Latinos Are the Largest Minority in the United States and
African Americans Will Never Regain This Position

On January 21, 2003, the U.S. Census Bureau officially announced that Latinos had surpassed African Americans as the largest minority group in the United States. This fact may be the hardest pill for African Americans to swallow even though the handwriting has been on the wall for some time now. Accepting this also means accepting the fact that it is now time to share center stage with another actor. This will be essential to fostering a positive ongoing relationship between Latinos and Blacks.

AXIOM 2

Latinos Have a History of Oppression

Latinos have a long history of oppression at the hands of white America. To highlight only a small part of this history, this oppression includes Mexicans' loss of rights under the Treaty of Guadalupe Hidalgo; the commonplace lynching of Mexicans in the late 1800s; the mistreatment of Mexican workers in the early 1900s; the forced repatriation of thousands of Mexicans in the 1930s; the abuses under the *bracero* program; and the institutionalized segregation in schools throughout the Southwest. It is therefore time for minorities to stop comparing their respective wounds and scars received at the hands of white society. Black suffering does not necessarily trump Latino suffering, just as Latino suffering does not necessarily trump Asian suffering. And there is certainly an argument that the collective suffering of all other minorities does not trump what happened to the Native Americans.

AXIOM 3

Latinos Are Not Responsible for the
Plight of African Americans

Latinos have never held the power and control that whites have in the United States, and they are not responsible for the historical oppression and suffering of African Americans. Slavery in the United States was imposed by white Americans, not Latinos. In fact, Latinos have a history of helping Black slaves to escape. Arnoldo de León, a Latino historian, describes this history.

> The slave plantations of central Texas served as one specific locale wherein the destinies of three different frontier groups played themselves out. There, in the 1850s, Mexicans and blacks joined together, bound by a common belief and trust in freedom and a common distaste for Anglo oppression. Mexicans, both natives of the state and other recent arrivals from Mexico, had established a quasi-underground railroad designed to facilitate the slaves' escape to Mexico. Defying slave codes and conventions forbidding fraternizing with the bondspeople, Mexicans braved both the threatened punishment tied to sabotaging the peculiar institution and the forbidding terrain on the way to the Rio Grande to assist runaways.[7]

African Americans cannot hold Latinos responsible for their historical social, economic, or political condition.

AXIOM 4

Because Latinos Are Not Responsible for the Plight of African
Americans, They Come to the Table with a Clear Conscience

Latinos are not responsible for the current condition of Blacks in the United States. As a student at the University of California at Berkeley I read a great many of the works of Black authors. I swept through the writings of Richard Wright, James Baldwin, Ralph Ellison, Claude Brown, Langston Hughes, Malcolm X, and a variety of lesser-known Black authors with a hunger to view the world from a nonwhite perspective. I read *Black Boy* with complete absorption and identified with the protagonist deeply even though my own life and condition were greatly dissimilar to his. Although I was not trapped in the South like the protagonist, I believed that I could at least empathize with what it was like to be treated by the "white world" of the South.

But I encountered no Latinos in the world of Black literature. The interplay between the actors in these pages was reserved for Blacks and whites—viewed solely in black and white. If I felt left out at times, and there were those times that I longed to catch a glimpse of a Latino in these pages, I was consoled by the fact that Latinos played no considerable role in the oppression of African Americans. There was no Latino Simon Legree, there was no Latino power structure that impinged on the lives of African Americans in a daily and negative way. Latinos were far, far away, in another land, living a life apart from the black-and-white vision of the world described by Black literature.

I did feel sympathy for white America. I understood how a white college student reading *Native Son* or *The Invisible Man* might writhe with discomfort at the turn of each page. It was, after all, "his people" who had created the plight of the Black man and forced him to share the guilt for this sin. But as a Latino I did not feel guilty. I could not because "my people" did not contribute to the oppression of Blacks that was so movingly and eloquently described by African American authors.

As a consequence, Latinos bring a different psyche to their interactions with Blacks than do whites. It is a psyche that is devoid of guilt and a need to compensate for past actions. The emotional playing field between the two groups is level, and as a result Blacks' expectations of Latinos must be markedly different from their expectations of whites. African Americans cannot expect that Latinos will respond to their condition in the same way as whites, and because of this African Americans must adjust their agenda accordingly.

AXIOM 5

Latinos Will Seek Different Benefits Than Blacks

At the risk of stating the obvious, immigrant Latinos come from foreign countries with different languages and different cultures. Language and cultural differences have been and will continue to be issues for Latinos. Whether it is manifested in the struggle over bilingual programs in schools or the development of a substantial and lucrative communications market, it is a fact of Latino existence. The needs of Spanish-speaking Latino children are different from those of Black children and Latinos will actively work to address those needs. Unfortunately, at times this will result in clashes with the needs of African Americans.

AXIOM 6

Latino Immigration Is a Fact of Life

Latino immigration has been ongoing almost from the day that the Southwest was ceded to the United States by Mexico. Latino immigration will continue as long as American business has a need for cheap labor and our neighbors to the south have workers in need of jobs. As Latinos achieve and move on to other locales, new Latino immigrants will replace them in the barrios. There is no sign that this flow will abate. Indeed, there is every sign that it will increase over the next several decades.

AXIOM 7

Immigrants Will Compete for Unskilled Jobs with
African Americans

The academic world is divided over whether immigrants take jobs away from unskilled African Americans. In either event, the perception is that they do. Whether in Los Angeles, Chicago, or the new locales of South Carolina and Georgia, the common lament of African Americans is that illegal immigrants are replacing them in unskilled positions. This refrain is repeated with such frequency and under such diverse circumstances that it hard to believe that it is not true at some level. And if it is believed to be true by African Americans, then it has to be addressed by both groups.

Things have changed indeed. Racial and ethnic relations are no longer a Black-White thing. Political parties now must recognize the ever-growing power of Latino voters, and society in general must fine-tune its ethnic screen to take into account the existence of a large and influential Latino population. The 2004 presidential election will serve as a test case of the effect of the new Latino numbers. It is already clear that President Bush considers the Latino vote to be an important element in his aspiration to be reelected. Al Sharpton has declared himself to be the only candidate who truly understands the "other America," which encompasses Blacks and Latinos. Any other candidate, whether Republican or Democrat, that surfaces before the next presidential election must also acknowledge the existence and power of the new Latino numbers and cater to some degree to the Latino agenda. In the area of ethnic relations the Latino population will continue to grow and have power to wield. And let there be no doubt that this power will be wielded. In the relations with African Americans a new dialogue must be opened, one with perspective and recognition of the Latinos' new numerical stature.

LATINOS AND TOMORROW'S AMERICA

When I first began researching Black-Latino relations in preparation for this book, I did so amid projections that Latinos would outnumber African Americans by the year 2005. In January 2003, shortly after the completion of the first draft of this book, the U.S. Census announced that Latinos had surpassed African Americans, citing figures of 37 million for Latinos and 36.2 million for African Americans.[8] In June 2003, barely six months after that blockbuster announcement, the U.S. Census announced that as of July 1, 2002, Latinos had increased their numbers by an additional 1.8 million.[9] The rate of Latino growth between April 1, 2000, and July 1, 2002, was 9.8 percent, while the rate of growth for the total population was only 2.5 percent. Additionally, the growth of the Latino population was almost evenly attributable between net international migration, which accounted for 53 percent of the growth, and birthrates, which accounted for 47 percent of the growth. These numbers confirm that the projections described in chapter 1 of this book were coming true and, apparently, at a quicker rate than had been predicted.

These numbers also confirmed that with each passing day the comparison between the numbers of Latinos and African Americans are being eclipsed by the larger question: What does the Latino population explosion mean for America? Indeed, when all is said and done, the swelling Latino tsunami in the United States will no doubt turn out to be the larger and more significant issue. While it is difficult to predict the exact impact the growth of the Latino population will have on America, the following are issues that will no doubt press themselves on the American public in general and public policy makers in particular.

DECONSTRUCTING THE "MINORITY" MONOLITH

For years the term *minority* has been used as a catchall term, an overarching word that incorporated all "peoples of color"—Blacks, Latinos, Native Americans, and Asians. *Minority* was a monolithic term whose very inclusiveness ignored the important differences between the racial and ethnic groups huddled beneath its nomenclature. The popular phraseology, found in newspaper and magazine articles, was either just "minorities" or "Blacks and other minorities," indicating that

Blacks, the group with the greatest profile, were accompanied by other minorities whose identity could be guessed at. These statements broadcast to the general population the belief that all groups were, to borrow a concept from the law in class-action suits, equally situated— that is, each group suffered equally at the hands of the majority, and the solution proposed for one group fit the rest of the other minorities. Perhaps the general public never truly accepted this characterization, but that was the manner in which ethnic groups were presented by the mass media. Certainly the "minority groups" never accepted this characterization. One need only refer to the various comments by African Americans and Latinos regarding each other throughout this book to conclude that they do not view each other as being either "the same" or equally situated. And one need only examine the history and contemporary condition of each ethnic and racial group to understand that, objectively, each has a unique history that has led them to a different place in contemporary America.

Latinos are asking, and through the political process demanding, that politicians and public policy makers consider their wants and needs separately from those of other "minorities." This demand for the deconstruction of the "minority" monolith springs from their history in the United States but also reflects what they perceive as a present and different condition in comparison with other minorities.

A segment of the African American intelligentsia, faced with the prospect that the historical Black-White dialogue about race is being destabilized by the infusion of the "Latino" element, has also challenged the "minority" monolith by arguing that Blacks are an exceptional minority among minorities—one so different that it stands unique and apart in terms of its history and treatment at the hands of "white" America. In academic literature it is sometimes referred to as "black exceptionalism." Cornel West, the renowned Black scholar, described this perspective by stating that "Black people in the United States differ from all other modern peoples owing to the unprecedented levels of unregulated and unrestrained violence directed at them."[10] And Angela P. Harris, a Black law professor, describes it as "the claim . . . quite simply, that African Americans play a unique and central role in American social, political, cultural and economic life, and have done so since the nation's founding."[11] Casting the Black experience in such graphic and separatist terms appears to be an attempt to preserve the Black-White analytical framework that has dominated race-relations scholarship for years and limits any role that Latinos may play in such a dialogue.

Whatever the reasons put forth by Latinos and African Americans for distinguishing their respective histories and contemporary conditions, the need to deconstruct the "minority" monolith is not only appropriate but necessary—the special demands made by Latinos, be they for bilingual education, employment, or immigration reform, cannot be lumped together with the separate demands made by African Americans. Politicians, institutions, and public policy makers must now approach Latinos with a singular perspective separate and apart from that used for other minority groups.

THE CHANGING LATINO VOTE

The deconstruction of the monolith is evidenced in the political arena where politicians now have to pay individual attention to Latino voters in ways they have not in the past. In Los Angeles, Compton, Houston, and New York City, the recent pattern has been the same—the Latino population increased dramatically but the number of voters lagged behind because the residency problems of many Latinos prevents them from voting. However, in each of these cases it was clear that the number of eligible Latino voters is changing and portends increased voting power among Latinos. A study conducted by the National Council of La Raza found that the number of Latino voters grew 15.5 percent from 1994 to 1998, an increase that reflected the 19.8 percent increase in Latino adult citizens during the same time frame.[12] And while Latinos do not always exercise their voting power in significant numbers, they do go to the polls in increased numbers when energized by a candidate such as Orlando Sánchez in Houston, or threatened by an issue such as Proposition 187 in California.

Furthermore, the assumption that Latinos (with the exception of Cuban Americans) will always vote Democratic has been challenged. The report issued by the National Council of La Raza noted that while Latinos continued to vote for Democratic politicians in 1998, they also responded to Republican George W. Bush, who managed to get 37 percent of the Latino vote when he was reelected governor of Texas.[13]

The Latino vote for Bush was no fluke. In a survey conducted by the Pew Hispanic Center, Latinos (native born and foreign born) were asked, "Which party do you think has more concern for Hispanics/Latinos—the Democratic party, the Republican party, or is there no difference?" While 45 percent of registered Latinos believed Democrats were more concerned compared to 10 percent who believed the same of Republicans, 40 percent saw no difference between the two parties, and 5 percent did not know.[14] The importance of these numbers is that 40 percent of the Latino voters did not automatically favor the Democratic party, revealing that if a Republican candidate presents an agenda that resonates with the Latino community, or, as in the case of Orlando Sánchez, presents himself as an attractive Latino candidate, then that candidate can make a significant inroad into what has traditionally been considered a Democratic vote.

As the numbers of Latinos continue to grow and their diversity increases, it can no longer be assumed that a Democratic candidate will automatically get the Latino vote, and what this signifies is that candidates will have to vie for the Latino vote with specific programs and policies that respond to their specific needs.

THE LATINO VOICE

For too long the Latino opinion has been ignored or assumed to be represented by the opinion of other minorities—the overarching minority monolith. Opinion polls frequently referred to what white and Black respondents thought of issues such as abortion, affirmative action, welfare, and myriad other important issues facing America. However, with a population of close to 39 million and growing, the Latino viewpoint must be gauged and reported separately from that of whites as well as other minority groups.

Institutions and organizations such as the Pew Hispanic Center, the National Council of La Raza, and the Tomás Rivera Institute have gone a long way in addressing this shortcoming and demonstrating a need to give voice to Latinos. For example, just before the United States took action against Iraq, the Pew Hispanic Center conducted a survey of Latinos and discovered that support for military intervention in Iraq was not as strong in the Latino community as it was among the general population.[15] The survey compared the findings of various polls (Gallup/CNN/*USA Today*/CBS/*New York Times*), which measured the general population's opinion with that of the Latino population and discovered that while between 60 and 70 percent of the general population supported military action only 48 percent of Latinos supported the invasion of Iraq. The survey also revealed that Latinos believed that the war could result in the "harassment" of Latinos by the police and the INS. Added to this concern was a worry that the war could lead to a loss of jobs, "Two-thirds of all Latinos fear that the country will experience difficult economic times and that they will be personally affected. Half express a great deal of concern that they might lose their jobs."[16]

The significance of the Pew Hispanic Center study was that its treatment of the Latino voice as one different from the white opinion and that it did not group their viewpoint with any other minority group. In so doing, it was able to identify differences between Latinos and the general population regarding possible military action in Iraq. The size of the Latino population as well as its diversity demand that its voice be heard and given the weight its numbers merit.

LATINOS AND TOMORROW'S AMERICA

It may appear prosaic if not downright silly that some Latinos point to the fact that salsa has replaced ketchup as the nation's favorite condiment as confirmation of Latino culture's influence on all aspects of American life. However, the influence of Latinos on American culture extends beyond mere food products and such popular culture idols as Jennifer Lopez, Ricki Martin, Cheech Marin, Paul Rodriguez, and the numerous other Latino entertainers who are on music labels and flash across television and movie screens. How can it be otherwise? With the Latino numbers streaking ever higher, the Latino influence is certain to pervade all aspects of American life.

Not only have school districts in such far-flung states as Georgia and North Carolina been forced to address the special needs of Spanish-speaking children and Latino voters by putting one of their own into office, but the impact of Latinos on the economy has recently been recognized. According to a news report, Latino consumer expenditures totaled $523 million in 2002, representing an increase of 243 percent from 1990. The same article reported that Latinos are expected to represent $1 trillion of spending by U.S. consumers, which would greatly outpace the predicted growth in total U.S. consumer spending.[17]

One of the principal traits that distinguishes Latinos from the rest of the population is the substantial number of persons who speak Spanish as their predominant language.[18] Business advertisers are aware of this phenomenon, and in 2001 it was estimated that $2.22 billion was aimed at Spanish-language media, and of this amount, almost 60 percent was devoted to advertising on Spanish-language television. "According to Nielsen Media Research, Hispanic Americans account for 18 percent of the highly coveted U.S. adult 18-to-34 television population. Last year, Hispanic Americans accounted for 84 percent of the growth in those combined television population categories," Fox News reported.[19]

All of this has led Gregory Rodriguez, a senior fellow at the New America Foundation think tank, to write, "having reached critical mass, Latinos are asserting their ethnicity more confidently than ever before ... their growing demographic presence is propelling American-born Latino political and cultural figures into the English-speaking mainstream."[20] The corollary to this statement is that as Latinos enter the "American mainstream" they will also influence it.

For those who fear that Latinos will "Latinize" America into a mini-replica of their countries of origin and thus render it unrecognizable from the nation created by our Founding Fathers, there is enough evidence to suggest that such fears are unfounded. Latinos, it appears, are typical of your average run-of-the-mill immigrants who want little more than to prosper under the political, economic, and legal systems in America. The difference is that unlike their European counterparts who have stopped arriving on America's shores, Latino immigrants continue to arrive in ever-increasing numbers. So what appears to be a reluctance to embrace "American society" and, in particular, its language, is an illusion. The Latino population is not static but represents a continuing replenishment from Mexico and South America.

How can we conclude otherwise when Latino immigrants not only freely acknowledge that economic opportunities in America are better than in their countries of origin but also express the belief that their children will get a better education than they received in their country of origin? And while a great number of Latinos do speak Spanish at home, they nevertheless believe that learning English is essential for success in America. The Pew Hispanic Center survey concluded that "about nine in ten (89 percent) Latinos indicate that they believe immigrants need to learn to speak English to succeed in the United States. Similar numbers of whites (86 percent) and African Americans (86 percent) agree." To prove this belief, the survey found that as few as 7 percent of the second-generation Latinos are "Spanish dominant," with the rest divided between bilingual (47 percent) and English dominant (46 percent).[21] It seems clear that the longer Latinos remain in the United States, the more English dominant they become.

Apart from English, Latinos differ somewhat from the general population in regard to such issues as divorce, sex between consenting adults, having children out of wedlock, and abortion. However, the differences are not unlike those found among white conservatives and white liberals.[22] Indeed, what is intriguing about Latinos, and in particular Mexican Americans, is their failure to create institutions or infrastructures that rival their American counterparts. Gregory Rodriguez observed this fact when he wrote:

> One national survey has shown that Mexican-Americans are far more likely to join a non-ethnic civic group than a Hispanic organization. There is no private Mexican-American college similar to Yeshiva University or Morehouse College. In Los Angeles, which has the largest Mexican population in the country, there is no ethnic-Mexican hospital, cemetery or broad-based charity organization. Nor does Los Angeles have an English-language newspaper for Mexican-Americans similar to the black *Amsterdam* and the *Jewish Forward* in New York.[23]

While Rodriguez's statement ignores the existence of the National Hispanic University, which has as its mission the goal of enabling "Hispanics, other minorities, women, and others to acquire an undergraduate degree or certificate using a multicultural educational experience to obtain a professional career in business, education, or technology" (admittedly a university that does not have the history of a Morehouse University), or the existence of *La Opinión,* the Los Angeles–based, Spanish-language newspaper (the African American newspaper has to be in English, since that is the language spoken and read by Blacks), his point is largely made—while Latinos may talk about holding fast to their "cultural identity," they also appear to have no problem accepting the general society.

Tomorrow's America will be an America greatly influenced by Latinos and their culture, but it will also be one based on the history of Latinos in the United States, in which Latinoism can be described as an ethnic patina set atop America's existing social, political, economic, and legal structures. And it is one I await with great anticipation.

Notes

INTRODUCTION

1. Roberto Suro and Audrey Singer, *Latino Growth in Metropolitan America: Changing Patterns, New Locations*, Center on Urban and Metropolitan Policy and the Pew Hispanic Center, July 2002 (Washington, D.C.: The Brookings Institution: Survey Series, Census 2000), p. 12.

2. Artellia Burch, "When Worlds Collide: Blacks Have Reservations About Influx of Hispanic Immigrants," *Charlotte Post*, March 10, 2001.

3. General Accounting Office, *Illegal Aliens: Significant Obstacles to Reducing Unauthorized Alien Employment Exist*, GAO/GGD-99-33. Washington, D.C., April 2, 1999, p. 5; Sam Fulwood III, "Work Document Idea Could Stir Wide Revolt; Congress Faces Pressure to Require Job Authorization Papers, But Many Predict Voter Outcry on Plan," *Los Angeles Times*, May 3, 1990, A5.

4. Sam Fulwood III, "Employer Sanctions Issue Straining Rights Coalition," *Los Angeles Times*, May 3, 1990, p. A1.

5. General Accounting Office, *Immigration Reform: Employer Sanctions and the Questions of Discrimination*, GAO/GGD-90-62-62. Washington, D.C., Mar. 29, 1990. The two prior reports were General Accounting Office, *Immigration Reform: Status of Implementing Employer Sanctions After Second Year*, GAO/GGD-89-16, Washington, D.C., Nov. 15, 1988, and General Accounting Office, *Immigration Reform: Status of Implementing Employer Sanctions After One Year*, GAO/GGD-88-14, Washington, D.C., Nov. 5, 1987.

6. The Leadership Conference on Civil Rights was founded in 1950 by A. Philip Randolph, Roy Wilkins, and Arnold Aronson. It consists of more than 180 national organizations representing people of color, women, children, labor unions, individuals with disabilities, older Americans, major religious groups, gays and lesbians, and civil liberties and human rights groups. Its prin-

cipal mission is to promote the enactment and enforcement of effective civil rights legislation and policy.

7. Sam Fulwood III, "Employer Sanctions Issues Straining Rights Coalition," *Los Angeles Times,* May 3, 1990, p. A1.

8. Hector Tobar, "NAACP Calls for End to Employer Sanctions," *Los Angeles Times,* July 12, 1990, p. B1.

9. Ibid.

10. Charles Kamasaki and Raul Yzaguirre, "Black-Hispanic Tensions: One Perspective," *Journal of Intergroup Relations,* Winter 1994–1995: 17–40, p. 36.

11. Keith Jennings and Clarence Lusane, "The State and Future of Black/Latino Relations in Washington, D.C.: A Bridge in Need of Repair," in James Jennings (ed.), *Blacks, Latinos, and Asians in Urban America: Status and Prospects for Politics and Activism,* (Westport, Connecticut: Praeger Publishers, 1994), p. 60. The difference in percentage of Latinos was based on a dispute among groups regrading the actual number of Latinos living in Washington, D.C. The 5 percent figure was based on the U.S. Census Bureau count of 32,710 Latinos, while the Office of Latinos Affairs, a Washington, D.C., community group, placed the number at 65,000, making the Latino population 10 percent of the total population of Washington, D.C. However, another Latino Community organization, the Latino Civil Rights Task Force, placed the Latino population at 85,000, making it 12 percent of the total D.C. population. Hence, the percentage range.

12. Ibid., p. 64

13. Ibid., p. 65

14. Ibid.

15. Ibid.

16. Ibid., p. 66.

17. Ibid., p. 68.

18. Kamasaki and Yzaguirre, "Black-Hispanic Tensions: One Perspective," presented at the 1991 Annual Meeting of the Political Science Association, Washington, D.C., August 29–September 1, 1991.

19. Kamasaki and Yzaguirre, "Black-Hispanic Tensions: One Perspective.

20. Ibid., p. 17.

21. Ibid., p. 20.

22. Ibid., p. 36.

23. Jack Miles, "Blacks vs. Browns," *The Atlantic Monthly,* October 1992, pp. 41–68.

24. Ibid., p. 51.

25. Ibid., p. 53.

26. Toni Morrison, "On the Backs of Blacks," *Time,* December 2, 1993, p. 57.

27. *Ronnie Patton et al. v. Del Taco, Inc. et al.,* Los Angeles County Superior Court (Unlimited Jurisdiction), no. BC 269 863, First Amended Complaint.

28. Ibid., pp. 46–47.

29. David E. Hayes-Bautista, Paul Hsu, Aidé Pérez, Miriam Iya Kahramanian, *The Latino Majority Has Emerged: Latinos Comprise More Than 50 Percent of All Births in California* (Los Angeles: Center for the Study of Health and Culture, Division of General Internal Medicine and Health Services Research School of Medicine, UCLA, February 5, 2003).

CHAPTER 1: THE LATINO TSUNAMI

1. Charles P. Henry, "Black-Chicano Coalitions: Possibilities and Problems," *Western Journal of Black Studies* 4, no. 4 (1980): 222–232, p. 223.

2. Edward Negrete and Susan Shimizu Taira, "The Voices of Blacks and Latinos: Understanding Racial Conflict," *California Politics & Policy* (1995): 65–73, pp. 65–66.

3. Campbell Gibson and Kay Jung, *Historical Census Statistics on Population Totals by Race, 1790 to 1990, and by Hispanic Origin, 1970 to 1990, for the United States, Regions, Divisions and States* (Washington, D.C.: U.S. Census Bureau Population, September 2002), pp. 1, 5–6.

4. The 1970 Census count for the Latino population was based on three different criteria. The first and second criteria were based on a 15 percent sample and the third criterion was based on a 5 percent sample. The first criterion was that portion of the population that reported Spanish as a mother language plus all other persons in families in which the head of family or wife reported Spanish as the mother language. The second criterion was that portion of the population that reported Spanish language and/or a Spanish surname in the states of Arizona, California, Colorado, New Mexico, and Texas; the pop-

ulation of Puerto Ricans by birth or parentage in New York, New Jersey, and Pennsylvania; and the population of Spanish language anywhere else. The third criterion was based on respondents self-identified as Spanish origin or descent. Ibid., Gibson and Jung, pp. 5–6. For purposes of this book, the number based on the 15 percent sample is used.

5. Ibid., Table 1.

6. Frederick W. Hollmann, Tammany J. Mulder, and Jeffrey E. Kallan, *Methodology and Assumptions for the Population Projections of the United States: 1999 to 2100.* Population Division Working Paper No. 38 (Washington, D.C.: U.S. Census Bureau, 2000).

7. Ibid., p. 15.

8. "U.S.-Born Hispanics Increasingly Drive Population Developments," *Fact Sheet* (Washington, D.C.: Pew Hispanic Center, January 2002).

9. Hollmann et al., *Methodology and Assumptions*, p. 17.

10. Frank D. Bean, Jennifer Van Hook, and Karen Woodrow-Lafield, *Estimates of Numbers of Unauthorized Migrants Residing in the United States: The Total, Mexican, and Non-Mexican Central American Unauthorized Populations in Mid-2001* (Washington, D.C.: Pew Hispanic Center, November 2001), pp. 2–3.

11. Robert Warren, *Annual Estimates of the Unauthorized Immigrant Population Residing in the United States and Components of Change: 1987 to 1997* (Washington, D.C.: U.S. Immigration and Naturalization Service, September 2000). The INS estimates that in 1996 the undocumented population was at 5 million and growing at an average rate of 275,000 per year.

12. Kitty Calavita, *Inside the State: The Bracero Program, Immigration, and the I.N.S.* (New York: Routledge, 1992), p. 1.

13. Philip Martin, *Guest Workers: New Solution, New Problems?* (Washington, D.C.: Pew Hispanic Center, March 21, 2002), p. 1.

14. Arthur F. Corwin and Walter A. Fogel, "Shadow Labor Force: Mexican Workers in the American Economy," in Arthur F. Corwin (ed.), *Immigrants— and Immigrants: Perspective on Mexican Labor Migration to the United States* (Westport, Conn.: Greenwood Press, 1978), pp. 257–304.

15. U.S. Census 2000.

16. Ibid.

17. Ibid.

18. Ibid.

19. Ibid.

20. Ibid. U.S. Census 2000. For a more detailed analysis of Latino migration to the Midwest, see Lourdes Gouveia and Thomas Sanchez, "Incorporation of Latinos/Immigrants in Rural Nebraska Communities: Grand Island and Schuyler," a report to the Texas A&M Research Foundation, July 21, 2000; see also Lourdes Gouveia and Donald D. Stull, "Latino Immigrants, Meatpacking, and Rural Communities: A Case Study of Lexington, Nebraska," Research Report No. 26. Julian Samora Research Institute. East Lansing: Michigan State University, August 1997.

21. Francisco L. Rivera-Batiz, *The Socioeconomic Status of Hispanic New Yorkers: Current Trends and Future Prospects* (Washington, D.C.: Pew Hispanic Center, January 2002), p. 24, Table 2.

22. Ibid., p. 24, and Table 3, pp. 4–5.

23. Roberto Suro and Audrey Singer, *Latino Growth in Metropolitan America: Changing Patterns, New Locations* (Washington, D.C.: Center on Urban and Metropolitan Policy and the Pew Hispanic Center, July 2002), p. 5.

24. Ibid., p. 6, Table 3.

25. Andrew A. Green, "Immigration in Arkansas" *Baltimore Sun,* April 17, 2002.

26. Barry Yeoman, "Hispanic Diaspora," *Mother Jones,* July/August, 2000. Viewed at http://www.motherjones.com/mother_jones/JA00/diaspora. html

27. U.S. Census 1990.

28. U.S. Census 2000.

29. Ned Celassock, "Latinos Now Filling Bottom-Rung Jobs, *Raleigh News and Observer* (Columbia, South Carolina), October 29, 2000.

30. Pat Butler, "Greenwood's New Accent," *The State* (Columbia, South Carolina), April 26, 1998.

31. Pat Butler, "New Immigrants Face Old Resentments," *The State* (Columbia, South Carolina), April 26, 1998.

32. U.S. Census 2000.

33. Joan Stroer, "Hispanic Population Will Overtake Ga. Blacks," February 17, 1999. Viewed at http://www.onlineathens.com/stories/o21799/new_0217 99001.shtml

34. Dahleen Glanton, "Hispanic Influx in Deep South Causes Tensions—with Blacks," *Chicago Tribune,* March 19, 2001. Viewed at http://www. usbc. org/info/popen/.301tensions.htm

35. Don Campbell, "The Coming Fight over Latino Power," *USA Today*, April, 23, 2001. Viewed at http://www.naleo.org/USATODAY010.htm

36. Roberto Suro, *Counting the "Other Hispanics": How Many Colombians, Dominicans, Ecuadorians, Guatemalans and Salvadorans Are There in the United States?* (Washington, D.C.: Pew Hispanic Center, May 9, 2001), adopted from Appendix A, Table 3.

37. Gloria Sandrino-Glasser, "*Los Confundidos:* De-Conflating Latinos/as Race and Ethnicity," *Chicano-Latino Law Review* 6 (Spring 1998): 78.

38. Arthur F. Corwin, "Early Mexican Labor Migration: A Frontier Sketch, 1848–1900," *Immigrants—and Immigrants: Perspectives on Mexican Labor Migration to the United States*, p. 31.

39. Carey McWilliams, *North From Mexico* (New York: Greenwood Press, 1968), p. 52.

40. Matt S. Meier and Felicano Ribera, *Mexican Americans/American Mexicans: From Conquistadors to Chicanos* (New York: Hill and Wang, 1993), p. 69.

41. Oscar J. Martinez, "On the Size of the Chicano Population: New Estimates, 1850–1900," *Aztlán: International Journal of Chicano Studies Research* 6, no. 1 (1975): 43–67.

42. The immigration was truly Latino. Joining the 8000 Mexicans who came to California during the Gold Rush were 5000 South Americans. See Leonard Pitt, *The Decline of Californios: A Social History of Spanish-Speaking Californians* (Berkeley: University of California Press, 1968), p. 52.

43. Corwin, "Early Mexican Labor Migration: A Frontier Sketch, 1848–1900," p. 27.

44. Ibid., p. 35, Table 3

45. Ibid., p. 34. For an even higher estimate, 381,000 to 552,000, see Martinez, "On the Size of the Chicano Population," p. 55.

46. Marion T. Bennett, *American Immigration Policies: A History* (Washington, D.C.: Public Affairs Press, 1963), p. 15.

47. Ibid.

48. Lawrence A. Cardoso, *Mexican Emigration to the United States, 1897–1931: Socio-Economic Patterns* (Tucson: University of Arizona Press, 1980), p. 22.

49. Mark Reisler, *By the Sweat of Their Brow: Mexican Immigrant Labor in the United States, 1900–1940* (New York: Greenwood Press 1976), p. 3.

50. Cardoso, *Mexican Emigration to the United States, 1897–1931*, p. 22.

51. See, for example, Stan Stein, *Fusang: The Chinese Who Built America: The Chinese Railroad Men* (New York: Harper & Row, 1979).

52. McWilliams, *North from Mexico*, pp. 168.

53. Reisler, *By the Sweat of Their Brow: Mexican Immigrant Labor in the United States, 1900–1940*, p. 4.

54. Arthur F. Corwin and Lawrence A. Cardoso, "*Vamos al Norte*: Causes of Mass Mexican Migration to the United States," *Immigrants—and Immigrants: Perspectives on Mexican Labor Migration to the United States, 1848–1900*, p. 46.

55. George J. Sánchez, *Becoming Mexican-American: Ethnicity, Culture, and Identity in Chicano Los Angeles, 1900–1945* (New York: Oxford University Press, 1993), p. 50.

56. Reisler, *By the Sweat of Their Brow*, p. 12.

57. Ibid.

58. Ibid., p. 13.

59. Ibid.

60. Cardoso, *Mexican Emigration to the United States, 1897–1931: Socio-economic Patterns*, pp. 35–36.

61. Ibid., 34–35.

62. Ibid., p. 44.

63. Bennett, *American Immigration Policies: A History*, pp. 26–28.

64. Reisler, *By the Sweat of Their Brow*, pp. 32–33.

65. Ibid., 38.

66. Ibid.

67. Arthur F. Corwin, "¿Quien Sabe? Mexican Migration Statistics," in *Immigrants—and Immigrants: Perspectives on Mexican Labor Migration to the United States*, p. 114, Table 3.

68. Reisler, *By the Sweat of Their Brow*, p. 56.

69. Corwin, "¿Quien Sabe? Mexican Migration Statistics," p. 114.

70. Ibid., pp. 116–117.

71. Ibid., p. 117.

72. Peter N. Kirstein, *Anglo Over Bracero: A History of the Mexican Worker in the United States from Roosevelt to Nixon* (San Francisco, Calif.: R and E Research Associates, 1977), p. 12.

73. Ibid., p. 13.

74. Richard B. Craig, *The Bracero Program* (Austin: University of Texas Press, 1971), p. 42.

75. Calavita, *Inside the State: The Bracero Program, Immigration, and the I.N.S.*, p. 21.

76. Ibid., Appendix B.

77. Ibid., Appendix A.

78. Ibid., p. 28.

79. Ibid., pp. 28–29.

80. Ibid., p. 32.

81. Ibid., Appendix A.

82. Ibid., p. 151.

83. Daniel James, *Illegal Immigration: An Unfolding Crisis* (Lanham, Md.: University Press of America, 1991), p. 24, Table 1.

84. Francisco L. Rivera-Batiz, Selig L. Sechzer, and Ira N. Gang (eds.), *U.S. Immigration Policy Reform in the 1980s* (New York: Praeger, 1991), p. 2.

85. Ibid., pp. 18, 30, 35.

86. Robert Manning, *Five Years After NAFTA* (Washington, D.C.: Center for Immigration Studies, March 2000), p. 4, Table 6.

87. Ibid., p. 14, Table 5.

88. Peter Brimelow, *Alien Nation* (New York: HarperPerennial, 1996), p. 75.

89. Consejo Naciónal de Población, *Migración México-Estados Unidos. Presente y futuro* (México, D.F.: Enero 2000), pp. 60–75.

90. Ibid.

CHAPTER 2: SOMEWHERE OVER THE RAINBOW COALITION

1. Maulana Karenga, "Black and Latino Relations: Context, Challenge, and Possibilities," in Ishmael Reed (ed.), *Multi-America: Essays on Cultural Wars and Cultural Peace* (New York: Penguin Books, 1998), pp. 194–195.

2. Kenneth J. Meier and Joseph Stewart, Jr., "Cooperation and Conflict in Multiracial School Districts," *Journal of Politics* 53, no. 4 (November 1991): 1123–1133, p. 1132.

3. Stokely Carmichael and Charles V. Hamilton, *Black Power* (New York: Vintage, 1967), p. 75.

4. Paula D. McClain, "The Changing Dynamics of Urban Politics: Black

and Hispanic Municipal Employment—Is There Competition?" *Journal of Politics* 55, no. 2 (1993): 399–414, p. 400.

5. Ibid., p. 411.

6. Ibid.

7. Jerry Yaffe, "Discrimination Against Hispanics in the Public Sector Work Force: Past, Present, and Future," *Journal of Intergroup Relations* 20, no. 1 (1993): 39–50, p. 40.

8. Jerry Yaffe, "Prospects and Barriers to Successful Latino and African-American Coalitions," *Harvard Journal of Hispanic Policy* 8 (1994–1995): 61–86, p. 66.

9. Ibid., p. 67.

10. Yaffe, "Discrimination Against Hispanics in the Public Sector Work Force, p. 43.

11. Ibid.

12. Yaffe, "Prospects and Barriers to Successful Latino and African-American Coalitions," p. 68.

13. Ibid.

14. Ibid.

15. Ibid.

16. Jerry Yaffe. "Institutional and Racial Barriers to Employment Equity for Hispanics," *Hispanic Journal of Behavioral Science* 16, no. 3 (August 1994): 211–229, p. 212.

17. Ibid., p. 213.

18. Victor Merina, "New Drive for County Jobs Set by Latino Group," *Los Angeles Times*, November 10, 1987, p. B3.

19. Ibid. Also see Scott Harris, "County's Health Services Probed for Bias After Latino Complaints," *Los Angeles Times*, November 6, 1987, p. B3.

20. Victor Merina, "County Figures Indicate Hiring Discrimination, Latinos Assert," *Los Angeles Times*, Feburary 25, 1988, p. B1.

21. Ibid.

22. Victor Merina, "County Jobs Pit Blacks Against Latino Workers," *Los Angeles Times*, February 28, 1988, p. B1.

23. Ibid.

24. Ibid.

25. Victor Merina, "'Cooling-off' Time Delays Affirmative-Action Report, *Los Angeles Times*, March 9, 1988, p. B1.

26. Victor Merina, "Supervisors Support Latinos in Clash over Hiring Goals," *Los Angeles Times,* July 13, 1988, p. B3.

27. Richard Simon, "County Accused of Anti-Latino Bias," *Los Angeles Times,* August 29, 1990, Part B, page 1, col. 2.

28. Frederick M. Muir, "Affirmative Action Chief Faces Bias Charge," *Los Angeles Times,* September 6, 1990, p. B3.

29. Richard Simon, "Torres Supervisors Clash Over Alleged Job Discrimination," *Los Angeles Times,* September 12, 1990, p. B3.

30. Yaffe, "Discrimination Against Hispanics in the Public Sector Work Force," p. 44, Table 1.

31. Ibid., p. 45, Table 2.

32. Richard Simon and Claire Spiegel, "County OKs Plan to Settle Charges of Job Bias Against Latinos," *Los Angeles Times,* March 12, 1992, p. B1.

33. Yaffe, "Discrimination Against Hispanics in the Public Sector Work Force," p. 46.

34. Simon and Spiegel, "County OKs Plan to Settle Charges of Job Bias Against Latinos; *Los Angeles Times,* September 12, 1992, p. B1.

35. Carla Rivera, "Latino Workers Sue County Over New Affirmative Action Rules," *Los Angeles Times,* February 22, 1995, B3.

36. Josh Meyer, "Panel Finds Bias at Hospital but Declines to Act; Health Care: Board Upholds Report on Racism at King/Drew Medical Center but Votes Down Doctor's Plea to be Reinstated," *Los Angeles Times,* January 18, 1996, p. B3.

37. Jeffrey L. Rabin, "Health Director Confronts Racial Parity," *Los Angeles Times,* February 18, 1996, p. B1.

38. James Jennings, "Conclusion: Racial Hierarchy and Ethnic Conflict in the United States," in *Blacks, Latinos and Asians in Urban America,* p. 146.

CHAPTER 3: WHO'S THE LEADER OF THE CIVIL RIGHTS BAND?

1. Kenneth J. Meier and Joseph Stewart, Jr., *The Politics of Hispanic Education: Un paso pa'lante y dos pa'tras* (Albany: State University of New York Press, 1991), p. xvii.

2. George J. Sánchez, *Becoming Mexican-American,* New York: Oxford University Press, 1993, p. 255.

3. Ibid., p. 257.

4. Charles Wollenberg, *All Deliberate Speed: Segregation and Exclusion in California Schools, 1855–1975* (Berkeley: University of California Press, 1976), p. 112.

5. Sánchez, *Becoming Mexican-American*, p. 258.

6. Wollenberg, *All Deliberate Speed*, p. 112.

7. Ibid., p. 113.

8. Ibid.

9. Gilbert G. Gonzalez, *Chicano Education in the Era of Segregation* (Cranbury, N.J.: Associated University Press, 1990), p. 72.

10. Ibid.

11. Wollenberg, *All Deliberate Speed*, p. 115.

12. Ibid., p. 116.

13. Gonzalez, *Chicano Education in the Era of Segregation*, p. 137.

14. Ibid., p. 141.

15. Ibid., p. 142.

16. Ibid., p. 143.

17. Wollenberg, *All Deliberate Speed*, p. 120.

18. Guadalupe San Miguel Jr., *Let All of Them Take Heed: Mexican Americans and the Campaign for Education Equality in Texas, 1910–1981* (Austin: University of Texas Press, 1987), pp. 114–115.

19. *Mendez et al. v. Westminster School District of Orange County et al.* (1946), 64 F. Supp. 544.

20. Ibid., p. 545.

21. Ibid., p. 546.

22. Ibid.

23. Ibid., p. 549.

24. Ibid., p. 551.

25. Wollenberg, *All Deliberate Speed*, p. 128.

26. Christopher Arriola, "Knocking on the Schoolhouse Door: *Mendez v. Westminster*: Equal Protection, Public Education and Mexican Americans in the 1940s," *La Raza Law Journal* 8, no. 2 (1995): pp. 166–207.

27. *Westminster School District of Orange County et al. v. Mendez et al.*, 161 F. 2nd 774 (9th Cir., 1947), 780.

28. Wollenberg, *All Deliberate Speed*, p. 132.

29. Gonzalez, *Chicano Education in the Era of Segregation*, p. 28.

30. "Segregation in Public Schools—A Violation of 'Equal Protection of the Laws,'" *Yale Law Journal* 56, no. 6 (1947): 1059–1067; see also, "Segregation in Schools as a Violation of the XIVth Amendment," *Columbia Law Review* 47, no. 1 (1947): 325–329.

31. Lester H. Phillips, "Segregation in Education: A California Case Study," *Phylon* 10, no. 4 (1949): 407–413, p. 407.

32. David Montejano, *Anglos and Mexicans in the Making of Texas: 1836–1986* (Austin: University of Texas Press, 1987).

33. Ibid., p. 191.

34. Herschel T. Manuel, *The Education of Mexican and Spanish-Speaking Children in Texas* (Austin: University of Texas Press, 1930), p. 60.

35. Guadalupe San Miguel, *Let All of Them Take Heed*, p. 56.

36. Ibid., p. 71.

37. Ibid., p. 77.

38. *Independent School District v. Salvatierra*, 33 S.W.2d 790 (Tex. Civ. App. 1930), cert. Denied, 284 U.S. 580 (1931).

39. Guadalupe San Miguel, *Let All of Them Take Heed*, p. 78.

40. Ibid., p. 121.

41. *Minerva Delgado et al. v. Bastrop Independent School District of Bastrop County, Texas, et al.* (D.C. Texas Western District), June 15, 1948, Civil Action No. 388.

42. Guadalupe San Miguel, *Let All of Them Take Heed*, p. 123.

CHAPTER 4: THE FOLLY OF PRESUMPTION

1. Jim Newton, "Speaker Villaraigosa Enters Race for Mayor," *Los Angeles Times*, October 17, 1999, p. B1.

2. Matea Gold, "Rivals in Mayor's Race Battle over Endorsements," *Los Angeles Times*, January 22, 2001, p. B1.

3. James Rainey, "Latino Candidates Running Despite Fear of Split Vote," *Los Angeles Times*, January 10, 2001, p. B1.

4. Ibid.

5. Matea Gold and Larry B. Stammer, "2 City Leaders Say They Regret Helping Dealer," *Los Angeles Times*, February 13, 2001, p. A22.

6. Matea Gold, "Villaraigosa Wins Key Labor Endorsement in Mayor's Race," *Los Angeles Times,* February 13, 2001, p. A1.

7. James Rainey, "The Times Poll: Hahn Takes Solid Lead in Race to Be Next Mayor," *Los Angeles Times,* March 4, 2001, p. A1.

8. Jeffrey L. Rabin, "Many of Hahn's Donors Benefit from City Hall; Politics: Lawyers Who Do Lucrative Work for the City Attorney's Office Are Among His Key Backers," *Los Angeles Times,* March 23, 2001, p. B1.

9. Matea Gold, "Los Angeles Elections; Anti-Villaraigosa Phone Calls Shake Up Campaign; Message Suggests He's Soft on Crime. Mayoral Rivals Deny Responsibility," *Los Angeles Times,* April 2, 2001, p. B1.

10. Matea Gold, "Kenneth Hahn's Legacy Serves His Son Well in Mayor's Race," *Los Angeles Times,* April 3, 2001, p. B1.

11. Ibid.

12. Ibid.

13. Matea Gold, "Campaign 2001: Mayor's Race Thrills and Frustrates L.A. Latinos," *Los Angeles Times,* April 5, 2001, p. B1.

14. Jeffrey L. Rabin and Jean Merl, "Mayoral Campaign Stirred by Indians' Last-Minute Ads Against Villaraigosa," *Los Angeles Times,* April 7, 2001, p. B7.

15. Hector Tobar and Carla Hall, "Los Angeles County Elections: Villaraigosa's Backers Revel in Historic Feat," *Los Angeles Times,* April 11, 2001, p. A20.

16. McWilliams, *North from Mexico,* p. 36.

17. Raphael J. Sonenshein, *Politics in Black and White: Race and Power in Los Angeles* (Princeton, N. J.: Princeton University Press, 1993), p. 26.

18. Sánchez, *Becoming Mexican American,* p. 90.

19. Sonenshein, *Politics in Black and White,* p. 48.

20. Ibid., p. 176.

21. Ibid., p. 45.

22. Ibid., p. 78.

23. Ibid., p. 86.

24. Ibid., p. 99.

25. Ibid., p. 110.

26. Ibid., p. 111, Table 7.7.

27. Ibid., p. 193.

28. Ibid., p. 206.

29. McClain and Stewart, *"Can We All Get Along?,"* p. 171.

30. Madison Shockley, "Commentary: Will This Fork in the Road Lead Black L.A. to a New Coalition?" *Los Angeles Times,* April 23, 2001, p. B7.

31. Sonenshein, *Politics in Black and White,* p. 263.

32. James Rainey, "Los Angeles: Campaign 2001; Candidates Work Each Other's Turf," *Los Angeles Times,* May 7, 2001, p. B3.

33. Susan Anderson, "The State/Mayoral Elections Surprise King Makers," *Los Angeles Times,* May 20, 2001, p. M2.

34. Steve Lopez, "Barbershop Perspective on the Mayor's Race," *Los Angeles Times,* May 21, 2001, p. B1.

35. Erin Texeira, "Generation Gap Seen in Black Support for Hahn; Politics: Some Observers Say Villaraigosa's Appeal to Younger Voters Could Run Counter to Older Generation's Long-Term Loyalties," *Los Angeles Times,* May 27, 2001, p. B1.

36. James Rainey and Matea Gold, "Campaign 2001; Hahn TV Ad Calls Rival Untrustworthy," *Los Angeles Times,* May 28, 2001, B1.

37. George Skelton, "Affection for Hahn a Hurdle Villaraigosa Couldn't Vault," *Los Angeles Times,* June 7, 2001, p. B7.

38. Roger Hernandez, "On the Way: Despite Defeat in Los Angeles, Hispanic Mayors Are the Wave of the Future," *Ventura County Star,* June 9, 2001.

39. Mickey Ibarra, "Second Place Isn't Good Enough," *Politico: The Magazine for Latino Politics and Culture,* August 2, 2002.

40. Martin Kasindorf, "Hispanics, Blacks Find Futures Entangled Immigration," *USA Today,* September 10, 1999.

CHAPTER 5: PASSED BY AND SHUT OUT

1. Barry Bearak, "4 Shot in Miami in 2nd Day of Racial Violence," *Los Angeles Times,* January 18, 1989, p. A1.

2. Michael Marriott, "Miami Officer Disputed on Shot That Led to Riots," *New York Times,* January 22, 1989, p. A18.

3. Barry Bearak and Eric Harrison, "Protest Seen Turning into Mayhem," *Los Angeles Times,* January 19, 1989, p. A1.

4. Eric Harrison, "Police, Cubans Blamed for Miami Riots," *Los Angeles Times,* January 20, 1989, p. A4.

5. Barry Bearak and Eric Harrison, "Protest Turning into Mayhem," *Los Angeles Times,* January 19, 1989, A1.

6. Alejandro Portes and Alex Stepick, *City on the Edge: The Transformation of Miami* (Berkeley: University of California Press, 1993), p. 76.

7. Ibid., p. 77.

8. Barry Bearak, "City Ponders Racial Unrest," *Los Angeles Times,* March 20, 1989, p. A1.

9. Alejandro Portes and Robert L. Bach, *Latin Journey: Cuban and Mexican Immigrants in the United States* (Berkeley: University of California Press, 1985), pp. 85–86.

10. Ibid., p. 85.

11. Ibid., p. 89.

12. James Kelley, reported by Bernard Diederich and William McWhirter, "Trouble in Paradise: South Florida Is Hit by a Hurricane of Crime, Drugs and Refugees," *Time,* November 23, 1981, p. 24.

13. Ibid.

14. "Miami: The Riot That Wasn't," *The Economist,* March 24, 1984, p. 27; Kurt Andersen, reported by William McWhirter, "Miami's New Days of Rage: Racial Violence Flares Again," *Time,* January 10, 1983, p. 20.

15. "Assessing Harm's Way in Miami: Officials Examine Police Performance During Riot," *Time,* January 17, 1983, p. 18.

16. William McWhirter, "Miami's New Days of Rage: Racial Violence Flares Again," *Time,* January 10, 1983, p. 20.

17. "Behind the Hibiscus and the Potted Palms," *The Economist,* July 19–25, 1986, p. 22.

18. Liz Balmaseda, "The *Contra* Rebels Run Their War from South Florida," *Newsweek,* May 26, 1986, p. 36.

19. Jeffrey Schmalz, "Miami, Saying It's Overburdened, Tells Nicaraguan to Stay Away," *New York Times,* January 14, 1989, p. A1.

20. Barry Klein, "Open Arms; Ticket Home: Hispanics, Haitians Get Different U.S. Treatment," *St. Petersburg Times,* February 7, 1989, p. 1A.

21. Barry Klein, "Panel Searches for Root Causes of Miami Riots," *St. Petersburg Times,* February 24, 1989, p. 1B.

22. Barry Klein, "Miami Riot Left Trail of Tension," *St. Petersburg Times,* February 27, 1989, p. 1B.

23. Ibid.

24. George Hackett and David L. Gonzalez, "Miami: 'We got Justice,'" *Newsweek*, December 18, 1989, p. 30.

25. Ibid.

26. Barry Klein and Kevin E. Washington, "Miami Officer Gets 7 Years in Shooting," *St. Petersburg Times*, January 25, 1990, p. 1A.

27. Maya Bell, "Miami Officer Who Killed 2 Blacks Gets 7 Years: Lozano Stays Free for Appeal," *Orlando Sentinel Tribune*, January 25, 1990, p. A1.

28. Maya Bell, "Miami—A City Torn over Mandela," *Orlando Sentinel Tribune*, June 27, 1990, p. A4.

29. Ibid.

30. Ibid.

31. Maya Bell, "Black Boycott Wounds Miami," *Orlando Sentinel Tribune*, September 16, 1990, p. D1.

32. Rick Bragg and Janita Poe, "Court Orders New Trial for Miami Officer," *St. Petersburg Times*, June 26, 1991, p. 1A.

33. Ibid.

34. Janita Poe and Rick Bragg, "Calm but No Peace," *St Petersburg Times*, June 29, 1991, p. 1B.

35. Eric Harrison, "In Wary Miami, A Day of Seeing and Being Seen," *Los Angeles Times*, May 30, 1993, p. A1.

36. Mireya Navarro, "Many Florida Blacks Say They Feel Passed Over by Prosperity," *Palm Beach Post* (Florida), February 18, 1997, p. A1.

37. Will Lester, "Race the Issue in Miami Appointment," *Stuart News/Port St. Lucie News* (Stuart, Florida), August 7, 1997, p. C6.

38. Bill Douthat, "Battle over Elian Aggravates Miami's Racial, Ethnic Rift," *Palm Beach Post* (Florida), April 16, 2000, p. A1.

39. Andrea Robinson, "Racial, Ethnic Tensions a Serious Problem, Residents Say in Survey," *Miami Herald*, December 12, 2002, p. B3.

CHAPTER 6: WHEN BLACKS RULE

1. Michele Fuetsch, "Candidate Would Be 1st Latino on Compton Council," *Los Angeles Times*, March 19, 1989, part 9, p. 1.

2. Ibid.

3. Ibid.

4. Michele Fuetsch, "Affirmative Action Plan Urges Compton to Triple Number of Jobs for Latinos," *Los Angeles Times,* April 6, 1989, p. I5.

5. Fuetsch, "Candidate Would Be 1st Latino on Compton Council," *Los Angeles Times,* March 19, 1989, I5.

6. Fuetsch, "Affirmative Action Plan Urges Compton to Triple Number of Jobs for Latinos," *Los Angeles Times,* April 6, 1989, I5.

7. Michele Fuetsch, "Compton School Chief Lands Top Job in Chicago," *Los Angeles Times,* October 14, 1989, p. B1.

8. Michele Fuetsch, "Latino Aspirations on Rise in Compton," *Los Angeles Times,* May 7, 1990, p. B1.

9. Ibid.

10. Ibid.

11. Michele Fuetsch, "Compton Latinos Allege Hiring Bias," *Los Angeles Times,* September 9, 1990, p. J7.

12. Ibid.

13. Michele Fuetsch and Lee Harris, "Elections Compton: Attorney Succeeds Father as Mayor; Government," *Los Angeles Times,* April 18, 1991, p. J1.

14. Michele Fuetsch, "Elections City Council; Bradley Victorious; Robbins Hangs on in District 4," *Los Angeles Times,* June 6, 1991, p. J1.

15. Mark Gladston, "Assemblyman Seeks Outside Help for Schools; Education," *Los Angeles Times,* April 5, 1992, p. J1.

16. Mark Gladstone, "State Scolds District on Students' Performance," *Los Angeles Times,* June 25, 1993, p. J1.

17. Howard Blume, "District Owes $2 Million to County, Board Learns," *Los Angeles Times,* February 25, 1993.

18. Howard Blume, "Compton Schools to Request State Loan," *Los Angeles Times,* March 23, 1993, p. B3.

19. Howard Blume, "School Given Failing Marks in Compton," *Los Angeles Times,* May 5, 1993, p. B1.

20. John Steward, "Crisis of Confidence," *Los Angeles Times,* September 2, 1993, p. J3.

21. Emily Adams, "Vote to Put Bradley Ally on Council Angers Latinos," *Los Angeles Times,* June 10, 1993, p. J1.

22. Ibid.

23. Howard Blume, "Ethnic Standoffs Continue to Plague City's High Schools," *Los Angeles Times,* November 18, 1993, p. J1.

24. Ibid.

25. Shawn Hubler, "Video Stirs Brutality Allegation," *Los Angeles Times,* August 3, 1994, p. B1; Richard Lee Colvin and Patrick J. McDonnell, "Grand Jury Probes Compton Police Beating," *Los Angeles Times,* August 5, 1994, p. B1.

26. Patrick J. McDonnell, "As Change Again Overtakes Compton, So Do Tensions," *Los Angeles Times,* August 21, 1994, p. A1.

27. Ibid.

28. Emily Adams, "Compton to Create Office for Racial Concerns," *Los Angeles Times,* September 22, 1994, p. B3.

29. Ibid.

30. John D. Wagner, "School Board Seeking Dymally Replacement," *Los Angeles Times,* October 13, 1994, p. J6.

31. John D. Wagner, "Outcry Forces Second Vote on Filling of Vacant School Board Position," *Los Angeles Times,* November 17, 1994, p. J3.

32. Ibid.

33. Ibid.

34. "School Board Appointment of Felon Put into Limbo," *Los Angeles Times,* November 19, 1994, p. B2.

35. "State Schools Chief Rejects Felon as Board Member," *Los Angeles Times,* February 8, 1995, p. B2.

36. Psyche Pascal, "Rejection of Appointee Irks Board," *Los Angeles Times,* February 9, 1995, p. J3. While Lankster's appointment to the school board was thwarted, he was popular enough to eventually be elected to the school board. Interview with Pedro Pallan, January 24, 2003.

37. Emily Adams, "Voters Reject Bid to Raise Mayor's Pay," *Los Angeles Times,* April 20, 1995, p. J3.

38. Darryl Fears, "Compton Latinos Still on Outside Looking In," *Los Angeles Times,* April 16, 1998, p. A1.

39. Ibid.

40. Legrand H. Clegg II, "Ethnic Politics in Compton," *Los Angeles Times,* April 26, 1998, p. M4.

CHAPTER 7: HOUSTON, WE HAVE A PROBLEM

1. Rachel Graves and Lori Rodriguez, "Candidates Rhetoric Rises in Affirmative Action Debate," *Houston Chronicle*, August 20, 2001, p. A17.

2. Joel Hochmuth, "The Politics of Ethnicity: The Growing Power of the Hispanic Vote," CNN.com, posted October 3, 2001.

3. Lori Rodriguez, "The Race for City Hall: Race Issue Underlies Campaign for Mayor," *Houston Chronicle*, September 9, 2001, p. A1.

4. Lori Rodriguez, "Sanchez Scores Win for Latinos: Hispanic Turnout in Election Hailed as a Benchmark," *Houston Chronicle*, December 9, 2001, p. A1.

5. Lori Rodriguez, "The Race for City Hall 2001; Hispanic Voters Moving Toward a New Political Era," *Houston Chronicle*, November 26, 2001, p. A1.

6. Richard Murray and Bob Stein, "Houston's Future After 9/11," http://www.uh.edu/cpp/Houston.pdf, p. 8.

7. Arnoldo de León, *Ethnicity in the Sunbelt: A History of Mexican-Americans in Houston* (College Station: Texas A&M University Press, 2001), p. 5.

8. Tatcho Mindiola Jr., Yolanda Flores Niemann, and Nestor Rodriguez, *Black-Brown Relations and Stereotypes* (Austin: University of Texas Press, 2002), p. 8.

9. Ibid., pp. 9–10.

10. Ibid., p. 10.

11. Ibid., p. 11.

12. Ibid.

13. Ibid., p. 12.

14. Alan Bernstein, "Top Issue in Runoff Is Turner; How Will Attacks on Him Affect Votes," *Houston Chronicle*, December 5, 1991, p. A1.

15. Murray and Stein, "Houston's Future After 9/11," p. 17.

16. Ibid., p. 11.

17. Ibid., p. 18.

18. Alan Bernstein and Jim Simmon, "Campaign Briefs: Raising Bail," *Houston Chronicle*, October 10, 1992, p. A31.

19. Alan Bernstein and Jim Simmon, "Candidate Raises Immigration Issue," *Houston Chronicle*, October 12, 1993, p. A4.

20. "Election '93 at a Glance," *Houston Chronicle*, November 3, 1993, p. A21.

21. "For Sanchez, Saenz; Endorsement for Two Citywide Council Positions," *Houston Chronicle*, October 17, 1995, p. A18.

22. Alan Bernstein, "Partisans Romp at City Hall as Non-Partisan Election Nears," *Houston Chronicle*, October 1, 1995, p. A42.

23. Alan Bernstein, "Two District E Hopefuls Will Seek Vote Recount," *Houston Chronicle*, November 9, 1995, p. A1.

24. Alan Bernstein, "Candidate's GOP Ties Hit in Council Race," *Houston Chronicle*, November 28, 1995, p. A13.

25. Alan Bernstein, "Sanchez, Boney Win Council Bids; Runoff Turnout Less Than 5%," *Houston Chronicle*, December 10, 1995, p. A1.

26. James T. Campbell, "Is the Coalition Ready for a Black Mayor," *Houston Chronicle*, January 6, 1997, p. A18.

27. Alan Bernstein, "Election '97; The Race for City Hall; Saenz Mayoral Bid Puts Focus on Hispanic Vote," *Houston Chronicle*, June 10, 1997, p. A17.

28. Julie Mason, "Election '97; The Race for City Hall; Contests for Mayor, Proposition A in Home Stretch; Passion over Affirmative Action Increases," *Houston Chronicle*, November 3, 1997, p. A1.

29. Steve Brewer, "Mfume Urges Voters to Defeat Proposition A," *Houston Chronicle*, November 1, 1997, p. A34.

30. Alan Bernstein, "Many Factors Will Sum Up Mayoral Victory," *Houston Chronicle*, November 16, 1997, p. A38.

31. Alan Bernstein, "Election '97; The Race for City Hall; Brown, Mosbacher Target Hispanic Votes in Runoff," *Houston Chronicle*, November 11, 1997, p. A19.

32. Alan Bernstein, "Election '97; The Race for City Hall; Lanier Pledges to Start Mending Affirmative Action; Large Black Turnout Was Extraordinary," *Houston Chronicle*, November 6, 1997, p. A1.

33. Ibid.

34. Alan Bernstein, "Election '97; The Race for City Hall; Saenz Throws Her Support to Mosbacher for Mayor," *Houston Chronicle*, November 18, 1997, p. A1.

35. Alan Bernstein, Salatheia Bryant and Lydia Lum, "Campaign Notebook," *Houston Chronicle*, November 27, 1997, p. A49.

36. Lori Rodriguez, "Assuring City's Hispanics Will Be Brown's Challenge," *Houston Chronicle*, December 14, 1997, p. A1.

37. Ibid.

38. Ibid.

39. Julie Mason, "Election Results Don't Bode Well for Brown in 2001 Re-Election," *Houston Chronicle*, November 14, 1999, p. A36.

40. "Hispanic Leaders Endorse Brown for Re-Election," *Houston Chronicle*, April 10, 2001, p. A16.

41. Ibid.

42. John Williams, "Sanchez to Toss Hat in the Ring for Mayor: Goal Is to Be First Hispanic Elected to Post," *Houston Chronicle*, April 22, 2001, p. A1.

43. Ibid.

44. John Williams, "Sanchez Announces Candidacy for Mayor; Brown Accused of Bad Management," *Houston Chronicle*, April 24, 2001, p. A17.

45. Lori Rodriguez, "Mayoral Rivals Promote Plans to Hispanics," *Houston Chronicle*, July 21, 2001, p. A27.

46. Ibid.

47. Rachel Graves, "Fight Looms as Mayor Seeks Tax Boost," *Houston Chronicle*, May 17, 2001, p. A1.

48. Rachel Graves and Lori Rodriguez, "Candidates' Rhetoric Rises in Affirmative Action Debate; Bell, Brown Support City's Program; Sanchez's Stance Vacillates," *Houston Chronicle*, August 20, 2001, p. A17.

49. Ibid.

50. Ibid.

51. Lori Rodriguez, "Sanchez's Mayoral Bid Targets Disparate Voters," *Houston Chronicle*, October 7, 2001, p. A1.

52. Lori Rodriguez, "Voter Drive Targets Latinos," *Houston Chronicle*, October 18, 2001, p. A31.

53. W. Gardner Selby, "What's Behind Hispanic Clout at Ballot Box?" *San Antonio Express-News*, November 8, 2001, p. 1A; John Williams, "Election 2001; Voter Turnout a Boon to Sanchez," *Houston Chronicle*, November 8, 2001, p. A23.

54. W. Gardner Selby, "What's Behind Hispanic Clout at the Ballot Box," *San Antonio Express-News*, November 8, 2001, p. 1A.

55. Salatheia Bryant, "Election 2001: Racial Pride to Play a Big Role in Runoff; For Many Voters, Serious City Issues Take a Backseat," *Houston Chronicle*, November 8, 2001, p. A28.

56. Ibid.

57. John Gizzi, "Republican Orlando Sanchez Loses Tight Mayoral Contest: Democrats Reprise Race-Baiting in Houston," OnLine Human Events, December 10, 2001, viewed at www.humaneventsonline.com/articles/12-10-01/gizzi.htm

58. Ibid.

59. Ibid.

CHAPTER 8: THE BIG *MANZANA*

1. Jonathan P. Hicks, "Platform Built on a Divided City; Ferrer Courts Voters He Says Giuliani Left Behind," *New York Times*, April 18, 2001, p. B1.

2. Mireya Navarro, "The Latino Candidate: You, Mine or Ours?; Ferrer Faces Diverse Hispanic Electorate," *New York Times*, May 6, 2001, p. A45.

3. Ibid.

4. Howard Jordan, "City Power: Who Deserves the Black-Latino Vote," *Newsday* (New York), March 8, 2001, p. A45.

5. Adam Nagourney, "Sharpton Gives Ferrer a List of Conditions," *New York Times*, May 9, 2001, p. B1.

6. Ibid.

7. Bob Herbert, "In America: Ferrer's Dilemma," *New York Times*, May 10, 2001, p. A33.

8. Joel Siegel, "Ferrer Uses 'Merit' System; Says He Won't Back Candidates on the Basis of Race, Ethnicity," *Daily News* (New York), May 10, 2001, p. 8.

9. Adam Nagourney, "Ferrer Refuses Endorsement Linked to Race," *New York Times*, May 10, 2001, p. B1.

10. Lenora Fulani, "City Power: Talk of Black-Latino Coalition Is Jive," *Newsday* (New York), May 15, 2001.

11. Bob Herbert, "In America: Trouble for Ferrer," *New York Times*, May 14, 2001, p. A15.

12. Adam Nagourney, "Dinkins Gives His Support to Green, Not Ferrer," *New York Times,* May 16, 2001, p. B3.

13. Joel Siegel, "Ferrer's Key Problem: Getting Latino Vote," *Daily News* (New York), May 20, 2001, p. 13.

14. Eric Lipton, "Sharpton and Three from Bronx Are Jailed in Vieques Protest," *New York Times,* May 24, 2001, p. A1.

15. Frank Lombardi, "Rudy Ratings Up with Latino Voters," *Daily News* (New York), June 7, 2001, p. 7.

16. Mirta Ojito, "Talking the Talk, Sometimes in Spanish," *New York Times,* June 19, 2001, p. B3.

17. Andy Newman, "Three Vieques Protesters Emerge from Prison after 37 Days," *New York Times,* June 30, 2001, p. B1.

18. Dexter Filkins and Adam Nagourney, "Sharpton Endorses Ferrer in Mayoral Race," *New York Times,* August 28, 2001, p. A1.

19. Michael Cooper, "The New York Primary; The Democrats: Ferrer and Green Divide the Spoils of Their Rivals," *New York Times,* September 27, 2001, p. D5.

20. Ibid.

21. Adam Nagourney, "Again, Democrats Find Giuliani at Center of the Race," *New York Times,* August 28, 2001, p. D1.

22. Adam Nagourney, "Ferrer and Green Battle in Debate over Claim of Divisiveness," *New York Times,* October 4, 2001, p. D1.

23. Jonathan P. Hicks, "Green's Campaign Angers Backers of Ferrer," *New York Times,* October 13, 2001, p. D3.

CHAPTER 9: VISIONS OF THE FUTURE

1. David O. Sears, *Final Report: Assessment of Interracial/Interethnic Conflict in Los Angeles,* UCLA Center for Study and Resolution of Interracial/ Interethnic Conflict, March 12, 2002, p. 3. Viewed at http://www.sscnet.ucla. edu/issr/crisp/report51.pdf

2. Ibid., p. 8.

3. Lee Romney, "Santa Ana Mayoral Candidate Puylido Opposes Prop. 187," *Los Angeles Times,* November 2, 1994, p. B1.

4. John W. Mack, "Proposition 187: Is Black-Latino Friction a Voting-Booth Issue? No: The Initiative's Backers Would Put All Minorities in the Same Boat. African Americans Won't Escape Harm," *Los Angeles Times,* October 24, 1994, p. B7.

5. Kevin Ross, "Proposition 187: Is Black-Latino Friction a Voting-Booth Issue? Yes: The Initiative Is Horrible Legislation, but It's Still a Focal Point for Legitimate African American Resentments," *Los Angeles Times,* October 24, 1994, p. B7. The Ross editorial comment was run alongside the Mack editorial comment, yet Yzaguirre and Kamaski made no mention of it in their post-script.

6. Ibid.

7. Arnoldo de León, *Racial Frontiers: Africans, Chinese, and Mexicans in Western America, 1848–1890* (Albuquerque, N.M.: University of New Mexico Press, 2002), p. 4.

8. Lynette Clemetson, "Hispanics Now Largest Minority, Census Shows," *New York Times,* January 21, 2003, p. A1.

9. "Hispanic Population Reaches All-Time High of 38.8 Million, New Census Bureau Estimates Show," United States Department of Commerce News, Washington, D.C. 20230. Viewed at http://www.census.gov/Press-Release/www/2003/cb03-100.html

10. Peter W. Wood, "Anti-Matters," *Partisan Review* 69, 1 (Winter 2002). Viewed at http://people.bu.edu/pwood/Antimatters.htm

11. Leslie Espinoza and Angela P. Harris, "Afterward: Embracing the Tar-baby-LaCrit Theory and the Sticky Mess of Race," *La Raza Law Journal* 10, no. 1, pp. 1585–1645.

12. Carmen T. Joge, "Latinos Vote in the '90s," *Issue Brief,* National Council of La Raza (October 2000), no. 4, p. 2.

13. Ibid., p. 4.

14. "National Survey of Latinos: The Latino Electorate" (Pew Hispanic Center/Kaiser Family Foundation, October 2002), p. 6.

15. "Summary of Findings: Survey of Latino Attitudes on a Possible War with Iraq Conducted February 13–16, 2003, Before Invasion of Iraq," April 2003, Pew Hispanic Center, a Project of the University of Southern California, Annenberg School for Communication. Viewed at http://www.pewhispanic.org/site/docs/pdf/Iraq2%20report.pdf

16. Ibid.

"The Streets Are Paved with 'Oro,'" FoxNews.com,
d at http://www.foxnews.com/story/0,2933,81019,00.

lie, Annie Steffenson, Jaime Valdez, Rebecca Levin, and
Jational Survey of Latinos" (Washington, D.C.: Pew His-
Henry Kaiser Family Foundation, 2002), p. 37.
Streets Are Paved with 'Oro.'"
odriguez, "150 Years Later, Latinos Finally Hit the
York Times, April 15, 2001. Viewed at http://www. new
cfm?sec=programs&pg=article&pubID=178&T2=Article
l., "2002 National Survey of Latinos," pp. 44–45.

odriguez, "Forging a New Vision of America's Melting Pot,"
New York Times, February 11, 2001. Viewed at http://www.newamerica.net/
index.cfm?sec=programs&pg=article&pubID=28&T2=Article

INDEX